March 7, 1990

I gaze upon the roast,
that is sliced and laid out
on my plate
and over it
I spoon the juices
of carrot and onion.
And for once I do not regret
the passage of time.
                    ~Mark Strand

Happy Birthday Sean

Steve

The Food of
Spain and Portugal

Con pan y vino
Se anda camino.

With bread and wine
One can travel life's road.

For my husband, Cesar Ortiz-Tinoco, who first set me off on the voyage of discovery that ended with this book.

THE FOOD OF
SPAIN AND PORTUGAL

THE COMPLETE IBERIAN CUISINE

Elisabeth Lambert Ortiz

Atheneum   New York   1989

Atheneum
Macmillan Publishing Company
866 Third Avenue, New York, N.Y. 10022

Library of Congress Cataloging-in-Publication Data

Ortiz, Elisabeth Lambert.
The food of Spain and Portugal/Elisabeth Lambert Ortiz.
p.   cm.
Includes index.
ISBN 0–689–12057–5
1. Cookery, Spanish. 2. Cookery, Portuguese.   I. Title.
TX723.5.S7075   1989
641.5946—dc19   88–13834
                                            CIP

Macmillan books are available at special discounts for bulk purchases for sales
promotions, premiums, fund-raising, or educational use. For details, contact:

Special Sales Director
Macmillan Publishing Company
866 Third Avenue
New York, N.Y. 10022

10 9 8 7 6 5 4 3 2 1

Printed in Great Britain

Contents

Acknowledgements

I have become indebted over the years to more people then I could possibly list for their generous sharing of knowledge of the cuisines of Spain and Portugal. To some, many dear friends, I am aspecially grateful.

Mr and Mrs Roberto Rendueles of Madrid
Mr and Mrs Asdrubal Salsamendi of Madrid
Professor and Mrs Miguel A. Marín of Barcelona
The late Rosa, Marquessa del Castellar of Barcelona and Mexico
Ms Suze Fisher who generously came with me on research trips in Portugal
Mr Patrick A. Gooche, Director, Foods from Spain, London
Ms Maria-José Seville, Gastronomy, Foods from Spain, London
Ms Gabriela Ferreira, Portuguese National Tourist Office, London
Mrs Teresa Martinho, Instituto de Promocãa Turistica, Lisbon
Mr Pedro Rebello de Andrade, Téchnico de Hotelaria, Lisbon
Mr Antonio Muchaxo, Director, Estalagem Muchaxo, Praia do Guincho, Cascais
Lis Leigh, food writer, for her generous help sorting out the influence of the Iberian cuisines on the cooking of Gibraltar.

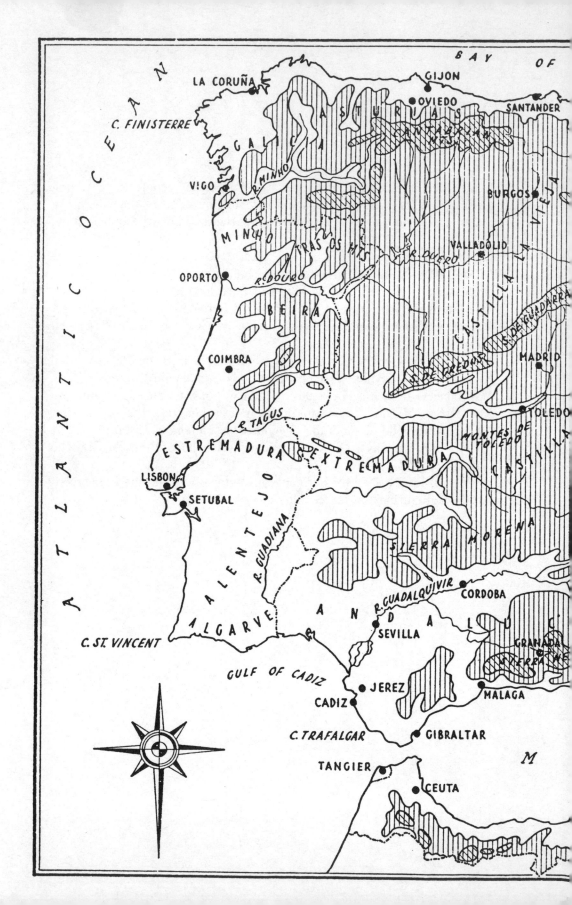

SCAY

BIARRITZ

SAN SEBASTIAN

TOULOUSE

NAVARRA

PERPIGNAN

ZARAGOZA

R. EBRO

CATALUÑA

BARCELONA

A R A G O N

UEVA

E

VALENCIA

C. JUCAR

L

A

N

C

I

A

BALEARIC   ISLES

PALMA

VALENCIA

MURCIA

C. LA NAO

M

E

D

I

T

E

R

R

A

N

E

A

N   SEA

ALICANTE

MURCIA

CARTAGENA

R

A

C. CATA

1

T

E

R

SPAIN
AND PORTUGAL

⊞⊞⊞   THE HIGH TABLELANDS

⊠⊠⊠   HIGH MOUNTAIN AREAS

〜〜〜   INTERNATIONAL FRONTIERS

SCALE

O MILES 50   100   150   200

O KMS 80   160   240   320

Introduction
Food and the History of Spain and Portugal

My interest in the cuisines of the Iberian Peninsula, Spain and Portugal, began on the other side of the world. It was when I first set out to learn about the cuisine of Mexico, a former Spanish colony, that I stumbled upon the most exciting event in the whole history of food and cooking. That first realisation was to send me off on a long voyage of discovery that now, after twenty-five years, ends with this book; though I know, of course, that I shall never stop learning about the history of food, or about cooking, an eternal, and eternally changing, art.

It began for me when I married and went to live in Mexico, where I spent several years. My husband, an official in the United Nations Secretariat and a Mexican national, is, roughly speaking, half-Spanish and half-Portuguese. I was eager to learn all I could about the exciting cuisine of his homeland, Mexico, which was the most foreign I had ever encountered, even though I had considerable working knowledge of cuisines in other parts of the world. There was not, at that time, a great body of kitchen literature to help me, so I took to the markets as a source of knowledge, where I met with great help, expertise, humour and affection. It soon became clear to me that while the cuisine was firmly rooted in its own soil, it was a colonial kitchen influenced by the foods that the Spanish conquerors of Mexico, the Caribbean, Central and South America had brought with them, now incorporated happily in the nation's earthenware cazuelas. I began to discover all I could about Spain and Portugal, and soon realized that the history of that Peninsular, with its dramatic series of changes, was essential to my understanding of its cuisine.

The Iberian Peninsula has been buffeted by invasions since the earliest times, beginning in 1100 BC when the Phoenicians carried their Semitic language and culture to Spain, founding Gadír, now modern Cadiz. Between 500 and 400 BC the Greeks colonized the coast and at the same time the Carthagians conquered much of Spain from north Africa. A little earlier, about 650 BC, the Celts had begun their invasions across the Pyrenees from the north. Then about 200 BC the Romans conquered Spain, adding the Peninsula to their Empire, and it was through them, in 100 AD, that Christianity was introduced.

This was not the end of the invasions and conquests. Although the Roman Empire offered centuries of stability, it too eventually felt the inroads of the tribes to its north, and as pressure grew on Italy itself, its

1

various provinces were increasingly left to themselves. About 400 AD the first pagan Germanic invasion of the Iberian Peninsula took place, ending less than 100 years later with the invading Visigothic tribes taking over completely. Under King Reccared the country, which then included Portugal, became converted to Christianity once more, only to fall prey to the Moslem invasion and conquest which was completed in 718. This was the most serious inroad yet made into Christian Europe by the expanding power of Islam, but almost immediately a Christian Visigothic leader, Pelayo, started the reconquest and founded the Kingdom of Asturias. Next it was the turn of Charlemagne to invade from the north in 778, but his Frankish forces were defeated by the Basques.

This extraordinary sequence of conquests might have obliterated any civilization in Spain and Portugal, and it is true that as the Dark Ages began, hordes of barbarians swept down from the north – Andalucía is actually named after the invading Vandals. But, strangely, while most of Europe struggled to keep civilisation alive, mainly through the libraries of the great monasteries, the Moslem countries reached unequalled peaks of learning and philosophy, especially in horticulture, architecture and mathematics. Nonetheless, civilization was not synonymous with the nationalities that made up Spain, and rebellion against the Muslim rulers was inevitable. In 961 Sancho the Great of Navarre set up the Kingdoms of Castille and Aragon and reduced the Moslem empire to a series of petty provinces. The turning point in the Moslem-Christian conflict came in 1085 when Alfonso VI of Castille, with the aid of the Christian Crusaders, captured Toledo. Soon after, in 1094 the celebrated El Cid took Valencia and by 1252, following the exploits of Ferdinand III, the reconquest was complete, with all the Peninsula free of Islamic domination except for Granada, which finally fell to their Catholic Majesties, Ferdinand and Isabella, in 1492. It was a year memorable for events both splendid and sordid, as it also saw the expulsion of the Jews from Castille and the discovery of the Americas by Christopher Columbus.

The ceaseless waves of invasion over the centuries that created the two races, Spanish and Portuguese, alike yet profoundly different, also brought their varied gifts to the kitchen. From their home in what is now Syria and Lebanon the Phoenicians brought saffron, the world's most expensive spice, and planted vines in what is now sherry country. The Romans planted olive trees, and anyone who has enjoyed the magnificently fruity oils of the peninsula might well think the Roman conquest worth the price as they lend an incomparable flavour to any food with which they are cooked. The Arabs introduced a great many good things, such as the short grain rice which they planted in Valencia, at the same time updating an irrigation system started by the Romans. Without this special stubby rice, a little like *arborio* Italian rice, *paella*, best-known of all the Spanish dishes, could not exist. They also brought almonds, citrus fruits including Seville oranges, sweet oranges and lemons all initially from China, the eggplant (or aubergine), spinach, cumin (a favourite flavouring), and sugar cane, and probably more, as over the nearly 800 years of Arab domination of most of Spain and Portugal, the Arab civilizations caused much movement of ingredients around the Mediterranean and beyond. Quinces, popular in both the countries, are an example. A native of south-west Asia, possibly Iran, where it still grows wild, it was greatly esteemed by the Romans who may have brought it with them wherever their conquests took them, but it was Shafer ben Utman al-Mushafi, the Vizir to Al Hakam the Second of Cordova around 980 AD, who wrote a poem extolling the fruit. To this day, quince paste is popular in the Middle East, the Iberian Peninsula and all of Latin America. Eggplant (aubergine) is an admired vegetable in a wide variety of dishes in Spain, as a salad, with meat, fish or shellfish. Almonds are used in both countries imaginatively and extensively, with borrowings from Middle Eastern cooking, especially when ground and used as a thickener for sauces for fish, and poultry.

The north of both countries is strongly influenced by the Celtic and Visigothic past, while Spain also has the Basques, a mysterious and ancient people of unknown origin, who also exist in France. Their language compounds the mystery as it has no known relationship with any other language. Their cooking is original and good, enjoying considerable fame throughout Spain. Pork, forbidden by Islam, was and is especially popular in the north. The Celts arrived with their pigs, still called the Celtic breed, a lop-eared beast that formerly inhabited Gaul and the British Isles, though cross-breeding has greatly changed it. Possibly their devotion to the pig strengthened the Celtic dislike of Islam, and the thought of roast suckling pig strengthened their resolve in battle. Today, as a result of this early invasion by Celt and pig together, there is a large Basque repertoire of hams and sausages.

Spain's great Imperial history begins with the death in 1504 of Queen Isabella who was succeeded by her grandson Charles V, and the launching of Spain under the leadership of the Hapsburgs. It was a tangled period of history with a great deal of political intrigue. From the point of view of the kitchen, Spain's culinary influence reached its apogee in Europe in the sixteenth and seventeenth centuries, when Spain ruled a large part of the Americas and more than half of Europe. Spanish chefs were imported by crowned heads, and the fashionable adopted Spanish cuisine. The esteem in which the cuisine was held was, of course, reinforced by the new foods from the Americas.

It was the search for spices that sent the explorers off in the first place, as well as the desire to know if the world was round. Fortunately it was. Columbus really found America for Spain in 1492 by accident, looking for a quicker route to the spice islands.

But it was Portugal that had ushered in Europe's Age of Discovery in the early fifteenth century. One of the most practical achievements of the nation was the invention of the *caravel*, a new type of ship which could sail both with and against the wind. Inspired by the King, Henry the Navigator, the Portuguese explored the West Coast of Africa and even ventured into the Atlantic, an act of great bravery in those almost unmapped times, when the unknown was peopled in the imagination by dreadful monsters. The undaunted Portuguese discovered Madeira, the Azores and the Cape Verde Islands. Vasco da Gama rounded the Cape of Good Hope in 1497 and reached the port of Calicut, near Goa. In doing so, of course, he was finding a route to the authentic Orient. There is no doubt that the search for spices was a large motivation. The only route overland was hazardous, lengthy and costly. Vasco da Gama, opening the sea route to India, made available a very popular spice, black peppercorns, probably the most widely used of all spices. Pepper, *Piper nigrum*, is indigenous to the southern part of the East coast of India, the Malabar coast still famed for the quality of its pepper, though the spice is now cultivated in a number of countries. The berries are picked green then dried until black and wrinkled. White pepper is picked a little later when the berries are turning red, with the skin, the pericarp, removed before drying. It is less pungent than black pepper. It was not until the 1970s that the French introduced the unripe, green peppercorns to the world as a new spice, proving the durable quality of this most popular, though by no means most expensive of the world's spices.

Pepper was not unknown to the west before the Portuguese sea route discovery. The Romans had reached India by land and sea routes in the first century AD. After the fall of the Roman Empire and the ensuing Dark Ages in Europe, Islamic Arabs dominated the trade routes. The port of Calicut had not seen a European ship sail into its harbour for 1,000 years, in fact Vasco da Gama and his crew were the first Europeans to sail direct to India from their home port. There were other explorer-navigators like Cabral, discoverer of Brazil, Bartolomeu Diaz, the first European to round the Cape of Good Hope (1486) which he called *Cabo Tormentoso*, the Cape of Storms, Sebastian del Cano and Fernão de Magalhães, known in Spanish as Fernando de Magellanes.

The rivalry between the two empires is exemplified in the epic voyage of Magellan. He believed he could reach the Spice Islands by going west, but Manuel 1, the King of Portugal, disagreed. Magellan went to Spain where King Charles 1, later the Emperor Charles V, listened to him and he set off with a fleet of five vessels and 265 men. After all manner of adventures he found the straits which bear his name almost at the tip of the South American continent which took him into the Pacific. Unfortunately he was killed in the Phillipines on the way back but the voyage was continued by del Cano, the Spanish captain of the *Victoria*, one of the ships under Magellan's command. Del Cano completed the first round the world journey with a cargo of nutmegs and cloves, which they had found in the Spice Islands. Driven by storms to seek refuge, they put in at the Cape Verde islands but managed to escape the irate Portuguese who felt the *Victoria* had been poaching in their territory. Del Cano and 18 men were all that returned from Magellan's expedition, but between them Spain and Portugal had changed our concept of the world, as well as satisfying the European passion for spices, peppercorns, cloves, nutmegs and cinnamon. The last is from Ceylon (now Sri Lanka), and is the bark of a native tree, a member of the laurel family. Sri Lanka cinnamon is the finest, but the trees also grow in South India and once a sea route to India was opened up, cinnamon became accessible. Charles V rewarded Del Cano with, among other things, a coat of arms featuring cloves and nutmegs.

Cloves, which are the dried, unopened flower buds of a tropical evergreen tree, have been popular since very early times in history. Indonesians, fine sailors, delivered cloves by sea to China and by 300 AD they had reached Rome. The fall of Rome and the Dark Ages that followed reduced this commerce to almost nothing and it was not until the Crusades that Europe redeveloped its taste for spices promoting the overland trade which in turn fuelled the search for new routes to the East.

As I have said, the two great empires that resulted from the discovery of the Americas were not friends. When they were unable to decide how to divide the spoils, it was Pope Alexander VI who sorted things out. By the Treaty of Tordesillas in 1494 Portugal got Brazil, and Spain the rest of the continent as well as Mexico in North America, and some of the Caribbean islands, including Cuba and Puerto Rico. Later Spain conquered the Philippine islands, consolidating the conquest about 1564. There was much coming and going between the Mexican port of Acapulco and the Philippines with very lively trade. Portugal's empire also comprised Macau in China, Goa in India, Mozambique and Angola in Africa and Timor, near Bali. All the countries of the two empires are now independent states, or no longer part of Spain or Portugal.

It cannot be emphasized too strongly that the importing of foods by Spain and Portugal from the Americas, was the single most significant development in European cuisine in the sixteenth and seventeenth centuries. What they found there was a New World of food. Throughout the long ages before Christopher Columbus discovered the Americas in 1492, agriculture had been developing in Mexico in isolation from the rest of the world, and its products were totally unknown. Agriculture had spread from the two great empires, Aztec and Maya, now modern Mexico and parts of Central America, to the Caribbean, Central America and into South America, where the great Inca Empire, now Peru, had brilliant agriculturists. When Spain and Portugal brought these products back, it was the most exciting time in the history of the kitchen, doubling the number of foods available to the world's cooks, and closing the only remaining gap in the world food map. The foods themselves were legion: there were all the members of the genus capsicum – the peppers (chillies), sweet, pungent and hot; maize (corn); all the common beans, *phaseolus vulgaris*, such as green beans and the dried kidney beans; tomatoes – both the now familiar red tomato and the small green husk tomato, still not as common; avocados; vanilla; pawpaws (papaya); chocolate; the squashes, including pumpkin and courgettes (zucchini); guavas; sapodillas, the fruit of the tree which produces the gum from which chewing gum is made, which had already been invented by the Mexicans and was used by them; pecan and pine nuts. Mexicans, Aztecs and Mayas domesticated the turkey, a bird unknown to Europe and Asia. In the high Andes, ancient Peruvians, whom we call Incas for convenience, cultivated potatoes in an astonishing variety of types, sizes and colours, some black, some purple, some white and others as yellow as sunshine itself. They also cultivated sweet potatoes, other root crops and new strains of corn from the Mexican original, including popcorn, and a purple corn that gives off its colour when simmered in water, the resulting liquid having a fresh and flowery lemony taste as well as a beautiful colour. They also cultivated many new types of peppers, some very hot like the *rocoto*, others full-flavoured and more gentle like *mirasol*. They also developed butter (lima) beans which, when fresh, are a sensible substitute for Old World broad beans, and they domesticated the guinea pig (*cuy*, pronounced kwee), which we think of as a pet, far removed from the cookpot, so endearing an animal it is. Brazil cultivated peanuts of a different genus from the almost identical peanuts of West Africa, cassava (manioc, gari), pineapples, passion fruit and Brazil nuts, among other things. The conquest brought about a unique meeting of foods, revolutionizing the world's kitchens. Out of this culinary wedding rose the modern Mexican kitchen, which sent me off to Spain to find out

what was Spanish, what Moorish, what Mexican in the cuisine, and later
to Portugal and the Middle East.

There had been much trade and commerce in the New World before
Columbus, and foods had spread to the islands of the Caribbean, south
to the tip of Chile and Argentina and back again. No wonder that cooks
in the Iberian Peninsula, given such a bursting larder, began the creation
of what has become the cuisines of Spain and Portugal.

Both nations introduced foods from one region to another with considerable enthusiasm, but it was more a matter of introducing ingredients, not
new cooking methods, which tended to remain intact; the new foods
finding their place without disturbing the established culinary order of
their new hosts. Some of these new ingredients were more immediately
and wholeheartedly adopted than others, notably the capsicums from
Mexico. When hot chilli peppers were introduced into India they met with
such a welcome and have become such an integral part of Indian cuisine
that some Indians still refuse to believe that capsicums are native Mexican.
They were of course so much easier and cheaper to produce and so much
hotter than the black peppercorns that gave hotness to Indian food, that it
is no wonder they established themselves with such ease. The Portuguese
introducing tiny, hot chillies into Africa were responsible for the creation
of Piri-Piri sauce, a very hot on-the-table sauce like Tabasco, without
which Portugal could not survive, any more than it could without Peruvian
potatoes, which are splendidly naturalized in their new home and eaten
with all main dishes. Neither Spain nor Portugal could exist without
tomatoes or sweet peppers, *pimientos* in Spain, *pimentas* in Portugal.
Portugal celebrates another Mexican contribution, maize (corn) in an
adapted form as *broa*, a greatly acclaimed robust corn bread that adds to
the enjoyment of stews in winter weather.

It was by no means a one-way traffic, as Spain rapidly introduced sheep,
cattle, pigs and goats into the New World as well as olive and walnut
trees, coffee, wheat, wine, rice, cinnamon, cloves, peaches, apricots, and
oranges. For a while the Spanish were enthusiastic about the new foods,
especially chocolate, but they longed for their own familiar dishes – wheat
bread, cheeses, pastries and so on. It could be said that it was the pig
which suffered most from the conquest. Mexico, which had previously
relied on the dangerous and wily wild boar, was more than enthusiastic
in adopting this fat and docile beast, while in Spain and Portugal where
pork had been forbidden by Islam, it was enthusiastically welcomed back
into the fold as itself when mature, as suckling pig, as bacon, and as salt-
cured, air-dried mountain ham, Spanish *serrano*, and Portuguese smoked
ham, *presunto*. Pork was also an ingredient in numerous sausages, smoked

and spiced like *chorizo (chourice)*, *longaniza (linguica)*, and *morcilla (morcela)* to give the Spanish and Portuguese names for very similar sausages. Ham is cooked with chicken, beef and pork, pork sausages and beans. The pig is welcome in a multitude of dishes. In 1497 Vasco da Gama brought back curry from India and today, in Minho province especially, curry powder is a common kitchen spice. Since all European food relied heavily on spices in medieval times, curry spices from India would not have seemed unusual. Delicate prawn (shrimp) curry points to the India connection. Goa was a Portuguese colony in southwest India until 1956, and Goanese food today is a blend of Portuguese and southern Indian influences. There are dishes like prawn (shrimp) curry, *Jhinga Kari*, using two of Portugal's favourite flavourings, ground cumin and fresh coriander; *Suvar mas ka Vindalu*, sometimes spelled *Vindaloo*, a very hot and spicy pork curry; *Cachumbar*, a tomato, onion and fresh ginger root salad which has a clear Portuguese influence; and *Beebeck*, a baked coconut batter cake, which owes something to the Portuguese love of egg-rich dishes. *Sorpotel*, a dish of pickled pork, pig's liver and heart and dried hot chilli peppers combined with all the usual Indian spices suggests a meeting of culinary minds.

Portugal introduced taro and pumpkin, both non-European, to Japan, as well as peppers. The Japanese have developed a hot chilli pepper, used fresh when green, dried when ripe and red. Called, appropriately, hawk's claw (*hontaka*), it can be used successfully to make *Piri-piri* sauce, which says something for its degree of heat. It was Portuguese monks in Nagasaki who, intent on observing the Lenten fast with an absence of meat, gave the Japanese the idea that flowered into *tempura*, batter-coated prawns (shrimps) and vegetables, the name a corruption of *Os Temperos*, the Ember (fast) days. Similar influences can be traced in Mozambique cooking from Africa, in dishes like *Peixe Lumbo*, fish and prawn (shrimp) stew where, as in Brazilian cooking, coconut plays an important role, as do tomatoes, hot dried red chilli peppers, sweet (bell) peppers and fresh coriander, all reflecting Portuguese influence. Another clear case of this is *Camarao Grelhado* with *Piri-piri* sauce, grilled or broiled prawns (shrimps) in hot chilli sauce.

Geography plays as large a role in the creation of a national cuisine as history does. Portugal, not as much of a string bean country as Chile, being less long, is nevertheless even less wide, 360 by 140 miles. Isolated by mountains and with the Atlantic as its western border for its whole length, it is no wonder it boasts a history of exploration, with the ocean luring the explorer to come and find out what lands exist beyond that mass of water. It is also no wonder that with such in extensive coastline the cuisine is equally famous for its fish and shellfish.

I shall never forget my first visit to a fish market in Portugal. It was in Lisbon and I could not believe that the huge fish I could see in such lavish quantity were indeed tamboril (monkfish). It strained credulity when I thought of the modestly sized fillets I was used to buying. There were swordfish and scabbard fish, piles of shiny green, yellow and silver sardines, blue-green and silver anchovies, sea bass, skate, turbot, skinny eels, decorous sole, huge grey-brown stone bass, and tuna. Then there were the shellfish, *percebes*, comical-looking goose-necked barnacles that are such fun to eat, squid, cuttlefish, octopus, giant crabs, clams, crayfish, lobsters and scallops.

I have always found it strange that with such an abundance of superb seafood the Portuguese and Spanish made for the Grand Banks off Newfoundland for cod which was dried and salted and brought home after long and perilous journeys. It remains an immense favourite even now throughout the Peninsula, and Portuguese cooks claim there is a different codfish recipe for every day of the year.

Portuguese food is essentially family food: simple, easy to cook, no difficult techniques to master, no hard-to-find ingredients. Cooks prefer to use the top of the stove, making cooking even easier. What makes it notably different from other cuisines, including that of Spain despite its Iberian quality, is the bold use of herbs and spices, and the imaginative putting together of foods in unusual combinations. Parsley (preferably the flat leafed kind) and coriander are favourite herbs; lemons are used in abundance, often with meats, beef for example. Equally lavishly used are olive oil, sweet and hot peppers, tomatoes, short and long-grain rice, and potatoes, without which no meal would be complete. It is a most accessible cuisine.

Because the country runs north – south and is mountainous, there is a great range of weather in addition to seasonal changes, and a great variety of food products. There are the firm, full-flavoured potatoes of the far north province of Minho, the glorious suckling pigs of Beira Litoral, the robust soups and dry soups of all the northern provinces, the dried salt cod dishes, lamprey if you are lucky enough to be in Douro at the right time of the year, the good meat stews and, of course, wickedly rich desserts. There are also the wines, for the north is fine wine country; its star, the port wine of the Douro, which has a vast and ancient reputation world-wide. A newer fame is now being enjoyed by a most delicious aperitif, *Porto Branco Seco*, dry white port, which I first tasted and fell in love with, on my very first trip to Portugal.

There are other attractive wines that enter into agreeable partnerships with the good food of the region. The altogether charming Vinho Verde Branco and Vinho Verde Tinto, both crisp, light, and just a tiny bit *pétillant*, come from Minho. Beira Alta is the home of Dão, best known of the Portuguese red wines, though the white is also good drinking. When in Coimbra or anywhere else in Beira, nothing is as good as the robust, fruity red Bairrada, with suckling pig, game such as partridge, rabbit or hare, domestic birds like duckling, especially *Arroz de Pato* (Duckling with Rice), meats like goat or lamb, or tripe for that matter.

Going south to Lisbon in Estremadura, Ribatejo and the Alentejos, there are other delights in food and drink. One of the nicest things in Portugal is that the small, ordinary restaurants, the *tascas*, have such very good food. They can be relied upon for this just as much as grander restaurants, and are sometimes even better. I have eaten superbly fresh fish in Cascais and Estoril, in simple restaurants, then enjoyed a grand lunch at the Estalagem Muchaxo in Guincho on the coast just up from Cascais where host and owner Antonio Muchaxo presides over the service of many fine wines as well as seafood dishes like percebes, clams, lobsters, and of course meat and poultry dishes, though it is the seafood dishes that are a triumph, especially when you sit, as we did, overlooking the rocky wave-lashed coast, just a few minutes drive from placid sandy beaches. I remember we finished a memorable meal with rich black coffee and the Algarve liqueur, Licor do Amendoa Amargo, made from bitter almonds. On another occasion, on the way to Sétubal on a hot sunny day, we stopped for a beer and drank chilled golden Sagres, sharp and refreshing, wonderful with shellfish and, at the Rostinguinha, a large but rustic roadside restaurant, we had grilled kid, *Cabrito na brasa*.

Further south in the Baixo Alentejo there are the cork trees, peeled every seven years for their cork. Newly peeled, they are a startling bright orange, then they fade to rust-red, making the cork forests an astonishing spectacle. There are many farms and wheat fields, rice growing in lagoons, and some very good wine and food. The region, with its prefix 'al' has, as one might expect, a strong Moorish influence like its neighbour, the Algarve. My favourite wine from the Alentejo is Vidigueira, though there are many others worthy of drinking. The reds are strong and fruity, deep red with an almost purple cast. The whites are equally full-flavoured.

A favourite soup, *Sopa à alentejana*, is really a version of garlic soup made different by the use of fresh coriander. The tomato soup is as hearty as the red wine. The dish I most enjoy and which should not be missed is *Porco com Amêijoas a Alentejana* "Pork with Clams". The clams lend a special flavour to the pork, and a bottle of Vidigueira turns the meal into a feast.

The desserts betray the Moorish influence more than anything else. Created by convent nuns, they are rich in eggs, sugar and almonds. The richest of all is probably *Touchinho-do-céu* (Heavenly Bacon), an almond cake using either no flour at all, or a very small amount. *Arroz Doce* (Sweet Rice) is an easy-to-make rice pudding that, despite its simplicity, is addictive. This is also the region of sweets more oddly named than Heavenly Bacon, like *Barriga de Freira* which translates into Nun's Belly, though I suppose the delicate-minded could call it Nun's Tummy! There is another dessert, from Trás-os-Montes and other provinces, that is an equal challenge – *Papos de Anjo* (Angel's Breasts). Because Portugal is not a very large country I could always ask if they had *Queijo da Serra*, a quite sublime cheese, which eaten with some red wine often kept me from a dessert, and be told, yes, we have it, even far from its mountain home in the north.

One runs out of Portugal with the Algarve and topples into the sea. The most Moorish part of Portugal, the Algarve is almost a twin to Andalucía, its very much larger Spanish southern neighbour, the last place on the Peninsula from which the Moors were expelled. It is a region of almond trees, wonderful fish soups and fish, figs, marzipan sunshine, white sandy beaches and dishes cooked in that ingenious, clam shell-shaped cooking vessel, the *cataplana*, the most famous of all these dishes being *Amêijoas na Cataplana* "Clams in a *cataplana*". Sausage, garlic, oil, tomatoes, onions, *presunto* ham, parsley, white wine and clams go into the *cataplana* and the dish is cooked over charcoal outdoors, or, if this is not possible, indoors over any source of heat. When the lid is opened, a wonderful smell emerges, redolent of the sea. The taste of the dish equals it.

Next door, Andalucía is the home of *gazpacho*, without doubt the best soup ever invented to suit a climate, but now popular the world over. The province is semi-arid and best suited to growing grapes and olives, but it is also blessed with an abundance of fish and shellfish. Sun-drenched and flower-filled and hot, it demands food that is light and cooling like *gazpacho*. Another splended creation which has also become a worldwide favourite, is *sangría*, a thirst-quenching summer drink of red wine and fruits. Another Andalucían creation is sherry, also appreciated the world over. It is one of the world's oldest wines and comes from Jerez, corrupted by the English into sherry. It existed before the Romans and survived the Moors. Shakespeare called it 'sherris sack' and even in his day, 'sherry' was a term in use. Phoenician settlers are credited with introducing the grapevines that, rooted in the chalky soil of Jerez and enjoying the predict-able climate where there is year-round sunshine, produce this versatile fortified wine, which makes an admirable aperitif.

Sherry is also good in cooking, lifting an ordinary sauce into a higher sphere, giving what could be a dull dish a golden flavour.

Sherry inevitably reminds me of its cousins, Port and Madeira, since dry port and dry Madeira are also available as aperitifs. *Sercial Madeira* is the driest, a fine aperitif and the classic accompaniment to turtle soup; *Verdelho* is also dry but a little sweeter; *Bual* is darker in colour and sweeter. Finally, *Malmsey* is a great dessert wine and after dinner drink.

While Portuguese meal hours put no strain on the visitor, with breakfast at about 8 a.m., lunch between 12.30 and 1 p.m., and dinner about 8 or 9 p.m., Spanish meal hours are greatly different from those of the English-speaking countries and many others, though they survive in Mexico. A second (11 a.m.) breakfast *almuerzo* follows the early one, the *tapas* are at 1 p.m. and lunch at 2 p.m., *merienda* (tea and cakes) at 6, *tapas* at 8 and dinner at 10 p.m. or later. It is a mystery to foreigners when Spanish people find time to do anything but eat! They do: even in the summer heat of Andalucía, cooks manage to produce dishes like fish soup with bitter (Seville) orange juice, refreshing salads, *Huevos a la Flamenca* (Baked Eggs with Ham), sausage and asparagus and notable seafood dishes.

Although the Greeks had colonies in Spain and about 200 AD Roman legions conquered the country, there is little culinary evidence of their occupation. Between 711 and 718 AD the Moorish invasion of Spain took place and had a profound and lasting influence on the cuisine. However, in 718, Pelayo, the Visigothic leader, who was a Christian, established the Kingdom of Asturias, and the Moors were never able to dominate the northwest, defeated in part by mountains and torrential rains. There is strong Celtic influence here and in Galicia. This is cider country and partly because of the climate, dishes are hearty, like the famous *Caldo Gallego*, a white bean, turnip greens and potato soup, and *Fabada Asturians*, a dried broad bean and sausage soup that is a meal in itself. There is abundant seafood, and *Caldereta Asturians*, a rich seafood stew, is also a complete meal.

Until the discovery of the Americas, Galicia was known as Finisterre, land's end. Here and in the Asturias the harsh, frequently damp climate encourages hearty appetites and dishes to satisfy them. There is *Merluza a la Gallega* (Poached hake with potatoes and tomato sauce), a delectable dish, and rabbit dishes like *Conejo a la Asturiana* (Rabbit, Asturian-style).

Catalonia, on the Mediterranean coast, has a kitchen that is full of excitements. There are large prawns (jumbo shrimps) cooked with brandy, almonds and a little grated bitter chocolate; *Mar i Muntanya* – Sea and Mountain; *allioli*, a mayonnaise whose prime ingredient is garlic, which is eaten with many things including salt cod and potatoes; and Romesco Sauce made with peppers, tomatoes and almonds, a noble accompaniment to snails, fish and shellfish. There is also one of the world's great spinach dishes in which the spinach is cooked with raisins, pine nuts and anchovies. All the seafood is notable. The best wines, red and white, are from the Penedés region.

It is said of the Spanish of the central plateau, both Old Castille and New Castille with the capital Madrid as its focal point, that they eat all day and part of the night. Their eating pattern is not really different from that in any other part of the kingdom. Perhaps the need is felt to combat the harsh winters and hot summers, but whatever the reason, it is in the captial city that the best tapas bars can be found, an invitation to eat and drink at any hour. The hors d'oeuvres are served with sherry and other wines in great variety and could easily replace lunch or dinner. Prawns (shrimps), clams, mussels and squid in various guises, as well as fish and salads, sausages and eggs are all used to make delectable small dishes. For heartier eating there is the famed *Cocido Madrileno*, a stew containing just about everything.

The cooking of Aragon and Navarre is characterized by sauces, the skilful blending of ingredients best exemplified in the *Chilindrón* dishes made from sweet red (bell) peppers, tomatoes, onion, garlic and *serrano* ham with chicken, lamb, veal, kid or rabbit. Rioja, a tiny province, produces the best peppers grown for the *chilindrón*, and the finest Spanish wines, the Riojas, to drink with any regional food. They have world fame and Marqués de Riscal would be grand with *Trucha a la Navarra*, trout stuffed with mountain ham, or with roast suckling pig, a famous dish in the plateau, especially in Madrid. Both red and white wines are produced in Rioja.

Valencia and Murcia are the provinces where rice dominates. This is the home of *Paella*, a rice, chicken and seafood dish named after the special shallow pan, a *paellera*, in which it is cooked, and for *Arroz con pollo*, Chicken with Rice, a much simpler form of the dish which is popular throughout Latin America. Peppers, saffron and tomatoes are key ingredients here with seafood and rice and, or course, the superb olive oil to be found everywhere in the peninsula.

Spanish cooking, like Portuguese is essentially family food. It is robust or light according to climate, there are no very difficult techniques to master and all the ingredients are easy to obtain. There are sensible substitutes for seafood with few exceptions. Freshness is greatly appreciated and cooks always prefer fresh local ingredients where possible, which keeps regional cooking alive, as even modern transportation cannot compete with the fish, shellfish, fruit or vegetable harvested on the spot. Basque cooks, both men and women, are noted for the excellence of the cooking and exemplify the attitude of the whole peninsula to the business of eating. Food is prepared with loving care, eaten without hurry, and accompanied by good wine, and above all, greatly enjoyed, so that the simplest of meals has all the ingredients of a feast.

Although it cannot be possible to encapsulate the whole of the cooking of the Peninsula in a single book, I hope I have succeeded in conveying the truth of the complex variety of dishes that make up these two delightful cuisines: never bland, never dull, never boring, and worth pursuing for the many good things waiting to be discovered. I hope that readers will enjoy cooking and eating these dishes, and wish them *buen provecho; bom proveito.*

Elisabeth Lambert Ortiz

Hams and Sausages

Pork curing and sausage making are highly developed arts in both Spain and Portugal, which is not surprising given the popularity of the pig in the kitchen. Most of them are not available outside the peninsula, but some are, and there are also some adequate substitutes. Some regional sausages are only available close to the villages where they are made, while others are universally used.

Local smoked bacon can be subsituted for Spanish *tocino* or Portuguese *toucinho*. Slab bacon, that is unsliced bacon, is often used in Spanish cooking and is available in supermarkets and butcher's shops, though it may have to be specially ordered. If it is not available, sliced bacon will do.

The most popular Spanish ham is *jamón serrano*, a cured ham best substituted by Italian *proscuitto*. Portugal's favourite, *presunto*, is a smoked ham, richly flavoured and quite dark in colour. It can best be substituted by Parma, Bayonne or Westphalian hams. Both hams are widely used in cooking but are also eaten thinly sliced with melon or fresh figs. The best *presunto* is said to come from the Lamego and Chaves regions of Tras-os-Montes in the north or Portugal.

In spite of the wealth of sausages made in the Peninsula, the cook outside the two countries can manage quite well on a limited number of them. *Chorizo* in Spanish and *chouriço* in Portuguese, very similar to each other, are the most popular of all. They can be eaten as an appetizer, sliced and cold, or fried, or cooked in a large number of dishes. Very garlicky and richly red from paprika, the sausage has achieved almost universal popularity and can be bought in many supermarkets and grocers as well as in speciality shops.

Next in popularity are *longaniza* and *linguiça*, again similar to each other. *Longaniza* is a long, thin, meaty pork sausage flavoured with rosemary and paprika; and *linguiça*, also long and thin, is flavoured with garlic and paprika. Both are used in cooking. Kielbasa (Polish boiling ring) a highly seasoned garlicky pork sausage is a reasonable substitute. *Morcilla* and *morcela* are very similar and are very like black pudding (blood sausage) which makes a good substitute. It is used in stews and with vegetables in Portugal, and when fried is a favourite accompaniment to eggs in Spain, where it is also used in cooking.

Paio and *salpicão*, both Portuguese, are thick smoked sausages made with large pieces of pork loin and seasonings. They are quite similar to *chouriço* though meatier.

Oils

Olive oils, in Spanish *Aceite de Oliva* and in Portuguese *Azeite de Azeitunas*, are richly aromatic and fruity with a beautiful golden-green colour. They are also very healthy oils. These are the cold pressed extra virgin oils. They may be too strongly flavoured for some tastes and there are lighter olive oils available in this case. Some cooks mix olive oil with peanut or corn oil to get an even lighter result but this inevitably removes much of the special flavour the oil gives to dishes. If Spanish or Portuguese olive oil is not available, use a fruity Greek or Italian oil.

Though the olive oils of the peninsula are similar, Portuguese oil is even more robust than Spanish, possibly because the olives are left to mature for a few days after harvesting before they are pressed. For those who relish a very full-flavoured oil, Portuguese oil is worth searching for. It adds an extra dimension to the dishes in which it is used.

The Cheeses of Spain and Portugal

Portugal produces a number of fine cheeses, mostly sheep or goat's milk cheeses, though there are good cow's milk cheeses as well. It would not be practical to list them all since many are made in local farming communities and are eaten in their own region. It is a pity that more of them are not available outside Portugal, especially the very fine *Queijo da Serra*.

There are innumerable fresh cheeses, *queijos frescos*, either sheep or goat's milk cheeses made into little cakes about 9cm-3½ inches in diameter. When mature they are firm with a strong flavour, when fresh they are soft and spreadable. Among these are *Tomar*, small nutty little sheep's milk cheeses from Tomar, about 75 miles north of Lisbon, *Rabacal*, made from a mixture of sheep's and goat's milk, sold both fresh and mature, and *Requeijão*, a sheep's milk cheese that is sold in small straw baskets lined with fig or cabbage leaves. Like some of the fresh cheeses in France, it is eaten as a dessert, usually sprinkled with sugar and cinnamon. The fresh cheeses are all good with bread or biscuits and fruit as a cheese course, or at any time as a snack.

Among the larger cheeses the most notable is *Queijo da Serra* from the Beira region of northeastern Portugal, made from the milk of long-horned sheep which graze in mountain meadows full of wild herbs, giving an exquisite flavour to the cheese, which is soft and buttery when young though still creamy when mature. Another of the notable cheeses is *Beja*, from the Alentejo, a semi-hard sheep's milk cheese weighing about 2.3 kg/5 pounds, which is matured for one or two years. *Serpa* is another Alentejo semi-hard sheep's milk cheese that is aged in caves and brushed with olive oil and paprika which gives the rind an orange colour. Its flavour is nutty. Like most Portuguese cheeses it is seasonal, made during the winter and spring. If eaten before it has matured the texture is buttery. *Evora*, another Alentejo sheep's milk cheese, is eaten both fresh and mature and is considered to be one of the best cheeses of the Alentejo, even rivalling *Queijo da Serra*, considered by most cheese lovers to be the finest in Portugal. These cheeses are excellent with a glass of wine as an appetizer, or as the cheese course of meal, with or without fruit. Cheese with *marmelada* (quince paste) is a popular dessert. This is equally popular in Mexico and South America where guava paste is also a favourite.

There is also *Queijo da Ilha,* a cow's milk cheese from the Azores that closely resembles Parmesan and can be used as grating cheese.

Every region of Spain has its special cheeses whether of sheep's, goat's or cow's milk, fresh or mature. Unfortunately they are not as well-known or as available outside Spain as could be wished, which is a pity as many are very good indeed. Possibly the best known cheese, available all over Spain is *Queso Manchego* from the La Mancha region of Castille. It is sold as a hard, sharp cheese, or mild and semi-soft according to how long it has matured. It makes a good appetizer with sliced *chorizo* sausage, or with ham. This is one of the Spanish cheeses that are exported. *Queso de Idiazábal* is an unusual cheese of smoked sheep's milk from the Basque country. It is sold as a fresh cheese and as a more mature cheese, both forms with a smoky taste.

From the Asturias comes the famous *Queso de Cabrales* made from a mixture of sheep's, goat's and cow's milk in farm kitchens, pressed into round shapes and salted and dried briefly, then stored in limestone caves to mature for two to three months, where it acquires a blue mould and a flavour not unlike Roquefort. Much of it is eaten locally, accompanied by red wine, the rest is wrapped in the leaves of a local tree and shipped to speciality shops all over Spain. *Queso de Roncal,* from the Pyrenees, is made from a mixture of sheep and cow's milk. A hard cheese, not unlike Parmesan, it is made into large cylinders weighing about 3.2kg/7 pounds.

Among the fresh cheeses is *Queso do Burgos* made with a mixture of cow, goat and sheep's milk near the city of Burgos in Old Castille. It is a great favourite, cut into thick slices, for dessert and may be served drizzled with honey and topped with walnuts. It is not unlike mozzarella.

For lovers of smoked cheese there is *Queso de San Simón* from Galicia. Made with cow's milk, it is pear-shaped and weighs about 1.4 kg/3 pounds. It is smoked during maturation.

The Wines of Spain and Portugal

Spanish wines are very old. It was in about 1100 BC that the Phoenecians, founding Gadir, now Cadiz, planted vines. Greeks, Carthaginians and Romans followed, planting more, though the barbarian invasions that followed the fall of Rome disrupted vine growing, destroyed vineyards and ended the production of wine. Fortunately the vine was stronger than the barbarians and persisted, so that today there is a great deal of very good wine produced in Spain.

Andalucía, where it all began, is notable for the production of sherry, a fortified wine, with grape brandy bringing up the alcoholic content. Sherry is a corruption of Jerez as the sherry vineyards lie around the town of Jerez-de-la-Frontera, south of Seville. The principal grape used is Palomino, one of the few wine grapes that are also good eating grapes.

There are four main types of sherry. The *Finos* which are pale and dry and *Manzanilla*, also pale and dry, are the best apperitif wines and should be drunk chilled. *Amontillado*, medium-dry, pale but slightly darker and slightly sweeter is still an acceptable aperitif wine, and *Oloroso* is an amber-coloured sweet dessert wine. There are also the sweeter sherries called cream sherry.

The same region produces brandy, and red and white table wines and in the nearby hill town of Montilla a sherry-like wine, *Montilla*. It may be dry, medium or sweet. The region also produces Málaga which may be sweet, semi-sweet, semi-dry or dry.

The Rioja regions in north-central Spain and the Penedés region of Catalonia are the two most important areas producing large quantities of top grade table wines, white, red and rosé. However, every region has its wines though these are not as readily available outside. The traveller will find them rewarding when visiting the country. There are the white wines of Valencia, more famous than its red wines, while the Valdepeñas region of Castille is famous for its light, fresh red wines made from a mixture of black and white grapes. The region also produces dry white wines and is known for its *anís* liqueur, sweet or dry, which is popular in Spain where it is drunk as it is, chilled, over ice or diluted into a long drink. It is also used in cooking.

There are also a number of good sparkling wines, mostly dry, from the Penedés regions which also produces some brandy.

The Asturias produces very dry strong (hard) cider that often replaces wine with meals and is used in cooking. A sparkling cider is often drunk instead of Spanish champagne.

Portugal produces good table wines, red, white and rosé, as well as the famous fortified wines, Port and Madeira. By Portuguese law, Port is defined as wine fortified by the addition of Portuguese grape brandy, and made from grapes grown in vineyards in the Upper Douro (Douro Alto) in the north of the country. It is shipped from Oporto the city in the mouth of the Douro river.

Porto Branco Seco, Dry White Port, makes a pleasing aperitif and should be served chilled. Ports lose colour the longer they are aged in wood which gives a good guide to Port types. Ruby Port is fairly sweet, Tawny Port, aged longer, is lighter in colour, drier and with a nutty flavour. However, for most cooking purposes these two are interchangeable.

Vintage Ports are very fine, often great wines to be drunk at the end of a meal with a good cheese of robust character, like Stilton, Roquefort or any cheese that is worthy of the wine.

Madeira comes from the tiny island of the same name. Like both sherry and Port there are a number of different types. The driest and best for drinking as an aperitif is *Sercial*, or Rainwater Madeira, a light Sercial. There is the semi-dry *Verdelho*, a sweeter wine, *Boal*, and the fine dessert Madeira, called Malmsey since it is made from the Malvoisie grape. It is a lovely wine, rich and generous with a fine bouquet. The Victorians, who greatly enjoyed good wine, would entertain mid-morning callers with a glass of Madeira and a slice of cake.

Among the most popular Portuguese table wines are the *Vinho Verdes*, literally green wines, from the north-west of Portugal. There are red and white *vinhos verdes*, light, sprightly wines that are a little *pétillant*. The white wine is particularly good with fish and shellfish. In addition to Port, the Douro produces some pleasant red wines and both whites and rosés. Sparkling wines of good quality are also produced. South of the Douro river is the Dão wine country producing red and white wines of excellent quality. Further south are the wines of Bairrada, in what is often called suckling pig country around the university town of Coimbra. A good robust fruity red *Bairrada* is excellent with roast suckling pig, or with game, or beef, or with the cheese course of a meal. The whites are spicy, and good with fish and shellfish. Some red and white wines of quality are produced in Colares near Lisbon, and there is an interesting white from Bucelas, also near Lisbon. The Algarve wines, red and white, make pleasant drinking when in the region. Portugal also produces a large quantity of rosé wine, the best known of which is probably *Mateus*.

Setúbal, south of Lisbon, produces *Moscatel de Setúbal*. A sweet wine, and good with dessert, it makes a pleasing aperitif if served well chilled. Liqueurs include *Amendoa Amarga*, made from bitter almonds, and a Madeira liqueur, *maracuja*, made from passion fruit.

My husband says that his grandfather taught him this Spanish rhyme, and it charmingly epitomizes the Iberian love of good wine.

Bueno es el vino	Good is the wine
Cuando el vino es bueno.	When the wine is good.
Bella es la copa	Beautiful is the glass
Cuando la copa es bella.	When the glass is beautiful.
Pero es más bella la copa	But the glass is more beautiful
Con buen vino,	With good wine,
Y es mas bueno el vino	And the wine is better
En bella copa.	In a beautiful glass.

Festivals in Spain and Portugal

I would like to close this Introduction to the food of Spain and Portugal with a glimpse of the enchanting and exciting festivals, characteristic of the Peninsular, in which food is so vital a part of the celebrations. There are innumerable festivals (*fiestas, festas*) in Spain and Portugal, small, medium and large, in cities, towns and villages. They are basically religious, centred on the Holy Family and the Saints. The range is enormous, from small village affairs honouring the patron saint, to grand affairs attracting visitors from all over the Christian world, like Holy Week and the Feria in Seville, or the celebration for St. Anthony, patron saint of Portugal's capital, Lisbon, on June 12, when the saint is celebrated by everyone eating grilled fresh sardines.

Festivals are marked by processions of costumed men and women carrying images of Christ and especially the Virgin, or the saints or relics, there is dancing and music, street decorations, elaborately lit at night, fireworks and special food as well as wine, for a wine-less festival would be no festival at all.

They are joyful noisy affairs and a great excuse for dressing up. There is a serious side to them apart from the purely religious aspect. There are, of course, the Brotherhoods whose members organize the processions and, with the aid of devout ladies look after the images, whose clothes wear out just as ours do, though perhaps not so fast. Some celebrate the harvest, such as the October saffron festival in Consuegra, New Castille where annually a Queen Dulcinea is chosen and crowned, her attendant men in colourful costumes with elaborate flower head-dresses. The chosen Queen then presides over a saffron-separating contest with busy fingers plucking out the orange stamens from the purple crocuses, the fastest being the winner. Some festivals go on for a week, though most are just for a day, a holiday from work. Celebrations in towns may be a little more formal, but in villages there is much singing, dancing and feasting. St. John's Eve (June 23) in Porto is quite a giddy affair with people dancing through the streets until all hours, hitting each other with leeks. There are popular festivals like the end of the academic year in mid-May in Coimbra, the university town in the province of Beira and once Portugal's capital.

Naturally enough there are many festivals celebrating the liberation of Spain from the Moors, such as the Moors and Christians festivals centred around St. George. It is a very popular festival with 32 towns and villages celebrating in the area between the cities of Valencia and Alicante alone. The festival at Alcoy on St. George's Day, April 23, is the most lavish and elaborate. St. George was the Crusader's saint believed to appear in the thick of battle on a white horse when most needed. He apparently helped mightily during the siege of Alcoy in 1276 when the Moors were routed and their leader, Al Azraq, killed. St. James, also on a white horse, would appear in battles against the Moors and he ultimately replaced St. George and become the patron saint of Spain. St. George returned to England supplanting Edward the Confessor to become the patron saint of that country. The mock battles between Moors and Christians in England became transformed, it is believed, into the Morris Men and the Moors and Turks of Mummer's plays. In the kitchen the concept also turns up, after the discovery of the Americas, in the dish *Moros y Cristianos*, credited to Cuba. In this dish, black beans, native to Mexico, are cooked and served with white rice. The dish is popular both in Spain and Latin America. Fiestas like this one are a mix of the religious and the secular. There is mass and a procession with a symbolic re-enactment of the event being celebrated. Keys of castles or fortresses or whatever else is appropriate are handed over in surrender, the participants in lavish costumes. In this case the Moors are in exotic fancy dress portraying the full panoply of the Orient at its most extravagant. Despite the warlike trappings this is an amusing and very lively festival. Quite often the festival runs to three days with the second day devoted to children, and holy images or relics are returned to their special places, and in the evening there are fireworks, inseparable from festivals. The third day is the day for battles and a colourful end to the fiesta. Not all the Moors and Christians festivals are as lavish or long as the one in Alcoy, but they are all spirited affairs and much eating, drinking and merrymaking goes on.

It would be impossible to list all the festivals of the peninsula in less than a book, and some may come as a rewarding surprise. Visitors report their delight at coming upon fiestas of quite a serious nature where fishermen give thanks to their patron Lady and pray for good luck throughout the coming year. There is one at the village of Culera in Andalucia paying homage to *la Virgen del Castillo*, a small image of Our Lady housed in a church on a hill overlooking the sea. Rice and squid cooked with onions and tomatoes is the sort of dish served for dinner while an *anís* flavoured sweet pastry is served with coffee for breakfast to wind up the solemn event. Fishermen clearly take no chances with the fickle and dangerous sea.

Another festival, serious in intent, is a harvest celebration in Tomar, a small town north of Lisbon in Portugal. Young girls, accompanied by father, brother or fiancé, walk in procession through the town with elaborate handmade crowns of bread with wheat ears and paper flowers as decorations. The crowns are as tall as the wearer and heavy, so that a male relative or fiancé is useful if the wind is frisky and tries to topple a crown. The girls do not walk in silence. There are bands and pipers, drummers, soldiers, standard bearers, oxen with gilded horns, and best of all, wine carts whose young drivers give the girls an occasional, and welcome, glass of wine to keep up their strength. Carrying about 30 pounds of bread on one's head makes considerable demands. After a ceremony choosing the most beautiful *tabuleiros* as the bread crowns are called, though the word literally means tray, the oxen are slaughtered and there is a ceremony in front of the church of St. John the Baptist, an ornate 15th-century building, to bless the bread, meat and wine. The following day the poor of the town are given gifts of food and then the solemn part is over and there are bullfights, the Portuguese type where the bull is allowed to survive, donkey cart races, dancing, eating, drinking and fireworks. The modern ceremony has its roots in a very old Roman ceremony giving thanks to Ceres for a good harvest.

Christmas in Spain and Portugal is the most important family festival of the year with a number of differing customs to mark the occasion. Epiphany, January 6, King's Day, when the Three Kings brought their gifts to the Christ Child is celebrated with gift giving to the children and a special sweet bread, *Rosca de Reyes* (Spain) and *Bolo Rei* (Portugal), (recipe page 255). It marks the end of the Christmas season.

Christmas Eve supper after midnight mass is always a grand affair. In Portugal the supper would probably include a salt codfish dish with potatoes, cabbage and hardboiled eggs, Octopus with Rice (recipe page 216), and a selection of cakes and desserts which will certainly include the great favourite, rice pudding, *Arroz Doce* (recipe page 274), dried fruits, nuts, wine and mulled port if the weather is cold, as it will be in the north. Christmas lunch will make use of leftovers, and start with the popular light chicken soup *Canja* (recipe page 48), there will be roast turkey or chicken, and uneaten desserts and cakes from the night before, or rather the early morning of Christmas day.

In Spain the Christmas Eve supper after midnight mass is also an elaborate affair with soup, fish, roast turkey or chicken, fruits, cheeses and *turrón*, an almond and honey nougat of Arab origin, most of it made in factories in Jijona near Alicante. It is eaten in large quantities, especially during the Christmas season.

1

Hors D'Oeuvres and Appetizers
Tapas/Acepipes

The custom of gathering before lunch or dinner for drinks and hors d'oeuvres reaches special heights in Spain with the endlessly imaginative *tapas*. These delicious appetizers may be produced simply at home or in *tapas* bars where the array of small dishes delights both eye and palate. They can be so delectable that an assortment of them usurps a meal and they become a light lunch or supper. They are a delightful way of entertaining friends, especially if the selection incudes some quite robust dishes to satisfy the appetite.

In Portugal there are always some nibbles served with drinks and often, in restaurants, the hors d'oeuvres are so rich and varied that there is a strong temptation to go no further than the hors d'oeuvres trolley.

These appetizers can be simple or complex, light or filling. They can be made in single servings or in larger quantities, whichever is more convenient. The category into which they fit is loosely defined so that many do double duty as salads, or first courses, and will be found in a number of different sections in cookbooks. Although they are flexible, they are bound to some extent by tradition, and it would be unthinkable to omit certain dishes from a party table. They could be called the friends of good conversation which they stimulate and never impede. There are no rules as to the order in which they should be eaten, and no rules as to which drinks to serve with them. Sherry, dry port, wine or beer are all suitable.

Most can be made quickly and easily. A great many can be served at room temperature and made ahead of time. Others can be partly prepared and finished at the last minute. There is an almost endless variety to choose from.

In Portugal small dishes of thinly sliced potatoes, fried in olive oil and lightly salted, are served in small bowls. They are infinitely superior to the usual potato crisps (potato chips), partly because of the nutty flavour of Portuguese potatoes and partly because of the excellence of Portuguese olive oil. Salt codfish cakes, stuffed eggs, black-eyed pea salad, fried almonds, tinned (canned) sardines, sardine butter to spread on crackers, cold meats and sausages, and dishes of black and green olives can all be served with pre-meal drinks.

Spanish potato omelette, cut into bite-size pieces, is almost obligatory for *tapas*, and so are nuts and olives. Salads, including the ubiquitous

Russian salad, canapés of sardine, tuna or chicken, cod fritters, garlic prawns (shrimp), clams and mussels may all be met with at the *tapas* bar or table.

Huevos Rellenos/Ovos Recheados
Stuffed Eggs

Stuffed eggs, popular the world over, are equally esteemed in Spain and Portugal. A favourite Spanish stuffed egg is made of the mashed yolks, cooked flaked salmon, a little tomato sauce, mayonnaise, salt, freshly ground pepper or a dash of cayenne, and finely chopped parsley.

In Portugal the yolks may be mashed with a little mayonnaise, mashed sardines or tuna, piled back into the whites and topped with a little chopped parsley, and a slice of black olive. Other garnishes are anchovy fillets, or strips of sweet red (bell) pepper.

Almendras Glaseadas
Glazed Almonds

Nuts are a favourite nibble with drinks and require little effort. Pine nuts and hazelnuts can be prepared in exactly the same way as almonds and set out in small dishes.

blanched almonds
olive oil

Spread the whole peeled almonds, or other nuts, out on a baking sheet. put into a preheated, moderate oven (180°/350f/gas 4) and toast until light brown, about 10–15 minutes. Take out and, when cool enough to handle, rub the nuts between the palms of the hands previously moistened with olive oil. Serve immediately or store in a tightly closed jar for a few days. They are best not kept for long.

Variation:Amèndoas Fritas (Fried Almonds) are a popular nibble in Portugal. Use peeled blanched almonds and sauté them in a heavy frying pan (skillet) with enough olive oil to cover the bottom of the pan. Do not have the oil too hot and take care not to burn the almonds. Sauté until lightly browned, then lift out and drain on paper towels, Sprinkle lightly with salt and pile into small bowls to serve.

Manteiga de Sardinha
Sardine Butter

To make sardine butter, a Portuguese favourite, drain tinned (canned) sardines, either in oil or tomato sauce, and mash with an equal amount of unsalted butter until smooth. Season with salt, freshly ground black pepper and a little lemon juice. Pack into small ramekins (crocks) and chill until ready to serve. Serve with bread or toast, or crackers.

   Instead of sardines, butter may be mixed with very finely chopped garlic, or finely chopped parsley. Bread is often spread with these butters to accompany first-course salads.

Olivos/Oliveiras
Olives

In Portugal black olives are preferred to green, but both the Spanish and the Portuguese esteem olives for *tapas* and as garnishes in many other dishes. For the *tapas* table choose olives of many kinds, black, large green, stuffed with pimiento or anchovy and so on. If liked, olives may be marinated. Ideally they should be prepared some days in advance as the flavour develops with time.

For **marinated black olives**, combine the olives in a jar with 2 cloves crushed garlic for each 500 g/1 pound olives, 1 teaspoon paprika, ¼ teaspoon ground cumin, 125 ml/4 fl oz (½ cup) olive oil and 2 tablespoons red wine vinegar. Salt will not be needed as the olives are salty. Refrigerate and shake the jar from time to time. Serve at room temperature.

For **marinated green olives**, combine about 500 g/1 pound olives in a jar with 4 cloves crushed garlic, 40 ml/2 fl oz (¼ cup) olive oil, 2 tablespoons white wine vinegar and ¼ teaspoon oregano. Refrigerate and shake to mix from time to time. The olives can be used in hours but have more flavour if left for a longer time.

Canapés

These bite-size morsels of bread or toast, topped with a variety of spreads, are always popular. Imagination and ingenuity combine to make them both appetizing and attractive.

For **anchovy canapés**, combine 1 tin (can) anchovy fillets (50g/2 oz), drained and chopped with ½ sweet red (bell) pepper, peeled seeded and finely chopped with 2 tablespoons finely chopped onion, freshly ground black pepper and 1 tablespoon mayonnaise. Chill lightly, then spread on slices of toast or sandwich bread with crusts removed, cut into triangles.

For **sardine canapés**, mash tinned (canned) sardines and spread on toast or sandwich bread. Garnish with chopped black or green olives and chopped hardboiled egg.

For **chicken canapés**, chop cooked leftover chicken until it is almost a purée. Stir in some chopped pine nuts, season with salt and pepper and add enough mayonnaise to make a spreading consistency. Spread on toast or sandwich bread with crusts removed. Garnish with chopped sweet red (bell) pepper and cut into triangles.

For **tuna canapés**, mash tinned (canned) drained tuna with finely chopped onion, chopped parsley, salt, freshly ground pepper, chopped sweet red (bell) pepper and enough mayonnaise to make a spreading consistency. Spread on toast or sandwich bread with crusts removed. Cut into triangles and garnish with a slice of hardboiled egg.

Fritos
Fried Things

Shellfish are the most popular ingredient for these little bites, served hot or warm. Cooked prawns (shrimp), clams, mussels, cockles, and scallops (raw) are rolled in plain flour, dipped in egg and fried in olive oil. Pour enough oil into a frying pan (skillet) to reach a depth of 5 cm/2 inches, just deep enough to cover the shellfish, and fry just until golden. Take care not to overcook the scallops. Serve on cocktail sticks (toothpicks).

Pinchos
Grilled (Broiled) Things

Chicken livers, sliced Spanish-type sausage, cubes of ham, button mushrooms, pieces of red or green sweet (bell) pepper, pieces of onion, small cooked artichoke hearts, lean pork or lamb, cut into 2 cm/¾ inch cubes and marinated overnight in olive oil with herbs such as thyme, cumin, and bay leaf, are threaded on small skewers, about 10 cm/4 inches long, alternating meat with vegetables, or simply using meat or chicken livers, or mushrooms, if preferred. Brush the foods with olive oil and grill (broil) or cook over charcoal, until browned, basting with the marinade from time to time.

Buñuelitos
Small Fritters

These little fritters can be made with a variety of fillings and are best made small enough to be eaten in a single mouthful, and served warm, rather than hot. The most popular fritter is made with salt codfish. The batter can, of course, be prepared ahead of time.

For the batter
125 g/4 oz (½ cup) plain (all-purpose) flour
½ teaspoon baking powder
¼ teaspoon salt
1 large egg, lightly beaten
water

Sift the flour, baking powder and salt into a bowl. Make a well in the centre and lightly mix in the egg. Add enough water, about 125 ml/4 fl oz (½ cup), to make a batter about the consistency of thin white sauce. Do not make it watery.

For *Buñuelitos de Bacalao* (Salt Cod Fritters), skin and bone 250 g/8 ounces dried salt cod. Soak in the usual way (page 66). Shred the cod finely with the fingers and add to the batter with 2 tablespoons chopped parsley, 2 cloves crushed garlic and freshly ground pepper to taste. Heat enough olive oil in a frying pan (skillet) to cover the bottom to a depth of 1 cm/ ½ inch). Drop the cod mixture by teaspoonfuls into the oil and fry until browned, turning once, about 8–10 minutes. Drain on paper towels and serve warm.

For *Buñuelitos de Jamon* (Ham Fritters) and *Buñuelitos de Pollo* (Chicken Fritters), heat 2 tablespoons olive oil in a small frying pan (skillet) and sauté 1 medium onion, finely chopped, until it is soft. Let it cool and mix with 250 g/8 oz (1 cup) chopped cured ham, (for ham fritters) or 250 g/8 oz (1 cup) chopped cooked chicken (for chicken fritters) and cook as for Cod Fritters.

There is really no limit to the fillings an imaginative cook can add to this simple batter, creating delicious mouthfuls.

Variation: *Pasteis de Bacalhau* (Codfish Cakes), sometimes called *Bolinhos de Bacalhau* (Codfish Balls), are even more popular than the fritters. Prepare 250 g/8 ounces dried salt codfish in the usual way (page 66) and simmer in water to cover for 15 minutes, or until tender. While the fish is cooking boil 300 g/10 ounces (about 2 medium) potatoes, in their skins, in cold water to cover. When the cod is tender drain it and make sure there are no bones or skin. Shred it with the fingers. Drain and peel the potatoes. Mash them and mix with the cod. Sauté 1 small onion, finely chopped, in 1 tablespoon olive oil. Cool and add to the cod mixture with 2 eggs, lightly beaten, 2 tablespoons finely chopped parsley, salt, if necessary, and freshly ground pepper. Shape the mixture with 2 tablespoons or roll into 2.5–5 cm/1–2 inch balls and fry in hot oil, about 5 cm/2 inches deep, in a frying pan (skillet), or cook in a deep-fat fryer at 190°C/375°F.

Variation: Spanish *Buñuelos de Bacalao* (Codfish Cakes) are very similar to the Portuguese ones. Cook the codfish and potatoes and mix as in the previous variation. Add 2 cloves garlic, crushed, 1 tablespoon chopped parsley, salt, if necessary, freshly ground pepper and 2 large egg yolks. Mix thoroughly and drop into hot oil by the heaped teaspoon until brown all over. Serve with a Tomato Sauce (page 244) or *Allioli* (Garlic Mayonnaise) (page 239).

Buñuelos de Bacalao
Salt Cod Fritters

Salt cod fritters as puffs, croquettes or balls, with slight variations in the seasoning, turn up in the United States, Britain and all over the Caribbean and Latin America, as well as in Spain and Portugal. They are a perennial favourite as a nibble with drinks.

MAKES ABOUT 30
250 g/8 ounces dried salt cod
375 g/12 ounces (about 2 medium) potatoes
1 clove garlic, crushed
1 tablespoon chopped parsley
salt and freshly ground pepper
2 eggs, lightly beaten
oil for frying

Soak the cod overnight in cold water to cover, changing the water several times. Drain and put on to cook in a saucepan with cold water to cover. Cover and simmer until the fish is tender, about 30 minutes. Drain, skin and remove any bones. Shred with the fingers as finely as possible. Set aside in a bowl.

While the cod is cooking, boil the potatoes in their skins until tender. When cool enough to handle, peel and put through a sieve into the bowl with the cod. Add the garlic, parsley, salt, if necessary, and pepper, mixing well. Add the eggs and mix until smooth.

Pour enough oil into a frying pan (skillet) to reach a depth of 5 cm/2 inches. Heat the oil and drop the cod fish mixture in by teaspoonfuls and sauté until lightly browned all over. Serve plain, warm, or with an *Allioli* dip or with Tomato Sauce.

Variation: *Bolinchos de Bacalhau* (Codfish Balls) soak and cook the cod and the potatoes as in the previous recipe and combine them in a bowl. In a small frying pan (skillet) heat 3 tablespoons olive oil and sauté 1 medium onion, finely chopped, until it is soft. Add 1 large clove garlic, chopped, and 2 tablespoons chopped parsley and sauté for 2 minutes longer. Season with salt and freshly ground pepper and ⅛ teaspoon cayenne, and add to the cod and potatoes together with 2 medium egg yolks, mixing well. Beat 2 medium egg whites until they stand in peaks and fold into the fish mixture. Pour enough vegetable oil into a frying pan (skillet) to reach a depth of 5 cm/2 inches. Heat the oil, drop the cod fish mixture in by teaspoonfuls and sauté until lightly browned all over. Drain on paper towels and serve warm, at room temperature.

Gambas al Ajillo
Garlic Shrimp

These garlicky prawns (shrimp) can be served in small, individual casseroles as *tapas* or as a first course. They can also be made in a large shallow casserole and served as a first course at the table. They are also good for a buffet with guests serving themselves.

SERVES 6
4 tablespoons olive oil
4 large cloves garlic, chopped
500 g/1 pound small/medium prawns (shrimp), shelled, thoroughly
defrosted if frozen
2 tablespoons lemon juice
2 tablespoons dry sherry
1 teaspoon paprika
1 small hot dried red chilli pepper, seeded and chopped
salt and freshly ground pepper
1 tablespoon chopped parsley

Heat the oil in a large, shallow, flameproof casserole, preferably earthenware, and sauté the garlic for 2 minutes. Add the prawns (shrimp) and
sauté for 1 minute longer. If using cooked frozen prawns (shrimp) do not
add them at this point. Add the lemon juice, sherry, paprika, chilli pepper
and salt and pepper to taste. Add the cooked frozen prawns (shrimp),
defrosted and cook just long enough to heat through, about 1 minute.
Sprinkle with parsley and serve.

Variation: For *Gambas en Allioli* (Prawns with Garlic Mayonnaise), mix
the cooked prawns (shrimps) with 250 ml/8 fl oz (1 cup) *Allioli* (Garlic
Mayonnaise) mound in a dish and sprinkle with chopped parsley.

Camarones en Salsa Mahonesa
Shrimps with Mayonnaise

Mayonnaise spiked with brandy as in this recipe is known in Columbia
and Chile as Salsa Golf, though why I could never discover. The Spaniards
claim that *Salsa Mahonesa* (Mayonnaise) was the creation of some culinary
genius in Mahón, capital of the Balearic island of Menorca. The shrimp
used are tiny though the larger ones, known in Britain as prawns, could
be used. This makes an excellent first course and is also good served with
other *tapas*.

SERVES 4
375 g/12 oz (2 cups) small shrimps
lettuce leaves
175 g/6 oz (¾ cup) Mayonnaise (page 238)
1 tablespoon tomato purée
2 teaspoons brandy, preferably Spanish

Pile the shrimps onto 4 small plates lined with lettuce leaves. In a bowl mix together the mayonnaise, tomato purée and brandy and pour over the shrimps. Chill in the refrigerator until ready to eat.

Variation: Mix together 125 g/4 oz (½ cup) each *Allioli* and Mayonnaise and pour over the shrimps.

Riñones a la Cántabra
Kidneys, Mountain-style

Cántabra, the small region to the north of Old Castille, has a great deal of character in its cooking. It is also influenced by the Basques, its near neighbours.

SERVES 4
4 lambs' kidneys, split open
2 rashers (slices) bacon, halved crossways
4 cherry tomatoes, or 2 small tomatoes, halved
2 chipolata sausages, halved
4 mushrooms, stems trimmed
olive oil
salt and freshly ground pepper

Thread the kidneys, bacon, tomatoes, sausages and mushrooms on to 4 small skewers. Brush with olive oil, season with salt and pepper and grill (broil) or cook over charcoal, for about 4 minutes on each side or until lightly browned but still juicy. Do not overcook.

Mejillones en Vinagreta
Marinated Mussels

500 g/1 pound cooked, shelled mussels
8 tablespoons olive oil
2 tablespoons red wine vinegar
2 teaspoons capers, chopped if large
2 tablespoons finely chopped onion
salt and freshly ground pepper
2 tablespoons chopped parsley
1 teaspoon paprika
dash of cayenne

Mix all the ingredients together and refrigerate overnight or for about 4 hours. Bring to room temperature before serving. If liked, the mussels and some of the marinade may be spooned into cleaned mussel shells or the mussels may be served in small bowls. For a buffet they may be served in a large bowl for guests to help themselves.

Variation: Use cooked, chopped octopus, cooked sliced squid, prawns (shrimp), small clams, or cockles.

Pimientos Mixtos
Mixed Sweet (Bell) Peppers

Choose red, green, yellow and orange peppers, peeled, seeded and sliced. Arrange the peppers in a dish, drizzle lightly with olive oil and garnish with drained, tinned (canned) anchovy fillets. Sprinkle with chopped parsley.

Pimientos Fritos
Fried Sweet Green Peppers

These small, sweet green peppers come into the market in spring and summer. The best are said to come from Galicia. They make a delicious appetizer, fried and eaten with the fingers. The small, tapering light green sweet Italian pepper is the best substitute, but any small, sweet green pepper can be used.

SERVES 4–6
500 g/1 pound small sweet green peppers
5 tablespoons olive oil
salt

Rinse and dry the peppers, leaving the stems on. Heat the oil in a large frying pan (skillet) and sauté the peppers over moderate heat until they are lightly browned all over. Lift out of the pan, sprinkle lightly with salt, and pile into a dish. Eat with the fingers, holding by the stem.

2

Soups
Sopas

Soups in Spain and Portugal are immensely popular and a great many of them are hearty as well. A *Caldo Gallego*, Galicia's famous dried white bean soup, *Sopa de Lentejas*, Spanish brown lentil soup, *Caldo Verde*, Portugal's green soup made with shredded kale-like cabbage, and *Sopa de Pedra*, a soup full of root and green vegetables and red kidney beans could all make a fine light meal if accompanied by crusty bread and a green salad, with dessert to follow. In the Peninsula soups are served as part of a meal, a testimony to robust appetites as well as to the esteem in which soup is held. There are, of course, ligher soups like *Canja*, Portugal's favourite chicken soup made with fresh mint and lemon, and the hot weather *Gazpacho*.

Gazpacho

This is a very ancient soup and, without any concrete proof, I believe it originated during the bitter centuries of struggle between the Spanish people and their Moorish conquerors. The *guerrillas* carrying, apart from their weapons, only wooden bowls and wine skins, would call at farmhouses and be given oil, vinegar, onion, garlic, water, bread and probably cucumber, out of which they made a soup. The soup flowered into something much more attractive after the *reconquista* when the Spanish, having become conquerors themselves, returned from Mexico bringing tomatoes and peppers, both of which originated in the Valley of Mexico but were unknown outside the Americas. In Andalucía, the most Moorish and most torrid province of Spain, *Gazpacho* reaches its peak, containing tomatoes, sweet green (bell) peppers, garlic, oil, vinegar, iced water and bread. It is known the world over as one of the most popular of all hot weather soups.

Gazpacho comes in so many forms that it could make a chapter on its own. There is the Malaga version, *Ajo Blanco con Uvas*, with almonds and peeled white grapes; *Gaspachuela*, also from Andalucía, is really a fish soup eaten at room temperature. It is made with mayonnaise. There is even a hot *Gazpacho* from Andalucía, almost a contradiction in terms, but useful if the weather unexpectedly turns chilly. Probably every region has its own version and it has spread to Portugal where there is a *Gazpacho* Alentejo-style as well as one from the Algarve.

The differences between one *Gazpacho* and another are usually not very great, and this gives cooks an opportunity to express creative individuality, adjusting quantities of bread, oil and other ingredients to suit personal taste.

Gazpacho Andaluz
Gazpacho, Andalucian-style

This is the classic *Gazpacho*, delicious on a hot summer day, especially for lunch. In the past this soup was laboriously made with a mortar and pestle, and there are traditionalists who still do it that way. However, a blender or food processor takes all the hard work out of it without spoiling the flavour.

SERVES 4
750 g/1½ pounds (about 6 medium) tomatoes, coarsely chopped
2 medium sweet green (bell) peppers, seeded and coarsely chopped
1 small onion, chopped
1 clove garlic, chopped
3 slices firm, day-old bread, crusts removed, soaked in water and
squeezed out
1 small cucumber, or ½ hot-house cucumber, peeled and coarsely
chopped
6 tablespoons olive oil
2 tablespoons white wine vinegar
salt
1 litre/1¾ pints (4 cups) iced water

For the garnish
2 slices firm bread, crusts removed, toasted and cubed
diced cucumber, green pepper, tomato and onion

In a food processor or blender combine all the ingredients except the garnish, and process until smooth. Do this in batches if necessary. Strain through a sieve, pressing down hard to extract all the liquid possible. Adjust the seasoning and chill.

To serve, pour the soup into bowls and pass the garnishes separately. If preferred, the bread may be sautéed in olive oil with crushed garlic, making garlic croûtons.

Ajo Blanco con Uvas
White Gazpacho with Grapes, Malaga-style

This is a very pretty *Gazpacho*, milky-white from the almonds instead of being the usual tomato red. The white grapes, which are really light green, make an attractive colour contrast as well as giving a slightly tart accent to the flavour. If seedless green grapes are not available, then use any white grapes, seeded.

SERVES 4

125 g/4 ounces (1 cup) blanched almonds, coarsely chopped
2 cloves garlic, chopped
4 slices firm day-old bread, crusts removed
6 tablespoons olive oil
2 tablespoons red wine vinegar
1 litre/1¾ pints (4 cups) iced water
salt
32 peeled, seedless white grapes

Combine the almonds and garlic in a food processor or blender and process until the almonds are very finely ground, almost paste-like. Meanwhile, soak the bread in cold water, and squeeze out. Add it to the food processor and process until smooth. With the motor running, pour in the oil in a thin stream, then add the vinegar, scraping down the sides of the bowl if necessary. Pour in the iced water, 50 ml/8 fl oz (1 cup) at a time. Season with salt.

Strain through a sieve, pressing down hard to extract as much liquid as possible. Chill thoroughly in the refrigerator. The soup should be very cold. Serve in soup bowls, each one garnished with 8 grapes.

Gazpachuelo
Fish Gazpacho

This *Gazpacho* is more closely related to the fish soups than to the classic *Gazpacho*. It is unusual and delicious.

SERVES 4

750 g/1½ pounds firm-fleshed white fish such as halibut or cod
700 ml/24 fl oz (3 cups) water
350 ml/12 fl oz (1½ cups) fish stock or clam juice
1 bay leaf
1 small onion, sliced
salt and freshly ground pepper
500 g/1pound potatoes, peeled and thinly sliced
350 ml/12 fl oz (1½ cups) Mayonnaise (page 238)
2 tablespoons lemon juice or white wine vinegar

In a saucepan or flameproof casserole combine the fish, water, fish stock, or clam juice, bay leaf, onion and salt and pepper to taste. Bring to a simmer and cook over low heat for 5 minutes. Transfer the fish to a bowl. Remove any skin and bones and cut into chunks. Pour over enough of the hot cooking liquid barely to cover the fish. Cover and keep warm.

Add the potato slices to the liquid remaining in the pan, cover and simmer until the potatoes are tender. Lift out the potatoes and add to the fish. Strain the cooking liquid, discarding the solids.

Have ready a warmed soup tureen. Add the mayonnaise, then beat in the lemon juice or vinegar. Reheat the strained broth and using a wire whisk gradually beat it into the mayonnaise. Add the fish and potatoes, mixing gently. Serve immediately in soup bowls.

Gazpacho Caliente Gaditano
Hot Gazpacho, Andalucia-style

As the word *Gaditano* indicates, this soup comes from Cadiz. It is really an unusual tomato soup made different by the addition of *pan moreno*, brown bread, preferably dark rye bread.

SERVES 4

500 g/1 pound (about 4 medium) tomatoes, peeled and chopped
6 cloves garlic, crushed
1 sweet green (bell) pepper, peeled, seeded and chopped (page 187)
4 tablespoons olive oil
salt and freshly ground pepper
1 teaspoon paprika
2 slices dark bread, preferably rye bread
1 litre/1¾ pints (4 cups) light chicken stock

In a food processor or blender combine the tomatoes, garlic, green pepper, oil, salt, pepper and paprika and process until smooth. Set aside.

Arrange the slices of bread in a large soup tureen. Heat the stock in a saucepan and pour some of it over the bread, mashing it until smooth. Put the tomato mixture into the pan with the remaining stock and heat through. Pour into the tureen and stir to mix.

Gaspacho Alentejano
Gaspacho, Alentejo-style

This is a Portuguese version of the Spanish *gazpacho*. It is a filling soup which might be classified as an *açorda* (dry soup) since it contains a large amount of bread.

SERVES 6
2 large cloves garlic, crushed
50 ml/2 fl oz (4 tablespoons) mild vinegar
50 ml/2 fl oz (4 tablespoons) olive oil
½ teaspoon oregano
salt and freshly ground pepper
500 g/1 pound (about 4 medium) tomatoes, peeled, seeded and finely chopped
½ hot-house cucumber, or 1 cucumber, peeled and diced
1 sweet green (bell) pepper, seeded and finely chopped
4 slices day-old firm white bread, Portuguese-type (see page 250), or French or Italian, crusts removed and cubed
700 ml–1 litre/24 fl oz–1¾ pints (3–4 cups) iced water

In a soup tureen combine the garlic, vinegar, oil, oregano, salt and a generous amount of black pepper. Mix thoroughly, beating with a whisk or fork. Add the tomatoes, cucumber, green pepper and bread. Stir to mix. Stir in the iced water and continue stirring until the soup is thick. Serve very cold.

Variation: For *Gaspacho do Algarve* Gazpacho, Algarve-style, use the same ingredients in the same amounts. Put the green pepper pieces into a food processor or blender with half the bread, the tomatoes, garlic and enough of the iced water to purée the mixture. Pour the mixture into a chilled soup tureen. Stir in the rest of the water, the oil, vinegar, oregano, salt and freshly ground pepper. Stir in the rest of the bread and garnish with the cucumber.

Sopa de Ajo al Huevo
Garlic Soup, Castilian-style

This is another very old traditional soup that may well have sustained the *guerrillas* fighting to liberate their country from the Arab invaders centuries ago. The simplest version is no more than bread, water, oil, garlic and salt. A more sophisticated version uses beef stock instead of water. Today's preferred version has beef stock, eggs and paprika. Other versions, and they are many, add a variety of ingredients, though the soup always remains an uncomplicated one, quickly made and very sustaining.

SERVES 4
4 tablespoons olive oil
4 large cloves garlic, peeled and left whole
4 thin slices French-style bread
1 tablespoon paprika
1 litre/1¾ pints (4 cups) beef stock
salt
4 large eggs

Heat the oil in a shallow, flameproof casserole, preferably earthenware. Add the garlic and cook over low heat until golden. Lift out and reserve. Add the bread slices and sauté until they are golden on both sides. Lift out and reserve.

Remove the casserole from the heat and stir in the paprika. Crush the garlic with a fork, mashing thoroughly. Add it to the casserole with the bread, broken up, and the stock. Season to taste with salt and pepper and cook slowly, covered, for 20 minutes.

Break an egg into each of 4 saucers and slide them, one by one, into the soup. Cover and cook just until the eggs are set, 3–4 minutes. The soup is often made in small individual earthenware dishes which make it easier to serve it without breaking the egg yolk.

A full bodied dry red wine is a fine accompaniment.

Variation: Make the soup in the same way but do not poach the eggs, instead break them into a bowl, season with salt and beat lightly, then pour over the soup. Sprinkle with 2 tablespoons breadcrumbs and drizzle with 1 tablespoon olive oil. Cook, uncovered, in a preheated, hot oven (230°C/450°F/gas 8) until a golden-brown crust is formed.

Variation: *Sopa à Alentejana* (Soup Alentejo-style) is the most popular form of garlic soup in the south of Portugal. Mash 4 cloves garlic with 1 teaspoon salt to a paste in a mortar. Mash in 4 tablespoons finely chopped fresh coriander, then slowly beat in 50 ml/2 fl oz (¼ cup) olive oil until the mixture is well blended. Halve 2 thick slices firm white bread, rub with a cut clove of garlic and fry in hot lard or olive oil until golden on both sides. Have ready 1 litre/1¾ pints (4 cups) boiling water, and 4 soup bowls. Divide the garlic–coriander mixture among the bowls. Add a slice of fried bread to each. Poach 4 large eggs and add one to each bowl. Pour on the boiling water and serve immediately.

Sopa de Tomate Alentejana
Tomato Soup, Alentejo-style

A light, delicate tomato soup this is not! It is hearty and robust as are many Portuguese soups, magnificent on a cold blustery day when food that is both filling and warming is needed. It is not possible to reproduce exactly the sausages that would be used in Portugal but adequate substitutes are available and given here.

SERVES 6
2 rashers (slices) bacon, chopped
250 g/8 ounces *morcella* sausage or (black pudding, blood sausage)
250 g/8 ounces any garlic-flavoured smoked pork sausage
1 large onion, halved and sliced
2 cloves garlic, chopped
1 bay leaf
900 g/2 pounds (about 8 medium) tomatoes, peeled, seeded and chopped
1 litre/1¾ pints (4 cups) water
salt and freshly ground pepper
6 fairly thick slices Portuguese-type bread, or any firm bread

In a large flameproof casserole or saucepan sauté the bacon until it has given up its fat. If necessary add a very little olive oil. Prick the sausages and add them. Sauté for a few minutes, then add the onion and garlic and sauté until the onion is soft. Add the bay leaf and tomatoes and stir to mix, then add the water and season with salt and pepper. Cover and simmer over low heat for 30 minutes.

Lift out the sausages and slice them. Put the bread into the bottom of a heated soup tureen. Return the sausages to the saucepan and simmer just long enough to heat them through, then pour the soup into the tureen.

If liked, put a slice of bread into the bottom of each of 6 soup bowls, divide the sausages among them and pour in the soup.

Caldo Verde à Minhota
Green Soup, Minho-style

Originally from the province of Minho, in the far north of Portugal, this hearty cold weather soup has become a general favourite to be enjoyed at all seasons. The green in the soup is *couve gallega* (Galician cabbage) which has large, deep green leaves and is more like kale than cabbage. The secret of success in making the soup lies in shredding the *couve* to almost grass-like fineness. Rolling up the leaves into a tube and then slicing them makes this quite easy. Each serving of soup is garnished with either sliced garlic sausage or *salpicão* (cured pork loin).

SERVES 4
4 tablespoons olive oil
1 medium onion, finely chopped
500 g/1 pound (about 3 medium) potatoes, peeled and thinly sliced
1.4 litres/2½ pints (6 cups) water
salt and freshly ground pepper
125 g/4 ounces *chouriço, chorizo* or other garlic-flavoured smoked pork sausage
250 g/8 ounces kale or collard greens

Heat 3 tablespoons of the oil in a large, heavy saucepan and sauté the onion until soft. Add the potatoes and sauté, stirring, for 3–4 minutes longer. Pour in the water, season with salt and pepper, bring to a simmer, cover and cook until the potatoes are very soft, about 20 minutes. Remove the pan from the heat and mash the potatoes into the soup.

Heat the remaining oil in a small frying pan (skillet) and sauté the sausage until lightly browned. Lift out and drain on paper towels, then add to the soup. Bring to a simmer and cook for 5 minutes longer.

Meanwhile, wash the kale or greens and cut away any coarse stems and veins. Stack the leaves, about 6 at a time, roll up and, using a very sharp knife, slice thinly. Add to the soup and cook, uncovered, for about 3 minutes, or until tender. Do not overcook. Serve in large soup bowls with good, chewy bread such as *Broa* (Corn Bread) and drink a crisp, light dry white wine.

Sopa de Pedra
Stone Soup

This quaintly named soup is another of the thick soups that characterize the Portuguese kitchen. Popular all over the country, the soup originated in Ribatejo province, famed for its horses, bulls and bullfighters, who, however do not kill the bull. Red kidney beans are the 'stones' of the soup.

SERVES 6
175 g/6 ounces (1 cup) dried red kidney beans
100 g/4 ounces smoked bacon in one piece
1 pig's ear
100 g/4 ounces *chouriço* or *chorizo* sausage or any smoked garlic-flavoured sausage
1 large onion, coarsely chopped
1 clove garlic, chopped
1 litre/1¾ pints (4 cups) chicken stock
1 bay leaf
Salt and freshly ground pepper
500 g/1 pound potatoes, peeled and diced
25 g/1 ounce (½ cup) chopped fresh coriander
2 small turnips, peeled and diced
2 medium carrots, scraped and diced
100 g/4 ounces cabbage, preferably Savoy, cored and thinly sliced

Soak the beans overnight in cold water to cover. Put the beans and the soaking water, adding a little more if necessary, into a large saucepan and bring to a simmer. Cook, covered, for about 40 minutes or until the beans are almost tender. Drain, discard the cooking water, and set aside. Rinse out and dry the saucepan.

Add the bacon to the saucepan and sauté until it has given off most of its fat, turning several times. If necessary add 1–2 tablespoons vegetable oil. Add the pig's ear, sausage, onion and garlic and sauté until the onion is soft, about 5 minutes. Add all the remaining ingredients, and simmer over low heat for 30 minutes. Lift out the bacon, sausage and pig's ear. Cut the bacon into dice, the pig's ear and sausage into slices. Return them to the soup, and simmer for 5 minutes longer. Discard the bay leaf. Serve the soup in big soup bowls accompanied by *Broa* (Portuguese Cornbread).

Caldo Gallego
Meat and Vegetable Soup

Hearty soups of meat and vegetables abound in Spain but *Caldo Gallego* is the one that has become world famous, a tribute to the good cooks of Galicia. The use of both ham and bacon in the soup has historic overtones. It is believed that converted Jews, after the *reconquista*, added pork wherever it was appropriate as proof of their fidelity to the Christian faith. I also suspect that the Spanish, after nearly eight centuries of non-pork-eating Islamic domination ate pork and bacon and pork sausages as a way of thumbing their noses at their erstwhile conquerors. These additions undoubtedly improve the flavour of this soup.

SERVES 6
3 litres/5 ½/pints (12 cups) water
250 g/8 ounces white haricot (navy or pea) beans
125 g/4 ounces lean smoked bacon or salt pork, in one piece
125 g/4 ounces cured ham, in one slice
1 ham bone
250 g/8 oz beef chuck
1 medium onion, thinly sliced
salt and freshly ground pepper
500 g/1 pound potatoes, peeled and quartered
4 small white turnips, peeled and halved
500 g/1 pound chopped green cabbage, kale, collard greens or Swiss chard, stems removed

In a large saucepan combine the water, beans, bacon or salt pork, ham, ham bone, beef and onion. Season with salt and pepper. Bring to a simmer over moderate heat and skim off any foam that rises. Cover and cook over very low heat for about 2 hours or until the beans are almost done. Add the potatoes, turnips and the chopped greens. Simmer until the potatoes and beans are both tender.

Lift out and discard the ham bone. Lift out the meats and cut each into small portions. Serve the soup in large soup bowls making sure that each bowl contains a little of everything. Drink a full-bodied dry red wine.

Sopa al Cuarto de Hora
Fifteen-minute Soup

Much Iberian food takes a long time to prepare and cook, so when a good dish comes along that only takes 15 minutes it is properly celebrated. The ingredients vary, but the soup is invariably good. This is one of many versions.

SERVES 6
4 tablespoons olive oil
½ medium onion, finely chopped
2 cloves garlic, chopped
4 thin or 2 thick slices day-old bread
50 g/2 ounces cured ham, diced
250 g/8 ounces (2 medium) tomatoes, peeled, seeded and finely chopped
700 ml/25 fl oz (3 cups) fish stock or clam juice
700 ml/25 fl oz (3 cups) water
salt and freshly ground pepper
½ teaspoon paprika
125 ml/4 fl oz (½ cup) dry sherry
24 clams or mussels in the shell, cleaned

For the garnish
1 hardboiled egg, chopped
2 tablespoons finely chopped parsley

Heat the oil in a casserole and sauté the onion until soft. Add the garlic, bread and ham and sauté for a few minutes longer. Add the tomatoes and sauté briefly, stirring. Stir in the stock or clam juice and the water and season to taste with salt and pepper. Add the paprika, sherry and clams or mussels.

Cook, covered, just until the clams or mussels open, about 5 minutes. The total cooking time should add up to 15 minutes. Garnish the soup with the chopped egg and parsley. Serve with crusty bread and drink a light dry white wine.

Variations: Use rice, about 3 tablespoons, instead of bread. Use about 500 g/1 pound fish, such as cod or haddock, filleted and cut into 2.5 cm/ 1 inch pieces. Add 250 g/8 ounces medium prawns (shrimps), peeled and halved, if liked. Vegetables such as green peas, about 175 g/6 ounces (1 cup), can also be added. This is a most flexible soup and depends largely on what the cook has in the kitchen.

Sopa de Lentejas Madrileña
Lentil Soup, New Castille-style

Lentil soup, which is highly nutritious, has been a family standby in Spain for ages. A big bowl of the hot soup is very welcome in cold weather, especially when accompanied by crusty bread.

SERVES 6
500 g/1 pound brown lentils
1.4 litres/2½ pints (6 cups) beef or chicken stock or water
1 sprig parsley
1 bay leaf
125 g/4 ounces smoked bacon, chopped
2 tablespoons olive oil
1 medium onion, finely chopped
1 medium or 2 small carrots, scraped and finely chopped
2 cloves garlic, chopped
250 g/8 oz (2 medium) tomatoes, peeled, seeded and chopped
1 tablespoon paprika
salt and freshly ground pepper

Wash and pick over the lentils and put them into a large saucepan with the stock or water, parsley, bay leaf and bacon. Bring to a simmer, cover and cook over very low heat.

Meanwhile, heat the oil in a frying pan (skillet) and sauté the onion until soft. Add the carrot, garlic and tomatoes and cook until the mixture is well blended. Off the heat stir in the paprika and season with salt and pepper. Add the mixture to the lentils and continue to cook until the lentils are soft, about 2 hours in all. Serve with a green salad and crusty bread and drink a full-bodied dry red wine.

Variation: For *Pure de Lentejas* (Lentil Purée) omit the bacon when cooking the lentils. When they are soft put them into a food processor or blender and reduce to a fairly smooth purée; they should retain some texture. Do this in batches and return the purée to the pan. Meanwhile, sauté the smoked bacon or salt pork, cut into cubes, in 1 tablespoon olive oil until crisp. Serve the soup garnished with the bacon or salt pork pieces and chopped parsley.

Canja
Chicken Soup with Mint and Lemon

This clear chicken soup, its delicate flavour sharpened by lemon juice and made fragrant with fresh mint, is popular all over Portugal. It may vary from place to place and cook to cook but fundamentally remains the same. Instead of rice, which is traditional, the soup may have small seed-like pasta.

SERVES 6

1.4–1.6 kg/3–3½ pound chicken
2 litre/3½ pints (8 cups) chicken stock or water
2 medium onions, finely chopped
1 teaspoon salt, or to taste
3 tablespoons short-grain rice
2 tablespoons lemon juice
6 tablespoons finely chopped fresh mint

Put the chicken into a heavy flameproof casserole into which it will fit comfortably. An oval casserole is best. Pour in the stock or water and add the onions and salt. Bring to a simmer, skim if necessary, cover and cook over very low heat so that the liquid barely moves for 30 minutes. Add the rice and cook for 30 minutes longer. Cool the chicken in the stock.

Lift out the chicken and remove the skin and bones. Cut the meat into strips about 5mm × 2.5 cm/¼ x 1 inch. Return the chicken to the casserole, stir in the lemon juice and reheat the soup. Put a tablespoon of mint into each of 6 soup bowls and pour the soup over them, distributing the chicken strips evenly. Serve with crusty bread. A crisp dry white wine is pleasant with this.

Sopa de Favas com Hortela
Broad Bean Soup with Mint

Tender young broad beans are used in this northern Portuguese soup, especially popular in the province of Trás-os-Montes. The beans are sliced, pods and all, cooked separately and added to the soup just before serving, or they may be cooked with the soup and puréed. If fresh young broad beans in the pod are not available, use shelled frozen beans and cook with the soup, then purée. Small lima beans are an acceptable substitute for broad beans. The mint garnish adds a refreshing flavour.

SERVES 6
2 tablespoons olive oil
1 large onion, chopped
1 clove garlic, chopped
2 medium potatoes, peeled and thinly sliced
500 g/1 pound broad beans or lima beans, preferably in the pod and thinly sliced, or frozen beans, defrosted
1 litre/½ pints (5 cups) chicken stock
salt and freshly ground pepper
3 tablespoons chopped fresh mint, to garnish.

Heat the oil in a saucepan and sauté the onion until soft. Add the garlic and sauté for 1 minute longer. Add the potatoes and continue to sauté for about 5 minutes longer, stirring from time to time. If young beans in the pod are not available, add the defrosted frozen beans and the stock, cover and simmer over low heat until the potatoes are tender, about 30 minutes. If using sliced beans in the pod, cook them in salted water for 15–20 minutes until tender, drain and set aside.

Strain the soup and purée the vegetables in a food processor or blender. Return the purée to the saucepan, stir to mix and heat through. If using beans in the pod, add them to the soup and cook for just long enough to heat them through. Serve the soup garnished with the chopped mint.

Sopa de Favas com Coentro
Broad Bean Soup with Coriander

Fresh coriander transforms this simple broad bean soup from Beira Baixa in Portugal into a subtle delight. It is easy to make. Frozen broad beans are an adequate substitute for fresh ones and if broad beans are not available, the best substitute is baby limas.

SERVES 4
500 g/1 lb (about 2½ cups) shelled broad beans or lima beans
2 medium potatoes, peeled and cubed
1 medium onion, finely chopped
2 tablespoons chopped fresh coriander
1 litre/1¾ pints (4 cups) chicken or beef stock
salt and freshly ground pepper
50 ml/2 fl oz olive oil

In a saucepan combine the beans, potatoes, onion, coriander and stock.

Bring to a simmer and cook over low heat, covered, for 15–20 minutes, or until the beans and potatoes are tender.

Transfer the vegetables to a food processor or blender and reduce to a smooth purée. Stir the purée back into the liquid. Heat it through, season with salt and pepper to taste and stir in the oil. Serve in soup bowls with rye bread, or other chewy bread.

Caldeirada à Pescador
Fish Stew, Ribatejo-style

The wonderful variety of fish that swim in Portuguese waters makes possible the fish stews, the *caldeiradas*, that deserve to be as famous as the *bouillabaisse* of the French Mediterranean, a magnificent bringing together of fish and shellfish, the exact contents depending on what the fishermen have caught that day. Be flexible when making the dish, using the best fish available. Serve it to friends for a weekend lunch and linger over it, sipping a dry white wine and enjoying this very good food.

SERVES 8–10
8 tablespoons olive oil
2 medium onions, finely chopped
1 sweet green (bell) pepper, seeded and chopped
1 sweet red (bell) pepper, seeded and chopped
500 g/1 pound (4 medium) tomatoes, peeled, seeded and chopped
2 cloves garlic, chopped
2 large sprigs parsley
1 large bay leaf
475 ml/16 fl oz (2 cups) fish stock
475 ml/16 fl oz (2 cups) dry white wine
salt and freshly ground pepper
1.8 kg/4 pounds mixed fish such as hake, haddock, cod, sea bass, etc., cut into bite-size pieces
700 g/1½ pounds small squid, body sac only, thinly sliced
18 clams in the shell, cleaned
18 mussels in the shell, cleaned
25 g/1 oz (½ cup) chopped fresh coriander

Heat the oil in a large flameproof casserole and sauté the onions and peppers for 5 minutes over moderate heat. Add the tomatoes, garlic, parsley, bay leaf, fish stock and wine and simmer, uncovered, over very low heat for 15 minutes. Season with salt and pepper.

Add the fish and cook for 4 minutes. Add the shellfish and cook for 4 minutes longer. Add the squid and cook for 1 minute longer. Sprinkle with the coriander. Serve from the casserole accompanied by a good crusty bread. Nothing more is needed than a crisp dry white wine.

Caldo de Pescado con Pimientos
Fish Soup with Sweet Red Peppers

This delightful fish soup from Andalucía is a prime example of the Spanish ability to incorporate foreign foods into the regional cuisine, naturalizing them so successfully they seem native-born. Here potatoes and sweet red (bell) peppers, both New World foods, combine with saffron, an early immigrant brought by the Phoenecians, and Spain's own splendid fish.

SERVES 4
375 g/12 ounces (about 3 medium) potatoes, peeled and sliced
salt
1 medium tomato, peeled, seeded and chopped
2 cloves garlic, crushed
⅛ teaspoon saffron threads, ground
⅛ teaspoon ground cumin
1 teaspoon paprika
4 tablespoons olive oil
1 litre/1¼ pts (4 cups) fish stock
250g/8 ounces monkfish, cut into 2.6 cm/1 inch slices
2 sweet red (bell) peppers, peeled and sliced (page 187)

In a small saucepan cook one of the potatoes (125 g/4 oz) in salted water to cover until tender. Drain, reserving the cooking liquid. In a blender or food processor combine the cooked potato, tomato, garlic, saffron, cumin and paprika with a little of the reserved potato stock and process until smooth. Scrape out into a bowl, stir in the oil and set aside.

Cook the remaining potatoes in the fish stock with any remaining potato stock. When the potatoes are tender add the fish, cook for 4 minutes, then stir in the reserved potato mixture and the sweet red peppers. Cook for 1 minute longer. Season to taste with salt and serve in soup bowls.

Açorda de Camarão
Dry Shrimp Soup

This is a very oddly named soup and nobody knows how or why this name came to be used for a number of bread-thickened soups. The use of the term *sopa seca*, dry soup, has spread to Mexico and applies to a rice, pasta, or tortilla dish served before the main course, after the 'wet' soup: again, nobody knows why. But since the dishes, whether in Portugal or Mexico, are appetizing and attractive, the origin of the name does not seem to matter a great deal. Chile's *Chupe de Pescado*, a fish stew, is thickened with breadcrumbs and is not dissimilar to the *açordas*, though bread does not play the star role as it does in the Portuguese dish. The most important thing in making this soup is to have a very well-flavoured stock. If it is not possible to make shellfish stock use a very rich fish stock which is improved by the addition of clam juice. The other key to the soup's success is to serve it very hot.

SERVES 6

For the shellfish stock
50 ml/2 fl oz (¼ cup) olive oil
shells from 900 g/2 pounds raw prawns (shrimps)
1 tablespoon brandy
2 medium onions, chopped
4 cloves garlic, chopped
250 g/8 ounces (about 2 medium) tomatoes, chopped
salt and freshly ground pepper
1.4 litres/2½ pints (6 cups) water

For the açorda
125 ml/4 fl oz (1½ cup) olive oil
2 medium onions, finely chopped
2 large cloves garlic, chopped
1–2 fresh hot chilli peppers, seeded and chopped, or seeded dry chilli peppers, crumbled, to taste
250 g/8 ounces (8 slices) day-old Portuguese, Italian or French bread, halved
900 g/2 pounds raw prawns (shrimps)
6 large eggs, at room temperature
25 g/1 ounce (½ cup) chopped coriander or flat-leaved parsley

To make the shellfish stock, heat the oil in a large saucepan and sauté the prawn (shrimp) shells until they turn pink, 2–3 minutes. Flame with the brandy. When the flames die down, add the onions and garlic and sauté until the onion is soft. Add the tomatoes, a little salt, pepper and the water. Simmer, covered, for 1 hour. Strain, rinse out the pan and measure the stock: there should be 1.1 litres/2 pints (5 cups). Reduce the stock if necessary over brisk heat. Taste for seasoning.

To make the *açorda*, heat half the olive oil in a frying pan (skillet) and sauté the onions, garlic and chilli peppers until the onion is soft. Set aside and keep warm.

Heat the earthenware or other casserole by filling it with boiling water, or heating it for a few minutes in a hot oven. Bring the shellfish stock to the boil. While it is heating, put the bread into the hot casserole and pour the remaining oil over it. Drop the prawns (shrimps) into the hot stock and cook just until they turn pink, no more than 3 minutes. Be careful not to overcook them as they toughen very quickly.

Strain the stock and add the prawn (shrimp) and reserved onion mixture to the casserole. Pour in the boiling stock and stir the dish quickly, then make 6 indentations and break in the 6 eggs. Sprinkle with coriander or parsley and serve immediately. To serve, stir all together to mix thoroughly and ladle into heated soup bowls.

If preferred, use poached eggs instead of raw eggs. If raw prawns (shrimps) are not available, thoroughly thaw and drain the best available frozen ones and add them to the stock for just long enough to heat them through, about 30 seconds.

Variations: For *Açorda de Mariscos* (Dry Seafood Soup), make in the same way as *Açorda de Camarão* (Dry Shrimp Soup) but use 500 g/1 pound cooked, shelled, mixed prawns (shrimps), mussels and clams and 500 g/1 pound monkfish, or other firm-fleshed white fish, cut into 2.5 cm/1 inch pieces and poached with the shellfish in shellfish or fish stock.

Variation: For the simplest of all the dry soups, *Açorda Alentejana* (Dry Garlic Soup, Alentejana-style), use chicken stock instead of shellfish stock, omit prawns (shrimps) and simply add 5 large cloves garlic, finely chopped and mixed with garlic and salt. Use poached eggs.

Sope de Tomate, Estilo Español
Tomato Soup, Spanish-style

This soup from Gibraltar shows a strong Iberian influence. It is very like a Portuguese *açorda* (dry soup) and is an excellent way of using up day-old bread. Topped with a fried or poached egg it makes a good light lunch or supper dish, though in Gibralter it would be served as a soup, which is fine for those with hearty appetites. The use of bread as a thickener is common in the peninsula, possibly because the bread is so good. It is similarly used in Spain's *Sopa de Ajo* (Garlic Soup) as well as in *Gazpacho*.

SERVES 4
4 tablespoons olive oil, or more to taste
1 medium onion, finely chopped
2 large cloves garlic, chopped
500 g/1 pound (about 4 medium) tomatoes, peeled, seeded and chopped
Salt, freshly ground pepper
250 g/8 ounces (8 slices, about) day-old firm white bread, or French or Italian bread, cubed
476 ml/16 fl oz (2 cups) chicken stock
4 large eggs, fried or poached

In a large frying pan (skillet), heat 3 tablespoons of oil and sauté the onion and garlic until the onion is soft. Add the tomatoes and continue to cook, over moderate heat until the mixture is thick and well blended. Season to taste with salt and pepper.

Stir in the bread cubes, the stock and the remaining tablespoon of olive oil. Cook, stirring until the mixture is smooth and thick. Add a little more olive oil, if liked. Serve the soup topped with a fried or poached egg.

3

Fish and Shellfish
Pescados y Mariscos/Peixes e Mariscos

It is said, with justification, that the fish and shellfish of Spain and Portugal are the great glory of their cuisines. There is a great abundance of seafood, not just in quantity but also in variety, from both the Atlantic Ocean and the Mediterranean Sea. Everyone in the Iberian Peninsula loves fish and all seafood is treated with respect, served beautifully fresh and cooked in many delectable ways. And of course there is the paradox that dried salt cod, which comes from the faraway Grand Banks off Newfoundland, is an equal favourite in both countries. Even the most resolute diner would be hard pressed to work his or her way through the huge repertoire of seafood dishes available in the Peninsula. The following selection is intended to whet appetites.

Zarzuela
Fish and Shellfish Medley

In Spain a *zarzuela* is a satirical light opera, full of fun and based on the lives of ordinary people. Immensely popular in the nineteenth century, it has never wholly lost its appeal and is now enjoying a revival. The dish *Zarzuela* is as lively as the operetta with its music, dance, singing and acting – a mixture, this time, of fish and shellfish. Some *Zarzuelas* contain only shellfish; others, like the one given, have both fish and shellfish. The first time I had *Zarzuela* was in Madrid in a small restaurant now, alas, closed. It was so good that the taste still haunts me.

SERVES 4–6
125 ml/4 fl oz (½ cup) olive oil
12 king prawns (jumbo shrimps) in the shell
1 medium onion, finely chopped
3 cloves garlic, chopped
2 tablespoons brandy, preferably Spanish
250 g/8 oz (about 2 medium) tomatoes, peeled, seeded and finely chopped
1 bay leaf
salt and freshly ground pepper
⅛ teaspoon ground saffron
1 teaspoon paprika
½ dried red chilli pepper, seeded
250 ml/8 fl oz (1 cup) dry white wine
8 fish steaks, about 2.5 cm/1 inch thick, from 2 kinds of white fish such
as haddock, halibut, hake, cod or bass
6 small squid, cleaned and sliced
12 clams, scrubbed
12 mussels, scrubbed
25 g/1 ounce (¼ cup) peeled, ground hazelnuts
1 tablespoon chopped parsley

Heat the oil in a large, shallow, flameproof casserole and sauté the prawns
(shrimps) just until they turn pink. Lift them out on to a platter. In the
oil in the pan sauté the onion and 1 of the cloves of garlic until the onion
is soft. Pour in the brandy and flame it. As soon as the flames die down,
add the tomatoes, bay leaf, salt, pepper, saffron, paprika, chilli, wine, white
fish and squid. Cook for 5 minutes, then add the clams and mussels and
cook, covered, over low heat for 5–10 minutes, or until the shellfish have
opened.

Lift out the fish on to a warmed platter, cover and set aside. Mix the
ground hazelnuts with the remaining cloves of garlic and the parsley. Stir
into the casserole. Return the prawns (shrimps) with any juices that may
have collected and cook just long enough to warm them through. Arrange
the contents of the casserole around the fish and pour the sauce over.
Serve with green salad, crusty bread and a light dry red wine or a medium-
dry white wine.

Amêijoas na Cataplana
Clams in a Cataplana

Cataplana cookery is an Algarve speciality and though *cataplanas* are now available outside Portugal, this is not the sort of equipment the average cook would find useful. It can be described as a clam-shaped copper (or less traditionally aluminium) pan, hinged at the back as a clam is, fastened by clasps on each side and with a handle on top and bottom. It seals so tightly it can be turned right over during cooking with no danger of spillage. However, a saucepan or flameproof casserole with a very tight-fitting lid can be used instead.

SERVES 4
900 g/2 pounds small clams in the shell
salt
1 tablespoon olive oil
1 tablespoon lard
2 medium onions, thinly sliced
1 clove garlic, chopped
85 g/3 ounces smoked ham, coarsely chopped
75 g/3 ounces *chouriço, chorizo*, or other garlic-flavoured smoked sausage
1 teaspoon, Piri-Piri Sauce, or other hot sauce, such as Tabasco, or 2 small, dried red chilli peppers, seeded
1 tablespoon chopped parsley

Thoroughly wash the clams in cold running water. Put them into a bowl with cold salted water to cover and let them stand for 3–4 hours to disgorge any sand. Rinse thoroughly.

Heat the oil and lard in the *cataplana* saucepan, or flameproof casserole and sauté the onion and garlic over low heat until the onion is soft. Add the ham, sausage, Piri-Piri Sauce, parsley, salt to taste and the clams. Cover the *cataplana* pan or casserole, and cook over moderate heat for 20 minutes. Serve immediately, straight from the cooking vessel. Accompany with a salad, and drink a crisp dry white wine.

Cangrejo/Carangeujo
Crab

The very first time I had a crab salad was in Falmouth in Cornwall when my mother and I overnighted on the way to join the rest of the family for the summer holidays. I was a late recoverer from mumps and held us all up. It was worth it for that freshly caught, freshly served crab whose flavour burst upon my six-year-old palate like hosts of angels singing. But that is an old, far-off tale and since then I vividly remember eating crab at a waterside restaurant in Barcelona, and again, this time with special delight, at the seaside resort of Figueira da Foz in Beira Litural in Portugal. The crab was plainly cooked and served cold, delicious for a sunny, seaside lunch. The Barcelona crab was part of a seafood platter, while the giant Portuguese crab, *santola* (spider or spiny crab), just right for two, came with salad and the inevitable potato chips (French fries) so loved by the Portuguese. I know of no better way to eat crab, especially when one is given a small wooden mallet and board for dealing with claws, and there is chilled, dry white wine, such as Vinho Verde, to accompany the meal. However, stuffed crab from the Basque country in Spain where the *centolla* is called *shangurro*, is also very good.

I never buy live crabs simply because I cannot kill them. I am told it is cruel to kill them by plunging them into boiling water, and that the humane way is to pierce them at several different angles with an awl in the central nervous centre which is located underneath the tail flap on the crab's underside. Alan Davidson, in his invaluable book *North Atlantic Seafood*, describes and illustrates this method for the brave. If you are like me, rely on your fishmonger, or buy frozen crab meat which is usually of excellent quality.

Santola Recheada Fria
Cold Stuffed Crab

SERVES 4

2 large crabs, or 500 g/1 pound crab meat, defrosted and picked over to remove any shell or cartilage

For live crabs
salt
1 teaspoon black peppercorns
1 clove
large sprig parsley
1 medium onion, halved and sliced
125 ml/4 fl oz (½ cup) dry white wine

For the dressing
2 large eggs, hardboiled
50 ml/2 fl oz (¼ cup) *aguardiente* or brandy
salt and freshly ground pepper
Piri-piri Sauce (page 246)
1 teaspoon Dijon-type mustard
1 tablespoon chopped gherkins
1 tablespoon chopped parsley

Kill the live crabs humanely, then drop them into a large saucepan of briskly boiling salted water and cook for 20 minutes, with the peppercorns, clove, parsley, onion and wine. Lift the crabs out with kitchen tongs and allow to cool.

Lay the crabs on their backs with the tail facing you. Twist off the claws and remove the meat, cracking the claws with a mallet or a nutcracker. Reserve any juices or creamy curd. Hold the top shell down with the fingers and lever the body section out, using the thumbs. Set aside. Remove and discard the stomach, which is at the head end. Remove any meat from the shell and add to the claw meat. Remove and discard the feathery gills from the body section. Open the section and remove any meat from the body cavities. Scrape out any meat from the shell, together with any coral.

Chop all the meat and mix with any juices or creamy curd from the claws. Add 1 hardboiled egg, chopped, to the crab together with the *aguardiente*, salt, pepper and Piri-piri Sauce to taste, the mustard and gherkins; mix well and pile back into the shells, or use scallop shells. Garnish with the other hardboiled egg, quartered, and sprinkle with chopped parsley. Treat the frozen crab meat in the same way, using scallop shells. Serve with toast and butter, or serve with a salad, potato chips (French fries) and *Pão* (Portuguese bread). Drink a crisp dry white wine such as Vinho Verde.

Shangurro
Stuffed Crab, Basque-style

The Bay of Biscay produces giant *centollas* (spider or spiny crabs), used in this traditional dish. The Basque name may be spelled *trangurro* or *changurro*. The crabs may weight 2.3 kg/5 pounds or more. They are an impressive sight, better met at table than in their watery habitat.

SERVES 4

3 tablespoons olive oil
2 medium onions, finely chopped
250 g/8 ounces (about 2 medium) tomatoes, peeled, seeded and finely chopped
2 tablespoons chopped parsley
250 ml/8 fl oz (1 cup) dry white wine
1 teaspoon sugar
salt and freshly ground pepper
dash of cayenne
meat from 2 large crabs, shells reserved, or 500 g/1 pound frozen crab meat, defrosted
50 g/2 ounces (½ cup) dry breadcrumbs
butter

Heat the oil in a frying pan (skillet) and sauté the onion and garlic over very low heat until the onion is soft. Add the tomatoes, increase the heat and cook until the mixture is thick and well-blended. Add the parsley, wine, sugar, salt and pepper to taste, and a dash of cayenne, and cook for 3–4 minutes over moderate heat. Add the crab meat, chopped or shredded, and cook for about 3 minutes longer.

Pile the mixture into the crab shells, or use 4 scallop shells. Each crab shell will serve 2. Sprinkle with the breadcrumbs, dot with butter and bake in a preheated moderately hot oven (200°C/400°F gas 6) for 10 minutes or until the top is lightly browned. Serve with a mixed green salad and drink a crisp dry white wine.

This dish can be served for 6, in scallop shells, as a first course.

Ensopada de Lulas
Squid Stew

The English translation, squid stew, does not begin to give an idea of how utterly delectable this dish is, nor could it be easier to cook. Squid – *calamares* in Spain and *lulas* in Portugal – come complete with their ink and are not at all difficult to handle. Usually sold cleaned, there may still be bits of the purple-coloured skin covering the body sac. It pulls away easily. Pull out the head and tentacles, the stiff quill and any white material that may be inside. Discard the quill, which looks like a piece of stiff, transparent plastic, and the white material. Cut off the tentacles, chop and reserve them. Remove and reserve the ink sac and discard the head. The squid is now ready to be cooked

SERVES 6
1.44 kg/3 pounds squid
175 ml/6 fl oz (¾ cup) olive oil
3 medium onions, finely chopped
1 clove garlic, chopped
3 sweet green (bell) peppers, seeded and sliced
500 g/1 pound (about 4 medium) tomatoes, peeled, seeded and chopped
125 ml/4 fl oz (½ cup) dry white wine
350 ml/12 fl oz (1½ cups) fish stock
salt and freshly ground pepper
1 tablespoon potato flour (starch) or plain (all-purpose) flour
3 slices bread, toasted and halved (*Pão* if possible)
1 tablespoon chopped parsley

Prepare the squid in the usual way, then cut them open into 2 separate halves. Cut them crosswise into 2.5 cm/1 inch clices. Set aside.

In a flameproof casserole heat the oil and sauté the onions, garlic and pepper until the vegetables are soft. Add the tomatoes and cook until the mixture is well blended. Add the wine and stock and season with salt and pepper. Add the sliced squid, and the ink squeezed out of the ink sacs, bring to a simmer, cover and cook until the squid is tender, 1–1½ hours, depending on the size.

Mix the potato flour (starch), or plain flour, with a little water and stir into the sauce. Simmer just long enough to cook the starch. Put the toasted bread into the bottom of a deep serving dish and pour the squid stew over it. Sprinkle with the parsley. Serve with boiled potatoes and salad. Drink a light red wine.

Variations: Eels (*anguillas/enguias*) can be cooked in the same way. Small, eels – about 15 cm/6 inch – should be left whole, large eels should be sliced.

Lulas Recheadas
Stuffed Squid, Portuguese-style

Squid is popular all over the Iberian Peninsula, and stuffed squid, with small variations in the stuffing and presentation, can be met with almost anywhere. They are not half as formidable to deal with as they first appear. They are cephalopods, head-footed shellfish, a name which aptly describes the way the tentacles and arms of these creatures spring directly from the head. They might have been designed by nature to be stuffed for when the head and tentacles are pulled away and the quill and any white material removed, the body sac positively invites a stuffing.

SERVES 3–6
6 medium squid, cleaned, tentacles chopped

For the stuffing
125 ml/4 fl oz (½ cup) olive oil
1 medium onion, chopped
1 medium carrot, scraped and chopped
375 g/12 ounces (about 3 medium) tomatoes, peeled, seeded and finely chopped
125 ml/4 fl oz (½ cup) lemon juice
salt and freshly ground pepper
50 g/2 oz (1 cup) fresh white breadcrumbs

For the sauce
2 onions, finely chopped
2 medium carrots, scraped and chopped
50 g/2 oz (4 tablespoons) butter
1 bay leaf
1 large sprig parsley
250 ml/8 fl oz (1 cup) fish stock
250 ml/8 fl oz (1 cup) dry white wine

In a frying pan (skillet) heat the oil and sauté the onion and carrot over moderate heat until the vegetables are soft. Add the tomatoes and cook until the mixture is thick and well-blended. Add the lemon juice, salt and pepper to taste and the breadcrumbs. Mix well. Add the chopped tentacles, cool the mixture and use to stuff the squid. Fasten the squid with wooden cocktail sticks (toothpicks) and set aside.

   To make the sauce, in a shallow casserole sauté the onions and carrots in the butter until the vegetables are soft. Add the bay leaf, parsley, stock, wine and salt and pepper to taste. Add the squid, bring to a simmer, cover and cook for about 1 hour or until the squid are tender. Lift out on to a warmed serving platter. Bring the sauce to a rapid boil, boil for 1–2 minutes, strain the sauce and pour over the squid. Serve with a mixed salad, boiled potatoes sprinkled with chopped parsley and a light red dry wine, or a medium-dry white wine.

Variations: For *Calamares Rellenos* (Stuffed Squid) from Spain, omit the carrot, tomatoes and lemon juice from the previous stuffing. Instead sauté 2 cloves garlic, 125 g/4 ounces cured ham, chopped, 1 tablespoon chopped parsley, ½ teaspoon paprika and 50 ml/2 fl oz (¼ cup) dry white wine, adding a little more if necessary. Stuff the squid with the mixture then simmer in 475 ml/16 ml fl oz (2 cups) fresh Tomato Sauce (page 244) for 1 hour, or until the squid are tender. Serve with a salad and drink a medium-dry fruity white wine.

Prawns/Shrimps
Camarones/Gambas

The shellfish called shrimps in the United States and prawns in Britain are the *gambas* of Spain and Portugal and the *camarones* of Spain. There is also a large member of the group called a *carabinero* in both countries though spelled slightly differently in Portugal as *carabineiro*. It is really not necessary to go into all the refinements of prawn/shrimp types in the Peninsula since for all practical purposes they are the same. There is an area of controversy: I do not de-vein this shellfish. Those who prefer to do so should continue.

Prawns/shrimps, whether served hot or cold, are ideal as accompaniments to pre-meal drinks or as first courses. They are at home with a great variety of dipping sauces and have a natural affinity for garlic which makes *Allioli* (Garlic mayonnaise) their perfect partner. For non-garlic lovers there is plain Mayonnaise and for everyone sauces like *Piri-piri* and *Romesco* or *Salsa Vinagreta* (Vinaigrette) (page 240). It is vital not to overcook this shellfish as it toughens and becomes dry and tasteless very quickly. Boiled shrimps take only 2–3 minutes to cook, according to size, and sauteed shrimp no longer unless recipe instructions specify otherwise.

Gambas com Caril
Curried Prawns (Shrimps)

The Portuguese picked up the concept of curry from their Indian colony, Goa, creating dishes of considerable distinction. For a livelier sauce, add a little *Piri-piri* to the finished dish. The curry flavour should be present, but muted, almost an echo on the palate.

SERVES 4
2 tablespoons olive oil
25 g/1 oz (2 tablespoons) butter
1 large onion, finely chopped
1 clove garlic, chopped
1 sweet red (bell) pepper, seeded and finely chopped
1 teaspoon curry powder
salt and freshly ground pepper
2 tablespoons plain (all-purpose) flour
125 ml/4 fl oz (½ cup) shrimp or fish stock
125 ml/4 fl oz (½ cup) milk
500 g/1 pound raw, peeled medium prawns (shrimps)
Piri-piri sauce to taste
lemon juice
250 g/8 oz (1 cup) long-grain rice, freshly cooked and hot.

Heat the oil and butter in a flameproof casserole. Sauté the onion, garlic and pepper over low heat until the vegetables are soft. Add the curry powder, salt, pepper and the flour and cook, stirring to mix, for 2 minutes longer. Stir in the stock and milk and cook, over low heat, stirring, until the mixture is smooth and well blended, 4–5 minutes.

Three minutes before serving add the prawns (shrimps), folding them into the sauce. Taste for seasoning and add Piri-piri sauce to taste. Stir in a generous squeeze of lemon juice. Have the Piri-piri sauce on the table to be added by those who like a very hot dish. On a serving dish make a circle of the rice and put the prawns (shrimps) in their sauce into the centre. Serve with salad and drink a crisp dry white wine such as a Vinho Verde.

Note: If using cooked frozen prawns (shrimps) let them defrost completely. If they seem at all watery put them into a sieve to drain. Fold them into the hot sauce, turn off the heat and let them stand, covered, for 2 minutes to warm through, then serve. This way they will not toughen.

Grilled Prawns (Shrimps)
Gambas Grelhadas

Spain and Portugal both have fine prawns (shrimps) and a common approach to cooking them. The most important thing is to avoid over-cooking. This is the simplest way and popular as an *acepipe* (hors d'oeuvre).

SERVES 6
500 g/1 pound medium or large raw prawns (shrimps), in the shell
salt
cayenne
1 tablespoon olive oil
40g/1½ oz (3 tablespoons) butter
lemon wedges

Season the prawns (shrimps) with salt and cayenne. Brush a grill rack (broiler) with olive oil and grill (broil) the prawns (shrimps) just until they change colour, a matter of minutes. Meanwhile, melt the butter and serve it with the shellfish, accompanied by lemon wedges.

Variation: For *Gambas al Ajillo* (Garlic Prawns/Shrimps), a Spanish dish, sauté the prawns (shrimps) in a mixture of 3 tablespoons each of butter and olive oil with 3 cloves crushed garlic, for 2–3 minutes. Add 3 tablespoons each of lemon juice and dry sherry, cayenne and salt. Sprinkle with chopped parsley and serve immediately.

Variations: For *Gambas Picantes* (Hot Prawns/Shrimps) from Portugal, sauté 6 cloves garlic, crushed, and 6 small, hot, dried red chilli peppers, seeded and crumbled, in 4 tablespoons olive oil. Add the prawns (shrimps), season with salt and sauté for about 2 minutes. Serve immediately.

Dried Salt Cod

In spite of the fact that the Iberian Peninsula has extensive sea coasts and magnificent fresh fish, dried salt cod, *bacalao* in Spanish, *bacalhau* in Portuguese, is a perennial favourite in both countries. About the time of the discovery of the New World Portuguese fishermen were making the long journey each spring to the Grand Banks of Newfoundland to fish for cod which they salted at sea and brought home each autumn sun-dried into the familiar stiff, pale yellow, board-like pieces that are salt cod, needing only prolonged soaking to turn them again into edible fish. They probably discovered the New World without knowing it. Salt cod is vastly appreciated in New England which these early Portuguese fishermen so narrowly missed, and in France where *la morue* is a gastronomic delight. The Portuguese are said to have 365 different ways to cook salt cod, which is a measure of their enthusiasm for the fish.

To prepare salt cod for cooking soak it for 24–36 hours in cold water, changing the water several times. If the cod is less heavily salted, Canadian salt cod for example, the soaking time can be shortened. Drain, rinse and blanch the cod, putting it into a saucepan with cold water to cover, and bringing it to a boil over high heat. Drain and remove any skin and bones. The cod is now ready to be used according to recipe instructions.

Bacalao a la Vizcaina
Salt Cod, Basque-style

There is a legend that the Basques are the descendants of Japhet, one of Noah's sons, who migrated to the valley of Roncal at the foot of the Pyrenees, from the mountains of Armenia where the ark had come to rest. The Basques point out that their language has nothing in common with Spanish, which they also speak, and that their cooking is superior. There is no doubt that they care greatly for food and drink, and that wherever they settle, even as far from home as Mexico, they set up restaurants serving their native cuisine. This is the most famous of the Basque salt cod dishes, though others, like *Pil-pil*, are memorable. The peppers used in the dish are sweet, dried, smooth-skinned, medium ones called *ñoras*, very like the Mexican *guajillo* or the tapering *choriceros*. In the United States a pepper giving the same taste and colour is the New Mexico dried sweet pepper. If dried sweet peppers are not available, fresh sweet red (bell) peppers are the best substitute.

SERVES 4
500 g (1 pound) dried salt cod
4 dried sweet red peppers, or 2 fresh sweet red (bell) peppers
4 tablespoons olive oil
4 medium onions, chopped
2 cloves garlic, chopped
1 tablespoon chopped parsley
2 hardboiled egg yolks
1 small hot dried red chilli pepper, seeded and crumbled.

Soak the fish in the usual way and blanch it. Remove skin and bones and cut it into 3.5 cm/1½ inch pieces. Soak the peppers, if using dried ones, in warm water for about 30 minutes. If using fresh peppers, seed and chop them.

Heat the oil in a frying pan (skillet) and sauté the onions, garlic and parsley over moderate heat until the onion is soft. Add the peppers and egg yolks and cook, covered, over very low heat for 5 minutes longer.

Transfer the mixture to a food processor or blender and reduce it to a purée. Return the mixture to the frying pan (skillet) and stir in 250 ml/8 fl oz (1 cup) water. Add the hot chilli pepper, cover and cook over very low heat for 15 minutes longer.

Spread a layer of the mixture in the bottom of a shallow, ovenproof casserole, preferably earthenware, cover with the cod and the rest of the mixture, sprinkle with a little olive oil and bake, uncovered, in a preheated moderate oven (170°325°F gas 3) for 30 minutes. Serve from the casserole with boiled potatoes and drink a dry white wine.

Bacalao al Pil-Pil
Simmered Salt Cod

This is a Basque speciality using a local cooking technique that involves olive oil heated to just below simmering point, and cooking the ingredients, covered, at a very low temperature, shaking the casserole from time to time to prevent the contents from catching on the bottom, and also to amalgamate the flavours. The oil marries with the ingredients to form a rich sauce.

SERVES 4
175 ml/6 fl oz (¾ cup) olive oil
4 cloves garlic, chopped
2 tablespoons chopped parsley
500 g/1 pound salt cod, soaked
freshly ground pepper (optional)

In a flameproof casserole, preferably earthenware, heat the oil and sauté the garlic over very low heat until golden. Add the parsley and cook for 2 minutes longer. Lift out the garlic and parsley with a slotted spoon and reserve.

Drain the soaked cod and remove any bones but do not skin it. Cut it into 8 equal-sized slices and pat dry with paper towels. Add it to the casserole, skin side down, cover and cook over very low heat, shaking the casserole from time to time, for 30 minutes.

Return the garlic and parsley to the casserole, season with pepper, if liked, cook for 1–2 minutes longer and serve from the casserole. The oil and fish will have formed a sauce. Serve with boiled potatoes and drink a full-bodied dry white wine.

Bacalao con Manzanas
Salt Cod with Apples

This is an unusual recipe from Navarre, the smallest of the kingdoms held by the Christians when Islam dominated the south, and whose cuisine is often confused with that of its neighbours, the Basques. It would not be surprising to find this dish in Normandy. The tartness of the unsweetened apples marries beautifully with the strongly flavoured fish.

SERVES 4

500 g/1 pound dried salt cod
900 g/2 pounds tart apples, peeled, cored and coarsely chopped
3 tablespoons olive oil
½ teaspoon salt
50 ml/2 fl oz (¼ cup) water

Prepare the cod in the usual way (page 66) and cut it into 2.5 cm/1 inch pieces. Set it aside.

In a flameproof casserole combine the apples with the olive oil, salt and water, cover and cook over very low heat until the apples are tender, about 20 minutes. Add the cod and simmer, uncovered, for 15 minutes longer. Serve with boiled potatoes, new if possible, and drink a dry white wine, or a rosé.

Bacalhau à Gomes de Sá
Salt Cod Casserole with Onions and Potatoes

This is the most famous of all the Portuguese salt cod dishes. It comes from Porto in the north and is believed to be the creation of a restaurateur called Gomes de Sá. Though it is popular in the north, it also appears on restaurant menus further south. It is an easy dish to make at home and deserves its fame.

SERVES 4

500 g/1 pound dried salt cod
4 tablespoons olive oil
1 large Spanish onion, thinly sliced
750 g/1½ pounds potatoes
16 pitted oil-cured black olives
25 g/1 oz (½ cup) chopped parsley
freshly ground pepper
2 large hardboiled eggs, quartered

Prepare the cod in the usual way (page 66) but instead of blanching it, put it on to cook in boiling water to cover and simmer gently for 15 minutes. Drain, cool, remove any skin and bone and flake the cod. Set aside.

Heat the oil in a heavy frying pan (skillet) and sauté the onion over moderate heat until soft. Do not let it brown. Transfer the onion rings to a bowl and set aside. Cook the potatoes, unpeeled, in salted water to cover until tender. When cool enough to handle, peel and slice thinly.

Grease a shallow casserole with oil and make layers of potatoes, parsley (reserving 1 tablespoon for the garnish), onion and cod, seasoning the layers with pepper, ending with onion rings. Bake in a preheated moderate oven (180°/350°F/gas 4) until lightly browned and heated through, about 35–40 minutes. Serve garnished with the hardboiled eggs and sprinkled with the reserved tablespoon of parsley. Serve with a dry red wine and a vegetable such as green beans, or a salad.

Bacalhau à Brás
Dried Salt Cod with Eggs, Onions and Potatoes

This is a recipe from Estremadura, the state where the Portuguese capital Lisbon is located. It is a favourite of mine and a favourite of those who usually find salt cod a little too strongly flavoured for their personal raste. It is splendid for an informal lunch or supper.

SERVES 4
500 g/1 pound dried salt cod
125 ml/4 fl oz (½ cup) olive oil
2 large onions, thinly sliced
2 cloves garlic, chopped
500 g/1 pound potatoes
8 large eggs, lightly beaten
freshly ground pepper
2 tablespoons chopped parsley
16 medium oil-cured black olives

Prepare the cod in the usual way (page 66). Shred it with the fingers and set it aside. Heat the oil in a large frying pan (skillet) and sauté the onions over low heat until golden. Add the garlic and sauté for 2–3 minutes longer. While the onions are cooking boil the potatoes, unpeeled, until tender. When they are cool enough to handle, peel and cut them into 1 cm/½-inch slices. Add them to the onions with the cod, stirring to mix. Cover and cook over very low heat for 15 minutes.

Add the eggs, pepper to taste and 1 tablespoon of the parsley. Cook, uncovered, over moderate heat, stirring from time to time, until the eggs are just set, about 3 minutes. Serve sprinkled with the rest of the parsley and garnished with olives. Serve with a mixed green salad and a drink a light red wine.

Lamprey
Lampreia do Mar

The lamprey, an antique creature resembling an eel, lives by attaching itself to other fish with the suction pad that serves it as a mouth and sucking the host's blood – an unpleasant habit, as some of its victims fail to survive. However, it gets its come-uppance when it is caught in the spring in the Minho river in northern Portugal, where it is regarded as a great culinary delicacy. It has been famed as such for centuries. England's Henry 1 is said to have died of a surfeit of lampreys, a dubious recommendation.

The season for lampreys in Portugal is a short one, ending in April, and they are not widely available there and less so elsewhere. The method of preparing it is difficult as the fish must be alive when bought and most recipes call for its blood, which in a way serves it right. One way and another it does not seem to me practical to try to give recipes. Far better to note that early spring is the time to travel to the north of Portugal, past Porto, and enjoy *Lampreia à Moda do Minho* (Lamprey, Minho-style).

Sardinhas Assadas
Grilled Sardines

Sardines are one of Portugal's favourite foods and the summer months are the favourite time to eat them when they are considered to be at their fat and sweetest best. Lisbon celebrates them on the eve of St Anthony's feast day (Festa de Santo Antonio) on 13 June, when Lisbon's patron saint is honoured with everyone's favourite food, cooked on small outdoor charcoal grills, especially in the ancient Alfama district with its steep, cobblestoned streets. Summertime beach resorts are good sardine territory too.

SERVES 4
16–24 medium fresh sardines
coarse salt
olive oil

Rinse the sardines, remove any scales and pat them dry. Sprinkle the sardines with coarse salt and leave them, spread out on a board or other flat surface, for 1 hour. When ready to cook, rinse the fish and pat them dry with paper towels. If using an outdoor grill, brush the grill rack and the sardines with olive oil and grill for about 3 minutes a side. If using an indoor oven grill (broiler) oil the sardines and cook them under, instead of over the heat in the same way. Pile them on to a large, warmed platter and place in the the centre of the table. Serve with 3 medium sweet green (bell) peppers, peeled, seeded and sliced, arranged on a dish, a dish of hot boiled potatoes, and a large bowl of salad: tomatoes and sliced onions on a bed of lettuce. Serve a fruity olive oil and a light vinegar to season the salad, and salt and pepper to be added as liked. Drink a light dry red wine or a crisp white wine.

Variation: An almost equally popular way of cooking sardines is *Sardinhas à Moda de Cascais* (Sardines, Cascais-style) which hardly differs from *Sardinhas à Moda de Setúbal* (Sardines, Setúbal-style). Flour the sardines lightly, then sauté them in hot olive oil for about 1 minute on each side. Drain the sardines on paper towels and arrange them in a shallow baking dish, preferably earthenware. Pour 475 ml/16 fl oz (2 cups) Tomato Sauce (page 244) over them, sprinkle with dry breadcrumbs and bake in a preheated moderate oven (190°C/375°F/gas 5), uncovered, for 25 minutes. Serve garnished with boiled potatoes. Accompany with a green salad and drink a fruity, full-bodied, dry red wine.

Rape con Piñones
Monkfish with Pine Nuts

Pine nuts are native to the Mediterranean region and, with different species, almost everywhere else. They are very popular in Catalan cooking. This recipe was given me by a Catalan friend who is particularly fond of the delicate flavour and gentle texture of the nuts.

SERVES 4–6
3 tablespoons olive oil
1 medium onion, finely chopped
1 clove garlic, chopped
2 tablespoons finely chopped parsley
500–750 g/1–1½ pounds monkfish fillets, skinned and cut into 2.5 cm/1 inch slices
plain (all-purpose) flour for dredging
salt and freshly ground pepper
1 tablespoon lemon juice
50 g/2 oz (½ cup) pine nuts
125 ml/4 fl oz (½ cup) beef or chicken stock
125 ml/4 fl oz (½ cup) dry white wine

Heat the oil in a flameproof casserole and sauté the onion, garlic and parsley over moderate heat until the onion is soft. Dredge the monkfish with flour, shaking to remove the excess, add it to the casserole, and sauté for 1 minute. Season with salt, pepper and lemon juice, stir to mix, add the pine nuts, stock and wine and simmer for 3 minutes longer, or until the fish is cooked through. Serve with rice and drink a light dry white wine.

Rape a la Costa Brava
Monkfish, Costa Brava-style

This Catalan dish comes from the Costa Brava named after the sea coast where the waves, in windy weather, can be strong enough to knock an unwary swimmer down. I first enjoyed it when a dear friend and great cook, Rosa, Marquesa del Castellar, cooked it for us, and later at the Hotel Santa Marta on the Costa Brava. It remains one of my favourite ways of cooking monkfish.

SERVES 4–6
1½ tablespoons olive oil
1 medium onion, finely chopped
750 g/1½ pounds monkfish fillets, skinned and cut into 2.5 cm/1 inch slices
250 g/8 oz shelled green peas, defrosted if frozen
2 sweet red (bell) peppers, peeled, seeded and cut into 5 mm/¼ inch strips
12 cooked shelled mussels
salt and freshly ground pepper
2 teaspoons plain (all-purpose) flour
1 tablespoon chopped parsley
⅛ teaspoon ground saffron
2 large cloves garlic, crushed
50 ml/2 fl oz (¼ cup) fish or chicken stock or water
250 ml/8 fl oz (1 cup) dry white wine
1 lemon, sliced

In a small frying pan (skillet) heat 1 tablespoon of the oil and sauté the onion until soft. Lightly oil a shallow, flameproof casserole or baking dish with the remaining oil and spread the onion on the bottom. Cover with the monkfish slices, the peas, peppers and mussels. Season with salt and pepper.

In a small saucepan mix together the flour, parsley, saffron, garlic, stock or water and the wine to make a smooth sauce. Season lightly with salt and pepper, bring to a simmer over low heat and cook, stirring, until the mixture is lightly thickened. Pour over the fish and vegetables and cover the dish with a lid or foil. Bake in a preheated moderate oven (180°C/350°F/gas 4) for about 15 minutes or until the fish has lost its translucent look. Serve garnished with lemon slices. Serve with potatoes, a salad and a full-bodied dry white wine or a rosé.

Rape a la Malagueña
Monkfish, Malaga-style

Freshly caught fish cooked with the light Andalusian touch typifies this aspect of Spanish cuisine. The rich, lobster-like texture of monkfish is enhanced by the almond, hazelnut and breadcrumb sauce.

SERVES 6

plain (all-purpose) flour for dredging
salt and freshly ground pepper
900 g/2 pounds monkfish fillets, skinned and cut into 5 cm/2 inch slices
4 tablespoons olive oil
12 blanched almonds
12 peeled hazelnuts
3 cloves garlic, chopped
50 g/2 oz (1 cup) fresh white breadcrumbs
1 tablespoon chopped parsley
⅛ teaspoon ground saffron
1 medium onion, finely chopped
250 g/½ lb (2 medium) tomatoes, peeled, seeded and chopped
125 ml/4 fl oz (½ cup) fish stock

Season the flour with salt and pepper. Dredge the monkfish with the flour, shaking to remove the excess. Heat 2 tablespoons of the oil in a large frying pan (skillet) and sauté the fish very briefly on both sides. Transfer the fish to a shallow casserole.

In the oil remaining in the pan sauté the almonds, hazelnuts, garlic, breadcrumbs and parsley. Transfer to a food processor or blender with the saffron and process until the mixture is finely ground. Scrape out into a bowl and set aside.

Wipe out the pan. Add the remaining 2 tablespoons oil and sauté the onion until soft. Add the tomatoes, season with salt and pepper and cook until the mixture is well-blended, about 5 minutes. Combine with the breadcrumb mixture and the stock. Pour the mixture over the monkfish in the casserole and bake in a preheated moderate oven (180°C/350°F/gas 4) for 10 minutes. Drink a dry white wine and serve with a green salad.

Variation: Monkfish is immensely popular in Catalonia and so are dishes using nuts in sauces. This recipe for *Rape en Salsa de Almendras* (Monkfish in Almond Sauce) is as close to the Malaga recipe above as brother and sister. Small differences in technique alter the flavour of the sauce very slightly. Which version came first? It is a puzzle which does not need to be solved as both dishes are very appetizing. Omit the hazelnuts; instead, use 50 g/2 oz (½ cup) flaked (slivered) almonds instead of whole almonds. Treat the fish in the same way as above. In a small pan heat 2 tablespoons olive oil and sauté a slice of firm white bread until brown on both sides. Add more oil if necessary. Lift out and chop coarsely. Add oil to the pan and sauté the almonds and just 1 clove of garlic until golden. Process the bread, almonds and garlic to a paste. Make the tomato, onion and saffron sauce, combine with the almond mixture and spread over the fish which has been put into an ovenproof shallow casserole with 1 tablespoon oil. Spread the mixture over the fish and cook in a preheated moderate oven (180°C/350°Fgas 4) for 10–15 minutes. The difference in the two dishes is subtle but it is worthwhile finding out which is preferred.

Rape a la Levantina
Monkfish, Valencia-style

There seems no end to the inventiveness of Spanish cooks, amply demonstrated in this monkfish recipe which is different from all the others yet just as delicious.

SERVES 2–3
500 g/1 pound monkfish fillets, cleaned, skinned and cut into 2.5 cm/1 inch slices
1 medium onion, chopped
1 clove garlic, chopped
1 tablespoon chopped parsley
⅛ teaspoon saffron ground in a mortar
1 tablespoon plain (all-purpose) flour
75 ml/3 fl oz (scant ⅓ cup) olive oil
250 ml/8 fl oz (1 cup) milk
salt and freshly ground pepper

Pat the monkfish dry with paper towels and arrange it in a shallow casserole.

In a blender or food processor combine the onion, garlic, parsley and saffron and process until smooth. Scrape the mixture into a small saucepan and add the flour. Gradually beat in the oil to make a smooth, thick mixture. Stir in the milk, season with salt and pepper and cook, stirring, over very low heat to make a medium-thick sauce.

Cool a little, then pour over the monkfish in the casserole. Bring to a simmer and cook, covered, over very low heat for about 10 minutes or until the fish is cooked through. Serve with a salad. Drink a light dry white wine.

Rape Gallego
Monkfish, Galicia-style

Galicia has a pleasingly different way of cooking monkfish, using almonds and saffron for flavouring.

SERVES 4

1 medium onion, finely chopped
750/g/1½ pounds monkfish, skinned, boned and cut into 8 slices
salt and freshly ground pepper
125 ml/4 fl oz (½ cup) olive oil
12 toasted almonds, finely ground
2 cloves garlic, crushed
⅛ teaspoon saffron threads, ground in a mortar
1 tablespoon finely chopped parsley
2 tablespoons fish stock or water
375 g/12 ounces (2 cups) freshly cooked green peas

Put the onion into a flameproof casserole, preferably earthenware and top with the monkfish slices. Season with salt and pepper. Pour in the oil, cover and cook over moderate heat for 5 minutes.

While the fish is cooking, mix together the almonds, garlic, saffron and parsley to a paste. Stir in the stock or water. When the fish has been cooking for 5 minutes, add this mixture on top of the fish. Add the peas, cover and cook for 3–5 minutes longer or until the fish is cooked through. Serve with a green salad and drink a light dry white wine.

Rape con Patatas
Monkfish with Potatoes

Monkfish is cooked in many ways in Andalucía. This is one of the simplest, in which the full flavour of the fish can be appreciated.

SERVES 4
750 g/1½ pounds monkfish fillets, skinned and cut into 5 cm/2 inch slices
salt and freshly ground pepper
plain (all-purpose) flour for dredging
4 tablespoons olive oil
2 medium onions, finely chopped
500 g/1 pound (4 medium) tomatoes, peeled, seeded and chopped
750 g/1½ pound potatoes, peeled and cut into 1 cm/½ inch slices
fish stock or water, about 250 ml/8 fl oz (1 cup)
1 sweet red (bell) pepper, peeled, seeded and sliced

Pat the monkfish slices dry with paper towels, season with salt and pepper and dredge with flour, shaking to remove the excess. Heat the oil in a casserole and sauté the fish over moderate heat for 1 minute on each side. Lift out and set aside.

In the oil remaining in the casserole sauté the onions until soft. Add the tomatoes, season with salt and pepper and cook for about 5 minutes or until the mixture is thick and well-blended Add the potatoes and enough stock or water barely to cover. Cover and simmer until the potatoes are almost tender. Add the fish and any liquid that has collected, cover and cook until the fish is cooked through, about 5 minutes. Serve garnished with the sweet red pepper strips. Drink a dry white wine.

Rape en Salsa de Piñones
Monkfish in Pine Nut Sauce

The use of nuts in sauces, a Moorish heritage, is popular in Spanish cooking, especially in the cuisine of Andalucía. Pine nuts are particularly delicious, adding both flavour and texture.

SERVES 4
750 g/1½ pounds monkfish fillets, skinned and cut into 5 cm/2 inch slices
salt and freshly ground pepper
3 tablespoons olive oil
1 medium onion, finely chopped
1 clove garlic, chopped
3 tablespoons pine nuts
250 g/8 oz (2 medium) tomatoes, peeled, seeded and chopped
⅛ teaspoon saffron threads, ground in a mortar
4 tablespoons fresh white breadcrumbs

Season the monkfish with salt and pepper. Pour 1 tablespoon of the oil into a shallow flameproof casserole. Set aside. Heat the remaining oil in a small frying pan (skillet) and sauté the onions until soft. Add the garlic and nuts and sauté for 1 minute longer. Add the tomato and cook, stirring from time to time, until the mixture is well-blended, about 5 minutes. Mix the saffron with the breadcrumbs and add to the pan, mixing well. Set aside.

Heat the oil in the casserole and sauté the monkfish slices for 1 minute on each side. Add the prepared sauce, cover and cook over low heat for another 8 minutes, or until the fish is cooked through. Serve from the casserole with a green salad and drink a light dry white wine.

Peixe Sapo Frito
Fried Monkfish

Monkfish, usually called *rape* in Spain, turns up in Galicia as *peixe sapo*, a name by which it is sometimes known in Portugal although *Tamboril* is more common. This is a delicious way to cook the firm-fleshed, flavourful fish and the dish has the virtue of requiring little or no preparation, and a very short cooking time.

SERVES 4
2 cloves garlic, crushed
1 tablespoon finely chopped parsley
2 tablespoons lemon juice
salt
750 g/1½ pounds monkfish fillets, skinned and cut into 5 cm/2 inch slices
plain (all-purpose) flour for dredging
2 eggs, lightly beaten
4 tablespoons olive oil

In a bowl mix together the garlic, parsley, lemon juice and salt to taste. Add the monkfish slices and mix thoroughly. Let the mixture stand for 30 minutes, or longer.

Lift out the fish and dredge with flour, then dip into the egg. Heat the oil in a heavy frying pan (skillet) and sauté the monkfish over moderate heat for 5 minutes, turning the slices once. Lift out on to a platter and serve with *Ensalada de Lechuga* (Lettuce Salad). Drink a light dry white wine.

Langosta del Pobre
Poor People's Lobster

Monkfish has the firm texture of lobster and a flavour quite akin to the magnificent shellfish, in fact it mimicks lobster. This recipe is a culinary joke but the resulting dish is certainly not to be laughed at. It combines the deliciousness of both monkfish and lobster in a single, simple dish.

SERVES 4

750 g/1½ pounds monkfish tail, skinned, boned and cut into 3.5 cm/1½ inch slices
6 cloves garlic, crushed
2 tablespoons olive oil
salt and freshly ground pepper
1 tablespoon paprika
125 ml/4 fl oz (½ cup) dry white wine

Put the monkfish slices into a bowl. Mix together the garlic, 1 tablespoon of the oil, salt, pepper and paprika and add to the fish, mixing to coat all over. Leave for 15 minutes for the flavours to blend.

In a casserole heat the remaining tablespoon of oil. Add the fish and seasonings and turn the pieces in the oil. Pour in the wine, cover and cook until the fish is cooked through, about 10 minutes. Serve with the pan juices. Accompany with a salad and drink a light dry white wine.

Merluza en Salsa Verde
Hake in Green Sauce

Hake, *merluza* in Spanish, is the country's most popular fish, abundant off the coast of Portugal and in the Bay of Biscay. It is a member of the Gadidae family which cod also belong to, so if hake is not available, use cod.

SERVES 4

4 hake or cod steaks, cut about 2.5 cm/1 inch thick and each weighing about 175 g/6 ounces
salt and freshly ground pepper
plain (all-purpose) flour for dredging
3 tablespoons olive oil
1 clove garlic
50 g/2 oz (1 cup) finely chopped parsley
250 ml/8 fl oz (1 cup) fish stock

Season the fish steaks with salt and pepper and dredge with flour, shaking to remove the excess. In a shallow flameproof casserole, preferably earthenware or in a frying pan (skillet) heat the oil with the garlic and sauté the garlic over low heat until golden-brown. Remove and discard. In the oil sauté the fish steaks over moderately high heat for 1 minute on each side. Lift out and set aside.

In the oil remaining in the pan sauté the parsley for 1–2 minutes, then stir in the fish stock. Return the fish steaks to the pan and cook, turning once, for 8 minutes or until cooked through. Serve with potatoes and a green salad. Drink a dry white wine.

Merluza a la Vasca
Hake, Basque-style

This is a more elaborate version of *Merluza en Salsa Verde* (Hake in Green Sauce) which is simple and quick. Garnished with asparagus, green peas and clams, it makes a good party dish.

SERVES 4

4 hake or cod steaks, cut about 2.5 cm/1 inch thick and each weighing about 175 g/6 ounces
salt and freshly ground pepper
plain (all-purpose) flour for dredging
4 tablespoons olive oil
3 cloves garlic, chopped
25 g/1 oz (½ cup) finely chopped parsley
125 ml/4 fl oz (½ cup) fish stock
125 ml/4 fl oz (½ cup) dry white wine
12 cooked asparagus spears
250 g/8 ounces (1½ cups) cooked green peas
24 small clams or mussels in the shell, or a mixture of both
2 hardboiled eggs, sliced

Season the fish steaks with salt and pepper and dredge with flour, shaking to remove the excess. In a shallow, flameproof casserole, preferably earthenware, or in a frying pan (skillet) heat the oil with the garlic and sauté the garlic over low heat until golden-brown. Lift out and discard the garlic. In the oil sauté the fish steaks over moderately high heat for 1 minute on each side. Lift out and set aside.

Stir the parsley into the oil remaining in the pan and fry for 1 minute.

Add the stock and wine and the reserved fish steaks and cook over low heat, turning once, for 6 minutes. Add the asparagus, peas and clams or mussels and cook for 2 minutes longer, or just long enough to heat through and make sure the fish is cooked and the shellfish have opened. Garnish with the slices of hardboiled egg and serve straight from the casserole, making sure that each serving has an equal amount of the garnish of asparagus, peas and shellfish. Serve with a green salad, and, if liked, plainly boiled potatoes. Drink a dry white wine.

Merluza Asturiana
Hake, Asturian-style

The northern province of Asturias which lies between the Basque country and Galicia is noted for the excellence of its strong, dry (hard) cider which is popular both as a drink and in cooking. There are also some fine apple dishes from the region so apples can keep one busy from the cider sipped before the meal in one of the local taverns, which are called *chigres*, to the main course and on to dessert.

SERVES 4
4 tablespoons olive oil
4 hake, cod or haddock steaks, cut about 2.5 cm/1 inch thick and each weighing about 175 g/6 ounces.
salt and freshly ground pepper
1 medium onion, finely chopped
2 cloves garlic, chopped
1 sweet red (bell) pepper, seeded and finely chopped
1 sweet green (bell) pepper, seeded and finely chopped
250 ml/8 fl oz (1 cup) strong, dry (hard) cider

Pour 1 tablespoon of the oil into a shallow ovenproof dish. Season the fish steaks with salt and pepper and bake, covered, in a preheated moderate oven (180°C/350°F/gas 4) for 15 minutes.

While the fish is cooking make the sauce. Heat the rest of the oil in a frying pan (skillet) and sauté the onion until soft. Add the garlic and red and green peppers and sauté until the peppers are soft. Stir in the cider and cook until the sauce is fairly thick. If liked, the sauce may be thickened with 2 teaspoons flour stirred into the pan and cooked for 2 minutes before the cider is added. Pour the sauce over the fish and continue cooking, covered, for 15 minutes. If preferred, the sauce may be puréed in a food processor or blender, though it is more attractive with flecks of red and green. Serve with new potatoes and a green salad. Drink dry (hard) cider, or a dry white wine.

Merluza a la Gallega
Hake, Galician-style

Potatoes, onions and fish combine with the paprika that is a feature of the cooking of this region, to admirable effect. A green salad is all that is needed to complete a satisfying meal.

SERVES 4
4 hake, cod or haddock steaks, cut about 2.5 cm/1-inch thick and each weighing about 175g/6 ounces
1 bay leaf
1 sprig parsley
¼ teaspoon thyme
salt and freshly ground pepper
1 tablespoon white wine vinegar
7 tablespoons olive oil
1 large onion, sliced
4 cloves garlic, chopped
3 tablespoons chopped parsley
4 medium potatoes, peeled and thinly sliced
1 tablespoon paprika or ½ teaspon cayenne

In a shallow flameproof casserole combine the fish steaks with the bay leaf, parsley sprig, thyme, salt, pepper and ½ tablespoon vinegar. Pour in enough water barely to cover, cover and poach over low heat for 5 minutes. Lift out the fish on to a platter, cover and keep warm. Strain and reserve the stock.

Meanwhile, heat 4 tablespoons of the oil in a frying pan (skillet) and sauté the onion until golden. Add the garlic, chopped parsley and potatoes and sauté for 1–2 minutes. Add 250 ml/8 fl oz (1 cup) of the reserved stock, cover and cook until the potatoes are tender, about 15 minutes. Drain and reserve the stock.

Reheat the fish in the casserole using the reserved stock. While the fish is reheating and finishing cooking, heat the rest of the oil, the rest of the vinegar and the paprika or cayenne in a small saucepan. Make a bed of the potato and onion mixture on a warmed platter, top with the fish steaks and pour the vinegar sauce over them.

Variation: For *Merluza con Cachelos* (Hake with Potatoes), cook as above but cook the potatoes separately. Add 500 g/1 lb (4 medium) tomatoes, peeled, seeded and chopped, to the onion mixture and cook until well blended, stirring from time to time. Pour this over the potatoes and fish, then sprinkle with the vinegar sauce as in the main recipe. Dry white wine is appropriate with both the main recipe and the variation.

Merluza con Vieiras
Hake with Scallops

This is another Galician recipe for hake which is very abundant in Spanish waters. The scallops are served with the orange tongue, but, if this is not available it does not matter. Be careful not to overcook the scallops which toughen with anything but the briefest cooking.

SERVES 4

5 tablespoons olive oil
1 medium onion, finely chopped
2 cloves garlic, chopped
1 teaspoon paprika
1 tablespoon chopped parsley
4 hake, cod or haddock steaks, cut about 2.5 cm/1 inch thick and each weighing about 175g/6 ounces
250 ml/8 fl oz (1 cup) dry white wine
salt and freshly ground pepper
4 large scallops
2 hardboiled eggs, chopped
8 asparagus tips

Heat 2 tablespoons of the oil in a frying pan (skillet) and sauté the onion until soft. Add the garlic and sauté for 2 minutes longer. Stir in the paprika and parsley and cook for 1 minute. Transfer the mixture to a bowl and set aside.

Wipe out the pan with paper towels. Heat the remaining oil in the pan and sauté the fish steaks briefly, about 1 minute on each side. Cover with the reserved onion mixture, pour in the wine, season with salt and pepper, cover and simmer for about 8 minutes or until the fish is cooked through. In the last 2 minutes of cooking top with the scallops. Serve with a scallop on each fish steak and garnish with chopped hardboiled egg and asparagus tips. Drink a dry white wine.

Merluza a la Andaluza
Hake, Andalucian-style

This is a very simple way of cooking hake which in Spain is sometimes called *pescada*, its Portuguese name, though *merluza* is more common. The garlic-flavoured oil does not overpower the delicate taste of the fish, just heightens it.

SERVES 4

750 g/1½ pounds hake (haddock or cod) fillets, skinned and cut into serving pieces
salt and freshly ground pepper
2 cloves garlic crushed
4 tablespoons olive oil and extra oil for greasing
50 g/2 oz (1 cup) fresh white breadcrumbs
2 tablespoons chopped parsley
4 tablespoons lemon juice
25g/1 oz (2 tablespoons) butter

Season the fish with salt and pepper. Mix the garlic and oil together and pour over the fish. Marinate for 1 hour.

Lightly oil a shallow baking dish and arrange the fish, with the oil and garlic, in it. Sprinkle with the breadcrumbs, parsley and lemon juice. Dot with the butter and bake in a preheated moderate oven (180C/350F/gas 4) until the fish is cooked through, about 15 minutes. Serve with rice or potatoes and a salad. Drink a light dry white wine.

Variation: This Galician dish, *Merluza a la Manera de Vigo* (Hake, Vigo-style), uses orange juice in much the same way as Andalucian cooks use lemon juice. Sauté 3 cloves garlic, chopped, and 1 tablespoon chopped parsley in 4 tablespoons olive oil for 1 minute. Add 4 hake or haddock steaks, each weighing about 175–250 g/6–8 ounces, seasoned with salt and pepper, to the pan and sauté quickly, turning once, for about 2 minutes. Sprinkle with 3 tablespoons fresh breadcrumbs, 125 ml/4 fl oz (½ cup) orange juice and 175 ml/6 fl oz (¾ cup) fish stock. Bring to a simmer, cover and cook over low heat for about 6 minutes or until the fish is cooked through. Serve with rice or potatoes and a green vegetable and drink a dry white wine.

Merluza Koskera
Hake with Mussels, Peas and Asparagus

Old Castille, home of many great Spanish dishes, is credited with this dish which treats a plentiful and popular fish as if it were a great rarity worthy of fine attention, which indeed it is. If hake is not available, use cod, or haddock, both members of the same family. Clams may be used instead of mussels.

SERVES 4

3 tablespoons olive oil
3 cloves garlic
1 small hot dried red chilli, seeded
4 hake (cod or haddock) steaks, cut about 2.5 cm/1 inch thick and each weighing 175–250 g/6–8 ounces
salt and freshly ground pepper
plain (all-purpose) flour for dredging
175 ml/6 fl oz (¾ cup) dry white wine
16 cooked mussels, cooking liquid reserved
2 tablespoons chopped parsley
8 cooked asparagus stalks
175 g/6 oz (1 cup) cooked green peas
2 large hardboiled eggs, quartered

Heat the oil in a shallow flameproof casserole, preferably earthenware, or use a heavy frying pan (skillet). Add the garlic and chilli and sauté over low heat until the garlic is golden. Lift out the garlic and chilli and discard. Season the fish steaks with salt and pepper and dredge with flour, shaking to remove the excess. Sauté the fish over moderate heat until golden on both sides. Add the wine and the liquid from the mussels, cover and cook until the fish is cooked through, about 5 minutes. Add the mussels, 1 tablespoon of the parsley, the asparagus and the peas and cook just long enough to heat them through.

Transfer the fish to a heated serving dish and garnish with the mussels, asparagus and peas. Pour the pan liquid over the fish, sprinkle with the remaining parsley and arrange the eggs decoratively on the dish. Drink a dry white wine.

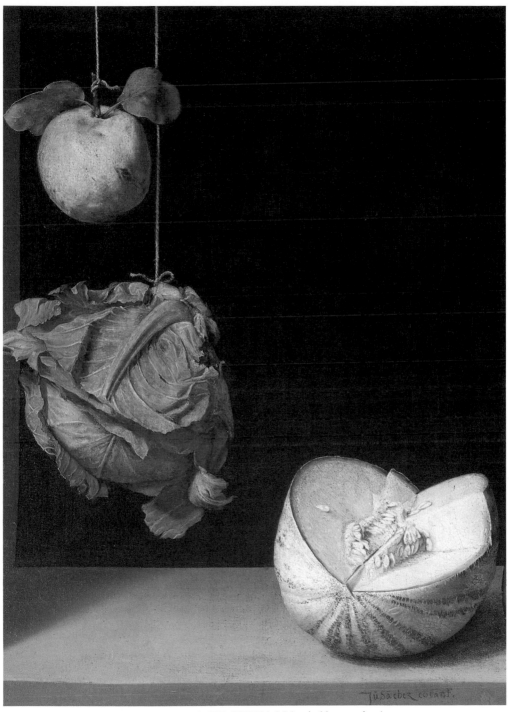

FRAY JUAN SANCHEZ COTAN. Melon, cabbage and quince.

EL LABRADOR. Traditional straw-covered flagon, bread and decorated water jug.

EL LABRADOR. Bread, artichoke, the ubiquitous lemons, and, rarely seen in art, a hearty, rich sausage.

LUIS MELENDEZ. A splendid display o

ods, including ham, cheese and a variety of

LUIS MELENDEZ. An uncommon and vivid depiction of fish.

LUIS MELENDEZ. *La Merienda* – The Afternoon Meal. One of the most sumptuous picnics ever shown in art, this contains the grapes, melons and peaches so prevalent in Iberian cuisine.

LUIS MELENDEZ. The citrus fruits essential to Iberian cuisine.

Filetes de Linguado á Portuguesa
Fillets of Sole, Portuguese-style

I remember with delight the beautiful sole I had daily for lunch or dinner, without boredom, when I was staying in Cascais. We would go down to the beach and watch the fishermen bringing in the catch, their nets full of fish. Then we would give ourselves time for a glass of dry port before going to our favourite restaurant at which the fish would have arrived. Our only problem was deciding how to have the fish cooked. This way, one of many, is delicious.

SERVES 4
750 g/1½ pounds sole or flounder fillets
salt and freshly ground pepper
125 ml/4 fl oz (½ cup) dry white wine
125 ml/4 fl oz (½ cup) fish stock
75g/3 oz (6 tablespoons) butter
1 medium onion, finely chopped
500 g/1 lb (4 medium) tomatoes, peeled, seeded and chopped
1 tablespoon chopped parsley

Season the fish fillets with salt and pepper and arrange them in a flameproof dish large enough to hold them in a single layer. Pour 50 ml/ 2 fl oz (¼ cup) each of wine and stock over the fish and dot with 25g/1 oz (2 tablespoons) butter. Bring to a simmer on top of the stove, cover and cook in a preheated moderate oven (180°C/350°F/gas 4) for 8–12 minutes, depending on the thickness of the fillets. Be careful not to overcook.

While the fish is cooking, make the sauce. In a medium saucepan heat 25g/1oz (2 tablespoons) more of the butter and sauté the onion until soft. Add the tomatoes and parsley and cook over low heat until the mixture is thick and well blended. Pour in the remaining wine and stock, and simmer for a minute or two, then stir in the rest of the butter. Taste for seasoning and add salt and pepper if necessary. Transfer the cooked fish to a warmed platter and pour any liquid into the saucepan. Reduce the sauce quickly over brisk heat just until it has a medium-thick consistency, then pour it round the fish and serve. A dry white wine and potatoes or salad accompany the dish.

Lenguados a la Riojana
Fillets of Sole, Rioja-style

The province of Rioja is noted for the excellence of its sweet peppers, whose flavour is held to be unexcelled. Peppers, even if not from Rioja, make this otherwise simple dish into a special one.

SERVES 2

2 sweet red (bell) peppers, peeled, seeded and cut into strips (page 187)
2 cloves garlic, left whole
½ dried hot chilli pepper, seeded and chopped
2 tablespoons olive oil
salt and freshly ground pepper
500 g/1 pound sole fillets, skinned
125 ml/4 fl oz (½ cup) fish stock

Sauté the red pepper strips, garlic and hot pepper in the oil in a large frying pan (skillet). Season with salt. When the garlic is lightly browned remove and discard it.

Season the sole fillets with salt and pepper and add to the pan. Cook for 1 minute on each side. Pour in the stock and cook for about 4 minutes longer, or until the fish is done. Serve with potatoes and a green salad and drink a dry white wine, preferably from Rioja.

Filetes de Lenguado con Champiñones
Sole with Mushrooms

The rich mushroom sauce makes this Galician dish into something elegant, worthy of a special occasion. Lemon sole, sand sole, plaice or flounder would be suitable. Dover sole would lift the dish to even greater heights.

SERVES 4

50g/2 oz (4 tablespoons) butter
½ medium onion, finely chopped
1 clove garlic, chopped
1 tablespoon plain (all-purpose) flour and extra flour for dredging
250 ml/8 fl oz (1 cup) fish stock
250 ml/8 fl oz (1 cup) dry white wine
2 tablespoons lemon juice
salt and freshly ground pepper
50 g/8 oz (2½ cups) thinly sliced mushrooms
4 sole fillets, skinned, total weight about 750 g/1½ pounds
2 egg yolks
1 tablespoon double (heavy) cream
2 tablespoons chopped parsley

Heat half the butter in a frying pan (skillet) and sauté the onion until soft. Add the garlic and sauté for 1 minute longer. Stir in the flour and cook, stirring, for about 2 minutes. Gradually stir in the stock, wine and lemon juice. Cook until the sauce is smooth. Season with salt and pepper. Add the mushrooms and cook over very low heat, uncovered, for 10 minutes. Set aside.

Season the flour with a little salt and dredge the sole fillets with it, shaking to remove the excess. Heat the remaining butter in another frying pan (skillet) and sauté the fish for about 2 minutes on each side, or until lightly coloured and cooked through. Lift out on to a warmed serving dish and keep warm. Meanwhile, beat the egg yolks with the cream and stir 2 tablespoons of the hot mushroom sauce into the eggs, then stir the mixture into the sauce and cook, stirring, for 1–2 minutes. Pour the hot sauce over the fish, sprinkle with the parsley and serve immediately. Rice is a pleasant accompaniment. Drink a dry white wine.

Besugo con Almendras
Bream or Porgy in Almond Sauce

León, one of the medieval kingdoms of Spain, often bracketed with Old Castille, is noted for the individuality of its cooking, which is rich and varied. A whole large bream is sometimes used for this dish from Léon and the fish is baked. Fillets, cooked on top of the stove, take far less time, making a simpler but equally delicious dish.

SERVES 4

900 g/2 pounds bream or porgy fillets, skinned
salt and freshly ground pepper
plain (all-purpose) flour for dredging, plus 1 tablespoon
4 tablespoons olive oil
25 g/1 oz (¼ cup) flaked (slivered) almonds
1 medium onion, finely chopped
2 cloves garlic, chopped
1 tablespoon chopped parsley
175 ml/6 fl oz (¾ cup) fish stock
175 ml/6 fl oz (¾ cup) dry white wine

Season the fish with salt and pepper and dredge with the flour, shaking to remove the excess. Heat 2 tablespoons of the oil in a large, heavy frying pan (skillet) and sauté the fillets over moderate heat for about 1 minute on each side. Lift out on to a platter and keep warm, covered. Wipe out the pan with paper towels.

Heat the remaining 2 tablespoons oil in the frying pan (skillet) and sauté the almonds until golden. Lift out with a slotted spoon and set aside. Add the onion to the pan and sauté until soft. Add the garlic and parsley and sauté for 2 minutes longer. Stir in the tablespoon of flour and cook for 2 minutes. Gradually stir in the stock and wine and simmer to make a smooth sauce.

Return the fish fillets to the pan, spoon the sauce over them and simmer, over low heat, covered, for 10 minutes. Serve sprinkled with the almonds.

Variation: For *Besugo con Piñones* (Bream with Pine Nuts) omit the almonds. Instead, grind 25 g/1 oz (¼ cup) pine nuts in a food processor or blender and gradually add the sauce, slightly cooled. Put the fish fillets back into the pan and pour the sauce over them. Cook, covered, over low heat for 10 minutes and serve sprinkled with 1 tablespoon chopped parsley.

Besugo a la Madrileña
Baked Bream (Porgy), Madrid-style

This was a favourite dish for the traditional Christmas Eve supper that took place after the celebration of midnight mass and signalled the end of the pre-Christmas fast. Fasting has now been abolished but many of the old traditions survive in Spain, this baked fish among them, since it is excellently flavoured and a pleasure to eat at any time of the year.

SERVES 4
1 large bream or porgy, about 1.8 kg/4 pounds, cleaned, with head left on
1 lemon, cut into 8 wedges
4 tablespoons lemon juice
4 tablespoons olive oil
salt and freshly ground pepper
250 ml/8 fl oz (1 cup) dry white wine
1 bay leaf, crumbled
1 tablespoon chopped parsley
2 cloves garlic, crushed

Make 4 diagonal cuts on each side of the fish and insert a wedge of lemon into each, skin-side up. Pour the lemon juice over the fish and let it stand for about 20 minutes. Pour 2 tablespoons of the oil into a shallow ovenproof dish. Season the fish with salt and pepper and put into the dish. Pour the rest of the oil and the wine over it. Add the bay leaf, parsley and garlic.

Bake in a preheated moderate oven (180°C/350°F/gas 4) for about 45–60 minutes, or until the fish is cooked through to the bone. Baste the fish frequently during the cooking, adding a little more wine if necessary. Serve with fried or baked potatoes, a mixed green salad and a dry white wine.

Besugo a la Guipuzcoana
Bream or Porgy, Basque-style

There is no exact equivalent in American waters for *besugo*, called red sea bream in English. However, sea bream in British waters and red porgy in American are very close equivalents. In this recipe the fish is either barbecued or grilled (broiled) whole.

SERVES 4
1 large bream or porgy, about 1.8 kg/4 pounds, with head left on
olive oil
salt, preferably coarse
3 cloves garlic, chopped
4 tablespoons lemon juice

Rub the fish generously all over with oil and season with salt. Spanish cooks say it should be hung up by the head while the barbecue is prepared.

For the barbecue brush a metal grill with olive oil and cook the fish for 10 minutes per 2.5 cm/1 inch of thickness. If grilling (broiling) the fish, preheat the grill (broiler) and cook the fish 7.5 cm/3 inches away from the heat for 10 minutes per 2.5 cm/1 inch of thickness.

While the fish is cooking, heat 2 tablespoons olive oil in a small frying pan (skillet) and sauté the garlic until golden. Pour in the lemon juice and stir to mix. Split the fish and pour the sauce over it. Serve immediately with crusty bread, a green salad and a dry white wine.

Trucha a la Navarra
Trout, Navarre-style

This is the most famous of all the Spanish trout dishes and wherever there are mountainous freshwater trout streams, as in Venezuela for example, the dish will appear on restaurant menus. The freshwater trout from Navarre's mountain streams produce the trout that inspired the dish.

SERVES 4
4 freshwater trout, each weighing about 250–375 g/8–12 ounces
salt and freshly ground pepper
4 thin slices cured ham
plain (all-purpose) flour for dredging
olive oil for frying, about 175 ml/6 fl oz (¾ cup)
lemon wedges, to garnish

Season the trout with salt and pepper. Stuff the cavities with the ham and secure the openings with wooden cocktail sticks (toothpicks). Dredge the fish with flour, shaking to remove the excess.

In a frying pan (skillet) large enough to hold the trout comfortably, heat the oil. Sauté the fish until brown on both sides and cooked through, about 5 minutes on each side. Serve immediately, garnished with lemon wedges, with potatoes and salad. Drink a dry white wine.

Variation: *Trutas a Moda de Bragança* (Trout, Bragança-style, does not differ greatly from Navarre-style. Cook the trout in the same way but do not stuff with cured ham. Instead, use 125 g/4 ounces *presunto*, or Parma, Bayonne or a Westphalian ham, chopped and sautéed in 1 tablespoon olive oil. Sprinkle this over the cooked trout and garnish with lemon wedges. Serve with potatoes. Drink a full-bodied dry white wine.

Truchas a la Catalana
Trout, Catalan-style

This is the Catalan way of cooking freshwater trout, and though it is not as famous as *Trucha a la Navarra* (Trout, Navarre-style) it is just as delicious.

SERVES 4
4 freshwater trout, each weighing about 250–300 g/8–10 ounces
salt and freshly ground pepper
plain (all-purpose) flour for dredging
6 tablespoons olive oil
2 medium onions,
finely chopped flat-leaved parsley
¼ teaspoon ground cumin
2 teaspoon red wine vinegar
125 ml/4 fl oz (½ cup) fish stock or water
lemon wedges, to garnish

Season the trout with salt and pepper and dredge with flour, shaking to remove the excess. Heat 4 tablespoons of the oil in a large saucepan that will hold the trout comfortably in a single layer and sauté the fish over moderate heat for about 5 minutes on each side, or until browned and cooked through. Lift out on to a warmed serving platter, cover and keep warm.

While the trout are cooking, make the sauce. Heat the remaining 2 tablespoons oil in a frying pan (skillet) and sauté the onions until soft. In a bowl combine the onions, garlic, parsley, cumin, salt and pepper to taste, vinegar and stock or water. Mix thoroughly and pour into a small saucepan. Simmer for 2–3 minutes and pour over the trout. Serve immediately, garnished with the lemon wedges. Drink a light dry red wine or a dry white wine.

Truchas a la Montanesa
Trout, Mountain-style

This recipe from the northern Spanish state of Cantabria makes an interesting change from the more usual dishes of trout sautéed in olive oil. The result is very delicate.

SERVES 4
4 freshwater trout, each weighing about 250–300 g/8–10 ounces
salt and freshly ground pepper
1 medium onion, finely chopped
1 bay leaf
175 ml/6 fl oz (¾ cup) dry white wine
fish stock or water
1 teaspoon plain (all-purpose) flour
1 teaspoon olive oil

Season the trout inside and out with salt and pepper and arrange in a frying pan (skillet) or a shallow casserole large enough to hold them comfortably in a single layer. Add the onion and bay leaf. Pour in the wine and enough stock or water barely to cover. Cover and simmer over low heat until the fish is cooked through, about 10–15 minutes. Lift out on to a warmed serving platter and keep warm.

Reduce the liquid in the pan over brisk heat to about 250 ml/8 fl oz (1 cup). Mix the flour with the oil and stir into the pan. Cook just long enough to thicken the sauce lightly. Pour over the trout and serve with boiled potatoes. Drink a dry white wine.

Lubina Albufera
Sea (Striped) Bass in Almond Sauce

This rich almond and garlic sauce with its Moorish overtones reminiscent of Middle Eastern cooks' foodness for nut-thickened sauces, is named after the huge lagoon in the rice fields of Valencia. There is a French sauce with the same name, called after Marshal Suchet who was made Duc d'Albuféra in 1812 after three victories in the French wars against Spain, including one in Valencia. It bears no resemblance to the Spanish sauce.

SERVES 4
6 cloves garlic
4 tablespoons chopped parsley
½ teaspoon fresh oregano or ¼ teaspoon dried
1 teaspoon chopped fresh mint or ½ teaspoon dried
4 tablespoons blanched ground almonds
½ teaspoon paprika
1 tablespoon olive oil and extra oil for greasing
2 tablespoons plain (all-purpose) flour
350 ml/12 fl oz (1½ cups) fish stock
salt
750 g/1½ pounds bass fillets

For the garnish
strips of sweet red (bell) pepper
8 cooked mussels (optional)
1 tablespoon pine nuts, sautéed in oil (optional)

In a food processor or blender, grind to a paste the garlic, parsley, oregano, 1 tablespoon of the almonds and the paprika. Set aside.

In a small frying pan (skillet) heat the oil, stir in the flour and the remaining almonds and cook over low heat, stirring, until golden. Stir in the garlic paste, then gradually stir in the stock and simmer until the sauce in smooth. Taste for seasoning and add salt if necessary.

Oil a shallow casserole or baking dish and arrange the bass fillets in it. Pour the hot sauce over the fish and cook in a preheated moderate oven (180°C/350°F gas 4) for 15–20 minutes, until cooked through. Serve straight from the dish, garnished with strips of pepper and, if liked, the mussels and pine nuts. Serve with a salad and drink a full-bodied dry white wine or a rosé.

Mero a la Valenciana
Grouper, Valencia-style

Mero, (grouper), is a highly esteemed fish in Valencia and indeed wherever the waters are warm enough to please this solitary fish. Bass is a good substitute, or tilefish in the United States, or other firm-fleshed, non-oily white fish. This simple recipe brings out the full, delicate flavour of the fish.

SERVES 4

750 g/1½ pounds grouper or other firm-fleshed, non-oily white fish, cut into 4 steaks
salt and freshly ground pepper
lemon juice or white wine vinegar
3 tablespoons olive oil
3 cloves garlic
Plain (all-purpose) flour for dredging, plus 1 tablespoon
1 tablespoon finely chopped parsley
⅛ teaspoon ground saffron
125 ml/4 fl oz (½ cup) fish stock or dry white wine or water

Sprinkle the fish steaks with salt and pepper and sprinkle with a little lemon juice or vinegar. Set aside.

Heat the oil in a frying pan (skillet) and sauté the garlic over very low heat until golden. Lift out with a slotted spoon and set aside. Pat the fish dry with paper towels and dredge with flour, shaking to remove the excess. Sauté the fish steaks in the garlic-flavoured oil until lightly browned on both sides and cooked through, about 10 minutes. Lift out, cover and keep warm.

While the fish is cooking, crush the reserved garlic cloves and mix with the parsley, saffron and salt and pepper to taste. Stir 1 tablespoon flour into the oil in the pan and cook, stirring, for 1 minute. Add the stock, wine or water to the pan and cook, stirring, until the mixture makes a smooth sauce. It should be quite thick. If it seems too thick, add a little more liquid. Stir in the garlic mixture and return the fish to the pan with any liquid that may have collected. Cook just long enough to heat through. Serve with a salad and drink a dry white wine.

4

Poultry and Game
Aves y Caza/Aves e Caça

Although Spain and Portugal are celebrated for their fish and shellfish, they have a great deal to offer in the field of poultry or more correctly, poultry and game – *aves y caza* in Spanish and *caça e capoeira* in Portuguese – as rabbit is always included as well as pheasants, partridges, quail and so on. Although there are many excellent ways of cooking chicken in Spain and Portugal, it is often easier to find good game than poultry, for the whole Peninsula is mountainous with many forests. The uplands are ideal country for large game (not included here), while in the foothills the smaller, feathered game flourish. Small furred game like rabbits also do very well indeed despite the farmer's gun, and so do hares. Ducks and geese take advantage of the extensive marshlands to the east and south and, since the Peninsula is on the migratory path of a great many different birds, the skies are often full of feathered game. Fortunately many of the birds are not designed for the cookpot, and large numbers of those that are, fly on unharmed, so a sensible balance between our needs and theirs is maintained. At present there is no mass-production of chicken on a large scale, although birds are available from small farms which supply markets. Farmers have always kept a few chickens, good for family Sunday dinner, and for their eggs, which may explain the number of imaginative recipes for cooking the birds.

Pechugas de Pollo en Salsa de Naranja
Chicken Breasts in Orange Sauce

Cooks in Valencia, the province of Spain famed for its oranges, have created a number of poultry dishes featuring the fruit. These recipes use the sweet orange, not the Seville (bitter or Bigarade) orange which was introduced by the Arabs into Andalucía from Asia, and is the orange used in the classic French dish *Caneton à l'Orange* (Roast Duck with Orange Sauce). It was not until the seventeenth century that sweet oranges ousted the Seville type, still widely used in Latin American cookery and British marmalade making. In this dish Moorish influence is clearly shown in the use of mint.

SERVES 4
4 chicken breasts, skinned and boned, each weighing 175–200 g/6–7
ounces
salt and freshly ground pepper
2 tablespoons clarified butter
250 ml/8 fl oz (1 cup) orange juice
2 tablespoons chopped fresh mint

Season the chicken breasts with salt and pepper. Heat the butter in a
frying pan (skillet) large enough to hold the chicken breasts in a single
layer. Add the breasts and sauté, turning once, until lightly coloured,
about 3–4 minutes.

   Pour in the orange juice, bring to a simmer, cover and cook over low
heat until the breasts are done, about 8 minutes longer. Be careful not to
overcook the breasts as they become dry and tasteless very quickly.
Transfer the breasts to a platter, cover and keep warm. Add the mint
to the pan and simmer for 1 minute. Pour over the breasts and serve
with rice. Drink a light, dry red wine.

Variation: For *Pechugas de Pollo con Naranjas* (Chicken Breasts with
Oranges), begin by making an orange sauce. Peel 2 oranges, removing as
much of the white pith as possible. Divide into segments and remove any
pips. Chop the orange segments coarsely. In a frying pan (skillet) heat
25g/1oz (2 tablespoons) butter, add the oranges and any juice that may
have accumulated, and simmer over low heat, stirring from time to time,
for 10 minutes. Strain through a sieve, pushing down hard with a ladle
to extract all the flavour. Season with salt and pepper. Set aside. In another
frying pan (skillet) heat 25g/1oz (2 tablespoons) butter. Season the 4
chicken breasts with salt and pepper and sauté in the butter for 3–4
minutes over moderate heat, turning once. Pour the reserved sauce over
the chicken, cover and cook over low heat until the breasts are done. Add
1 tablespoon chopped mint to the pan and simmer for 1 minute longer.
Serve with rice. Drink a rosé or light dry red wine.

Pollo con Langosta
Chicken with Lobster

This is an exotic and expensive Catalan dish, called in the local language,
Mar i Muntanya (Sea and Mountain). The sauce combines almonds,
hazelnuts, saffron and bitter chocolate, unlikely and unusual. However,

the blend of flavours works, though it is not a dish for everyday, indeed not a dish for anything but a very special occasion.

SERVES 4

a 1.1–1.4 kg/2½–3 pound chicken, cut into serving pieces
salt and freshly ground pepper
pinch of ground cinnamon (optional)
4 tablespoons olive oil
a 900 g/2 pound lobster, divided into the tail, large claws, head and small claws
lobster liver (tomalley)
2 medium onions, finely chopped
2 tablespoons finely chopped parsley
1 bay leaf
½ teaspoon thyme
500 g/1 pound (4 medium) tomatoes, peeled, seeded and chopped
250 ml/8 fl oz (1 cup) dry white wine
2 tablespoons *aguardiente* or brandy
⅛ teaspoon ground saffron
2 cloves garlic
25 g/1 oz (⅛ cup) each hazelnuts and blanched almonds, finely ground
2 teaspoons grated bitter chocolate

Season the chicken pieces with salt and pepper, and a pinch of cinnamon if liked. Heat the oil in a large frying pan (skillet) and sauté the chicken pieces until golden on both sides. Transfer to a flameproof casserole. Put the head and small claws of the lobster into a saucepan with salted water to cover, cover and simmer for 30 minutes. Strain and reserve the cooking liquid. In the frying pan (skillet) sauté the lobster tail and claws over fairly high heat until they turn pink. Add to the chicken pieces.

In the oil remaining in the pan sauté the onion until soft. Add 1 tablespoon of the parsley, the bay leaf, thyme and tomatoes and cook until the mixture is slightly thickened. Add the wine and *aguardiente* or brandy, season with salt and pepper and simmer until reduced by half. Remove and discard the herbs and pour over the chicken and lobster in the casserole. Bring the liquid to a simmer, cover and cook over very low heat.

In a food processor or blender, combine the garlic cloves, saffron, remaining tablespoon of parsley, the nuts and the chocolate. Add the lobster liver (tomalley) and 250 ml/8 fl oz (1 cup) of the reserved lobster stock and process to a purée. Pour the mixture into the casserole and continue cooking until the chicken is tender, about 15 minutes.

To serve, remove the lobster shell from the tail and large claws and cut the meat into even slices. Distribute equally among 4 warmed dinner plates. Add a chicken piece to each plate and pour the sauce over. Serve with a salad and a full-bodied dry white wine.

Pollo Tomatero
Chicken with Tomatoes

When summer tomatoes are at their sweetest, ripest and most abundant best I like to cook this dish for a long, lazy summer lunch, or informal supper. It is from the Basque country, home of much good cooking.

SERVES 4
a 1–1.4 kg/2½–3 pound chicken, quartered
salt and freshly ground pepper
3 tablespoons olive oil
125 g/4 ounces cured ham, chopped
1 medium onion, finely chopped
2 cloves garlic, chopped
500 g/1 pound (4 medium) tomatoes, peeled, seeded and chopped
1 teaspoon sugar

Season the chicken pieces with salt and pepper. Heat the oil in a deep frying pan (skillet) and sauté the chicken pieces, turning until golden-brown and tender. As the breasts cook more quickly than the legs, cook the legs first and for a longer time, in all about 30 minutes, with 15 minutes for the breasts. Lift out to a serving dish, cover and keep warm. Add the ham to the pan and sauté until lightly browned. Add to the chicken.

In the oil remaining in the pan, sauté the onion until it is soft, adding a little more oil if necessary. Add the garlic and sauté for 2 minutes longer. Add the tomatoes and the sugar, season with salt and pepper and cook until the mixture is thick and well-blended. Return the chicken and ham to the pan and cook for a few minutes to heat the chicken through and blend the flavours. Serve with rice or potatoes, and a salad. Drink a light dry red wine, or a rosé.

Pollo a la Española
Chicken, Spanish-style

This is another of the easy-to-cook chicken dishes in which the Spanish kitchen abounds, this time from New Castille. The pine nuts give a pleasantly crunchy texture to the sauce.

SERVES 4

a 1.2–1.4 kg /2½–3 pound chicken, cut into serving pieces
salt and freshly ground pepper
plain (all-purpose) flour
4 tablespoons olive oil
1 medium onion, finely chopped
50 g/2 ounces *serrano* or *prosciutto* ham, chopped
1 clove garlic, chopped
2 tablespoons finely chopped parsley
2 teaspoons chopped fresh basil
1 bay leaf
125 ml/4 fl oz)½ cup) dry white wine
125 ml/4 fl oz (½ cup) chicken stock
50 g/2 oz (½ cup) pine nuts

Season the chicken pieces with salt and pepper and dredge with flour, shaking to remove the excess. Heat the oil in a heavy frying pan (skillet) and sauté the chicken pieces until golden-brown on both sides. Transfer them to a flameproof casserole. In the oil remaining in the pan sauté the onion until soft. Add the ham and garlic and cook for 2–3 minutes longer. Add to the casserole with the parsley, basil, bay leaf, wine, stock and pine nuts. Cover and cook over low heat until the chicken is tender, 30–45 minutes.

Transfer the chicken pieces to a warmed serving dish and, using a slotted spoon, lift out the other ingredients and add them to the chicken. If the sauce in the casserole is very abundant, reduce it over brisk heat. Taste for seasoning and add salt and pepper if necessary. Pour the sauce over the chicken and serve with potatoes and a salad. A dry light red wine is good with this.

Variation: For an elegant dish to serve 4, use skinned and boned chicken breasts. Cut a slit in each of 4 breasts and stuff with a slice of serrano or prosciutto ham. Secure with wooden cocktail sticks (toothpicks). Heat the oil and sauté the onion until soft. Add the garlic and sauté 2 minutes longer. Add the chicken breasts, 50 ml/2 fl oz (¼ cup) each dry white wine and chicken stock, parsley, basil and pine nuts and cook, covered, for 10–12 minutes or until the chicken breasts are done. Serve them with the sauce poured over, after removing the cocktail sticks (toothpicks).

Polle en Chilindrón
Chicken with Sweet Red (Bell) Peppers

This is from Aragon where chicken, pork and lamb are cooked *en chilindrón*, that is, with sweet red (bell) peppers, an example of the cross-fertilization that comes to cuisines from conquests, wars and exploration. Some good always comes from bad happenings and the *chilindrón* dishes are an example of this, as the sweet red (bell) peppers came to Spain from Mexico, the original home of all the members of the capsicum family, sweet, pungent and hot.

SERVES 4
a 1.1–1.4 kg /2½–3 pound chicken, cut into serving pieces
salt and freshly ground pepper
4 tablespoons olive oil
1 medium onion, finely chopped
1 clove garlic, chopped
2 sweet red (bell) peppers, seeded and cut into 5mm/¼ inch strips
50 g/2 ounces *serrano* or *prosciutto* ham, chopped
250 g/8 ounces (4 medium) tomatoes, peeled, seeded and chopped

Season the chicken pieces with salt and pepper. In a large frying pan (skillet) heat the oil and sauté the chicken pieces until golden on both sides. Lift out into a flameproof casserole. In the oil remaining in the pan sauté the onion until soft. Add the garlic and sauté for 2 minutes longer. Add the peppers and ham and continue to cook until the peppers are soft. Add the tomatoes and cook until the mixture is well blended.

Add the mixture to the casserole, season to taste with salt and pepper, cover and cook over low heat for 30 minutes or until the chicken is tender. The sauce should be quite thick.

Variation: If liked, add a small, hot seeded red chilli pepper chopped, to the sauce. Halved, pitted green and black olives, about 8 of each, can be added to the sauce during the last few minutes of cooking.

Pepitoria de Gallina
Casseroled Chicken

This chicken dish from New Castille translates literally into a medley of fowl, which fails to explain what the dish is composed of. It is a casseroled chicken enriched by the addition of hazelnuts, the yolks of hardboiled eggs, and ham. A delicious medley.

SERVES 4–6
a 1.4–1.6 kg/3–3½ pound chicken, cut into serving pieces
salt and freshly ground pepper
125 g/4 ounces smoked ham, cubed
3 tablespoons finely chopped parsley
250 ml/8 fl oz (1 cup) chicken stock
3 cloves garlic, crushed
12 toasted hazelnuts, ground
2 hardboiled egg yolks
⅛ teaspoon ground cloves
1 large egg yolk, lightly beaten

Pat the chicken pieces dry with paper towels and season to taste with salt and pepper. Heat the oil in a frying pan (skillet) and sauté the chicken pieces over moderate heat until golden brown on both sides. Add the ham and 1 tablespoon of the parsley and sauté for 1–2 minutes longer. Transfer the chicken and ham mixture to a flameproof casserole. Pour in the chicken stock, bring to a simmer, cover and cook over low heat until the chicken is tender, about 45 minutes.

While the chicken is cooking, mix the garlic, hazelnuts, hardboiled egg yolks, cloves and the remaining parsley together in a small bowl. Stir until the mixture is smooth. When the chicken is tender, stir in the mixture and simmer for 5 minutes longer. Stir in the egg yolk and cook, stirring, until the sauce has lightly thickened. Serve immediately with rice or potatoes and a green salad. Drink a light dry red wine.

Pollo en Chanfaina
Chicken with Vegetables

Cataluña was once part of France and even today there are echoes of Provençal cooking in the province. This Catalan dish is reminiscent of ratatouille. Whatever its origins, it is a delightful dish, especially for summer dining.

SERVES 4–6
4 tablespoons olive oil
a 1.6 kg/3½ pound chicken, cut into serving pieces
2 medium onions, finely chopped
3 cloves garlic, chopped
2 medium aubergines (eggplants), cubed
2 red or green sweet (bell) peppers, seeded and sliced
500 g/1 pound (4 medium) tomatoes, peeled, seeded and chopped
1 bay leaf
1 sprig thyme or ¼ teaspoon dried thyme
salt and freshly ground pepper
125 ml/4 fl oz (½ cup) dry white wine
bread triangles fried in olive oil, to garnish

Heat the oil in a heavy frying pan (skillet) and sauté the chicken pieces until golden on both sides. Lift out into a flameproof casserole. In the oil remaining in the pan, sauté the onion until soft, add the garlic and sauté for 2 minutes longer. Add the aubergine (eggplant) cubes and peppers and sauté for 5 minutes longer. Add the tomatoes, bay leaf, thyme and salt and pepper to taste. Stir in the wine and add the mixture to the casserole, smothering the chicken with the vegetable mixture. Cover and simmer over low heat for about 45–60 minutes or until the chicken is tender. Serve garnished with triangles of fried bread. Drink a light dry red wine.

Pollo con Setas a la Navarra
Chicken with Mushrooms, Navarre-style

Simplicity and economy characterize much of the cooking of Spain. Here the chicken's liver is used to enrich the sauce and mushrooms are used lavishly when they are in season. An ordinary dish is transformed into a luxury one.

SERVES 4–6
a 1.4–1.6 kg/3–3½ pound chicken, cut into serving pieces
salt and freshly ground pepper
4 tablespoons olive oil
8 cloves garlic
500 g/1 pound mushrooms, sliced
1 chicken liver, halved
250 ml/8 fl oz (1 cup) dry white wine

Season the chicken pieces with salt and pepper. In a frying pan (skillet) heat the oil and sauté the garlic cloves over low heat until golden. Do not let them burn or they will taste bitter. Lift them out into a bowl.

In the oil remaining in the pan sauté the chicken pieces until golden on both sides. Transfer them to a flameproof casserole. Add the mushrooms to the pan and sauté them over moderately high heat until lightly browned, stirring from time to time. Add them to the casserole. In the oil remaining in the pan, sauté the chicken liver until it is browned on the outside, but still pink within, adding a little more oil if necessary.

In a food processor or blender reduce the garlic cloves and chicken liver to a paste. Add to the casserole with the wine. Bring to a simmer, cover and cook over very low heat until the chicken is tender, about 45 minutes. If necessary, add a little more wine during cooking. Season with salt and pepper. Serve with potatoes and a salad and drink a light dry red wine.

Frango com Ervilhas
Chicken with Peas

This Portuguese dish is of the utmost simplicity but that does not mean it is dull or ordinary. The combination of onions, stock and dry Madeira, or even better, dry Port, create a delicious flavour enhanced by the addition of fresh young peas.

SERVES 4–6
a 1.4–1.6 kg/3–3½ pound chicken, cut into serving pieces
salt and freshly ground pepper
2 tablespoons olive oil
25 g/1 oz (2 tablespoons) butter
2 medium onions, finely chopped
½ teaspon chopped fresh oregano or ¼ teaspoon dried
250 ml/8 fl oz (1 cup) chicken stock
50 ml/2 fl oz (¼ cup) dry Port or dry Madeira
175 g/6 oz (1 cup) fresh green peas or if frozen, defrosted

Season the chicken pieces with salt and pepper. Heat the oil and butter in a flameproof casserole and sauté the chicken pieces until golden on both sides. Lift out on to a plate and reserve. In the fat remaining in the casserole sauté the onions until soft. Stir in the stock, wine and oregano.

Return the chicken pieces to the casserole with any juices that may have collected. Cover and simmer over low heat until the chicken is tender, 45–60 minutes. Season to taste with salt and pepper. Fifteen minutes before the chicken is done, add the peas. Serve with fried potatoes and drink a light dry red wine.

Pollo a la Extremeña
Chicken, Extremeña-style

This Spanish province facing, though not on, the Atlantic, seems to have no end of imaginative chicken dishes, making this most versatile of birds not only useful but festive.

SERVES 4–6
a 1.4–1.6 kg/3–3½ pound chicken, cut into serving pieces
salt and freshly ground pepper
2 tablespoons olive oil
1 medium onion, finely chopped
grated rind of 1 lemon
3 tablespoons honey
½ teaspoon dried rosemary, crumbled
dry white wine

Season the chicken pieces with salt and pepper. Heat the oil in a frying pan (skillet) and sauté the chicken until golden on both sides. Lift out into a flameproof casserole. In the oil remaining in the pan sauté the onion until soft. Add it to the casserole.

In a small saucepan combine the lemon rind, honey and rosemary and warm the mixture through. Season with a little salt. Pour the mixture over the chicken and cook over very low heat until the chicken is tender, about 45 minutes. If the chicken seems to be drying out, add a little dry white wine and continue cooking.

Pollo con Jamón Serrano
Chicken with Mountain Ham

This splendid mountain ham is not often available outside Spain. Our best substitute is Italian *prosciutto*, salted, air-cured ham which has a similar flavour. It adds something special to this chicken dish from Extremeña.

SERVES 4–6
a 1.4–1.6 kg/3–3½ pound chicken, cut into serving pieces
125 g/4 ounces serrano or prosciutto ham, cut into thin strips
2 tablespoons olive oil
2 medium onions, finely chopped
500 g/1 lb (4 medium) tomatoes, peeled, seeded and chopped
125 ml/4 fl oz (½ cup) brandy, preferably Spanish
salt and freshly ground pepper

Lard the chicken pieces under the skin with the strips of ham. Heat the oil in a frying pan (skillet) and sauté the chicken pieces until golden on both sides. Lift out into a casserole.

In the oil remaining in the pan sauté the onions until soft. Add the tomatoes and cook until the mixture is well-blended, about 5 minutes. Stir in the brandy, season with salt and pepper and pour over the chicken pieces. Bring to a simmer, cover and cook over low heat until the chicken is tender, about 45 minutes. Serve with rice or potatoes and a salad. Drink a light dry red wine.

Pollo al Estilo Murciano
Chicken, Murcian-style

Influenced by both Valencia and New Castille, the Murcian cuisine from a very small province is highly original. It has a sophisticated simplicity that makes apparently routine dishes taste wonderful. This chicken dish is a good example of the cooking.

SERVES 4
4 tablespoons olive oil
2 large or 3 medium sweet red (bell) peppers, seeded and cut into strips
a 1.6 kg/3½ pound chicken, cut into serving pieces
500 g/1 pound (4 medium) tomatoes, peeled, seeded and chopped
salt and freshly ground pepper
1 teaspoon sugar

Heat the oil in a large frying pan (skillet) and sauté the pepper strips until soft. Lift them out onto a dish with a slotted spoon and set aside.

In the oil remaining in the pan sauté the chicken pieces until golden on both sides. Put the tomatoes into a deep casserole. Season them with salt, pepper and the sugar. Add the chicken legs, then top with the breasts.

Cover and cook over low heat until the chicken is tender, about 45 minutes. Add the pepper strips and cook for 5 minutes longer, to blend the flavours. Serve with potatoes and a green salad. Drink a light red wine.

Pechugas de Pollo con Piñones
Chicken Breasts with Pine Nuts

The technique of adding nuts to main dish sauces is popular all over Spain and is a heritage from the time when the country was under Arab domination. This luxurious-tasting dish is made special by the delicate crunchy flavour of pine nuts. It has the added advantage of needing little preparation time.

SERVES 4
about 2 tablespoons olive oil
4 chicken breasts, skinned and boned
1 medium onion, finely chopped
1 clove garlic, chopped
1 medium sweet red (bell) pepper, seeded and chopped
1 teaspoon plain (all-purpose) flour
2 tablespoons chopped parsley
50 g/2 ounces (½ cup) pine nuts
125 ml/4 fl oz (½ cup) dry white wine

Heat the oil in a frying pan (skillet) and sauté the chicken breasts for 1 minute on each side. Transfer the breasts to a shallow flameproof casserole large enough to hold them in a single layer.

In the oil remaining in the pan, sauté the onion, garlic and pepper until soft, adding a little more oil if necessary. Stir in the flour and cook for about 1 minute. Add the parsley and pine nuts and the wine, stirring to mix. Season with salt and pepper, bring to a simmer, cover and cook over very low heat for 15 minutes. Pour the sauce over the chicken breasts and cook 10 minutes longer.

Perdices Estofados
Stewed Partridges

The name of this dish from Old Castille does not convey the beauty of it, which gives a great reward at the table for little work in the kitchen. It will serve 4 if preceded by a fairly hearty first course, or 2 diners with robust appetites.

SERVES 2–4
2 partridges, halved, each weighing about 500 g/1 pound
salt and freshly ground pepper
2 tablespoons olive oil
1 large onion, chopped
8 cloves garlic, left whole
1 clove
1 bay leaf
250 ml/8 fl oz (1 cup) dry white wine
500 g/1 pound (about 3 medium) potatoes, peeled, sliced and fried
375 g/12 ounces (about 4 cups) mushrooms

Season the partridges with salt and pepper. In a large flameproof casserole, preferably oval, that will hold the birds comfortably, heat the oil and sauté the partridges until lightly browned all over.

Add the onion, garlic, clove, bay leaf and wine, bring to a simmer, cover and cook over low heat until the partridges are tender, about 1 hour, adding more wine during cooking if necessary. Five minutes before serving add the potatoes and the mushrooms. Serve with a green salad and drink a light dry red wine.

Variation: For an exotic version of the dish add 1 teaspoon grated bitter chocolate to the sauce, just before serving, stirring until it has dissolved.

Oca con Peras
Baby Goose with Pears

This is a famous Catalan dish, known in the local language as *L'Oca Amb Peres*. Unfortunately baby goose is not generally available but a duckling is an admirable substitute.

SERVES 4

a 1.8–2 kg/4–4½ pound duckling or baby goose, quartered
4 tablespoons olive oil
1 medium onion, chopped
2 cloves garlic, chopped
1 tablespoon plain (all-purpose) flour plus extra for dredging
250 ml/8 fl oz (1 cup) chicken stock
2 tablespoons pine nuts
75 g/3 oz (½ cup) seedless raisins
1 tablespoon finely chopped parsley
4 small, firm pears, peeled

Pull away and discard any surplus fat from the duckling or baby goose. Prick the pieces all over with a fork to help release the fat. Heat 1 tablespoon of the oil in a heavy frying pan (skillet) and brown the duckling or baby goose on both sides. Put into a large casserole that will hold the pieces comfortably.

In the oil remaining in the pan sauté the onion and garlic until the onion is soft. Stir in 1 tablespoon flour and cook for 2 minutes, then stir in the stock and cook until the mixture is smooth. Pour over the duckling or baby goose in the casserole. The liquid should come about one-third of the way up the bird. Add a little more stock if necessary. Cook in a preheated moderate oven (180°C/350°F/gas 4) for about 1½ hours, or until almost done. Stir in the pine nuts, raisins and parsley and cook for 10 minutes longer.

While the bird is cooking, dredge the pears in flour and sauté in a frying pan (skillet) in the remaining 3 tablespoons oil, turning to colour lightly all over. Add to the casserole with the bird and cook for 10–15 minutes longer. Serve straight from the casserole, placing a quarter of the duckling or baby goose on each plate with a pear. Serve with a green salad and drink a light dry red wine.

Pato con Aceitunas a la Andaluza
Duckling with Olives, Andalucian-style

Olive trees may have been introduced into Andalucía by Phoenician traders as early as 1100 BC or, not much later from a historical point of view, by Greek colonizers about 500 BC or by the Romans. In any event it would be impossible to think of this part of Spain without its olives which have a special affinity for duckling.

SERVES 4
a 1.8–2 kg/4–4½ pound duckling, quartered
salt and freshly ground pepper
1 tablespoon olive oil
1 medium onion, finely chopped
2 medium carrots, scraped and thinly sliced
2 cloves garlic, chopped
2 teaspoons plain (all-purpose) flour
125 ml/4 fl oz (½ cup) dry sherry
350 ml/12 fl oz (1½ cups) duck or chicken stock
1 teaspoon tomato purée
1 bay leaf
1 tablespoon finely chopped parsley
24 unstuffed pitted green olives, sliced

Pull away and discard any surplus fat from the duckling. Prick the pieces all over to help release the fat. Season with salt and pepper. Heat the oil in a heavy flameproof casserole large enough to hold the duckling pieces comfortably. Brown the duckling pieces on both sides over moderate heat. Lift out on to a platter and set aside. Pour off all but 2 tablespoons fat from the casserole.

Add the onion and carrots to the casserole and sauté until the vegetables are soft. Add the garlic and sauté for 2 minutes longer. Add the flour and cook, stirring, for 1 minute. Pour in the sherry and stock, and stir in the tomato purée. Add the bay leaf and parsley, and return the duckling to the casserole with any juices that may have collected. Bring the liquid to a simmer, cover and cook over low heat for about 1½ hours, or until the duckling is tender.

While the duckling is cooking, soak the olives in cold water for 10 minutes. Drain and simmer in a little stock for 5 minutes and set aside. Lift out the cooked duckling to a warmed dish and keep it warm. Strain the liquid in the casserole through a fine sieve set over a bowl, pressing down with a ladle or a wooden spoon to extract all the flavour. Return the liquid to the casserole, add the olives and the duckling pieces, cover and simmer just long enough to heat the olives through. Serve with rice and a salad and drink a full-bodied dry red wine.

Pato con Judias a la Catalana
Duckling with Beans, Catalan-style

This is a robust dish lifted out of the ordinary by the charming Catalan habit of adding nuts and saffron to what might otherwise be a rather pedestrian sauce.

SERVES 4

375 g/12 oz (2 cups) white haricot or Great Northern beans
a 1.8–2 kg/4–4½ pound duckling, quartered
salt and freshly ground pepper
plain (all-purpose) flour for dredging
1 tablespoon olive oil
125 g/4 oz (8 slices) bacon, chopped
2 medium onions, finely chopped
125 ml/4 fl oz (½ cup) duck or chicken stock or water
125 ml/4 fl oz (½ cup) dry red wine
1 tablespoon tomato purée
25 g/1 oz (¼ cup) dry red wine
1 tablespoon tomato purée
25 g/1 oz (¼ cup) pine nuts
⅛ teaspoon saffron, ground
2 cloves garlic, crushed
1 bay leaf
1 sprig thyme or ¼ teaspoon dried
¼ teaspoon oregano
1 tablespoon finely chopped parsley

Wash and pick over the beans and put them to soak in cold water overnight. Drain and put into a saucepan with fresh water to cover and 1 teaspoon salt. Bring to a simmer, cover and cook over low heat until the beans are tender, 1½–2 hours. The time will vary. When cooked, set aside.

Pull away and discard any surplus fat from the duckling. Prick the pieces all over to help release the fat. Season with salt and pepper and dredge with flour, shaking to remove the excess. In a large heavy frying pan (skillet) heat the oil and sauté the bacon until crisp. Add the duckling and brown the pieces all over. Transfer to a flameproof casserole.

In the fat remaining in the pan sauté the onions until soft. Add them to the casserole with the wine, stock or water, and tomato purée and simmer until the duck is almost tender, about 1½ hours.

In a bowl mix together the pine nuts, saffron, garlic, bay leaf, thyme, oregano and parsley and stir into the casserole. Cook for 15 minutes longer, then add the strained beans and cook for another 15 minutes, or until the duckling is tender. Serve straight from the casserole and drink a full-bodied dry red wine.

Pato Montanesa
Braised Duckling, Mountain-style

This simple Galician dish is made special by its garnish of button mushrooms, small white onions and new potatoes.

SERVES 4

a 1.8–2 kg/4–4½ pound duckling, quartered
1 tablespoon olive oil
1 medium onion, finely chopped
2 teaspoons plain (all-purpose) flour
250 g/8 oz (2 medium) tomatoes, peeled, seeded and chopped
125 ml/4 fl oz (½ cup) dry sherry
250 ml/8 fl oz (1 cup) duck or chicken stock
salt and freshly ground pepper
1 tablespoon paprika

For the garnish
25 g/1 oz (2 tablespoons) butter
16 small new potatoes, freshly cooked
16 small white onions, about 2.5 cm/1 inch, freshly cooked
16 button mushrooms

Pull away and discard any surplus fat from the duckling. Prick the pieces all over to help release the fat. In a large frying pan (skillet) sauté the duckling pieces in the olive oil until browned all over. Lift out into a casserole. In the fat remaining in the pan sauté the onion until soft. Stir in the flour and cook for 1–2 minutes. Add the tomatoes and sherry, stir to mix and add the stock, salt, pepper and paprika, mixing thoroughly. Cook for 1–2 minutes, then add the duckling pieces, cover and simmer gently until the duckling is tender, about 1½ hours.

When ready to serve put the duckling on a warmed platter and surround with the mushrooms sautéed in the butter over moderately high heat for 5 minutes, the new potatoes and the onions mixed quickly in the butter remaining in the pan in which the mushrooms were sautéed. A full-bodied dry red wine is a good accompaniment.

Pato a la Vasca
Duckling, Basque-style

Basque cooking is renowned for its excellence, and often produces the simplest and most delicious Spanish dishes.

SERVES 4
a 1.8–2 kg/4–4½ pound duckling, quartered
salt and freshly ground pepper
1 tablespoon olive oil
125 ml/4 fl oz (½ cup) dry white wine
beef, chicken or duck stock
1 teaspoon chopped tarragon
½ teaspoon chopped thyme
1 clove
2 medium onions, finely chopped
1 tablespoon plain (all-purpose) flour
1 teaspoon white wine vinegar (optional)

Pull away and discard any surplus fat from the duckling. Prick the pieces all over with a fork to help release the fat. Season with salt and pepper. Heat the oil in a large frying pan (skillet) and sauté the duckling pieces until lightly browned all over. Lift out into a flameproof casserole and pour in the wine and enough stock to come about one-third of the way up the duckling. Add the tarragon, thyme and clove. Cover and cook over low heat until the duckling is tender, or cook in a preheated moderate oven (180°C/350°F/gas 4) for about 1 hour and 20 minutes.

In the fat remaining in the frying pan sauté the onions until soft. Stir in the flour and cook for 2 minutes longer. When the duckling is tender remove from the heat, pour off the stock from the casserole into a jug, spoon off the excess fat and add the liquid to the frying pan (skillet), stirring constantly to make a smooth sauce. There should be about 330 ml/12 fl oz (1½ cups). If necessary make up the quantity with extra stock and wine. Season to taste with salt and pepper. Pour the sauce over the duckling in the casserole and simmer just long enough to heat the dish through. Stir in the vinegar if liked. Serve with potatoes and a salad. Drink a full-bodied dry red wine.

Pato en Salsa de Almendras
Duck in Almond Sauce

This is a Catalan dish using nuts to thicken the sauce, in this case almonds. It is an Arab culinary influence from the days before the *reconquista* which cooks have sensibly retained since it is one thing to throw out an invader, another to throw out valuable contributions to the kitchen.

SERVES 4

a 1.8–2 kg/4–4½ pound duckling, cut into serving pieces
1 tablespoon lard or oil
duckling liver
1 onion, coarsely chopped
2 cloves garlic, chopped
500 g/1 pound (4 medium) tomatoes, peeled, seeded and chopped
salt and freshly ground pepper
50 g/2 ounces (½ cup) blanched almonds
50 ml/2 fl oz (¼ cup) dry sherry
1 tablespoon chopped parsley
duck or chicken stock if necessary

Pull away and discard any surplus fat from the duckling. Heat the lard or oil in a large frying pan (skillet) and brown the duckling pieces all over. Lift out and set aside. Sauté the duckling liver briefly, turning once. Lift out and set aside. Pour away all but 1 tablespoon fat from the pan and sauté the onion until soft. Add the garlic and sauté for 1–2 minutes longer. Add to the liver.

Put the duckling pieces into a flameproof casserole large enough to hold them comfortably. Add the tomatoes, season with salt and pepper, cover and cook over low heat until the duckling is tender, 1–1½ hours.

Toast the almonds on a baking sheet in a preheated moderate (180°C/350°F/gas 4) oven for 10 minutes or until lightly coloured. In a blender or food processor grind the almonds. Add the liver, chopped coarsely, the onion and garlic and process to a heavy paste. Scrape out the mixture into a bowl and add the sherry.

When the duckling is tender, stir in the liver and almond mixture and simmer for 5 minutes. Stir in the parsley and simmer for 1 minute longer. If at any time during the cooking the duckling seems at all dry, add a little duck or chicken stock: this will depend on the juiciness of the tomatoes. Serve with rice and a salad and drink a full-bodied dry red wine.

Pato a la Gallega
Duckling, Galician-style

This is a very rich duckling dish from Galicia with an amalgam of flavours, a delicious blend of duck, vegetables, herbs, wine and chestnuts.

SERVES 4–6
a 2 kg/4½ lb duckling
salt and freshly ground pepper
225 g/8 ounces bacon, chopped
3 tablespoons lard or butter
225 g/8 ounces small white turnips, peeled and sliced
225 g/8 ounces carrots, scraped and sliced
12 spring onions (scallions), trimmed, using some of the green part
250 ml/8 fl oz (1 cup) dry white wine
50 ml/2 fl oz (¼ cup) *anis* liqueur (optional)
bouquet garni (sprig thyme, oregano, bay leaf, parsley tied together with a piece of cotton thread)
2 cloves garlic, chopped
24 cooked, whole chestnuts
chicken stock

Season the duckling inside and out with salt and pepper and put into a large, deep, flameproof casserole with the bacon and lard or butter. Brown the duckling on both sides over moderate heat. Add the turnips, carrots, onions, bouquet garni and garlic. Cover and cook in a preheated moderate oven (160°C/325°F/gas 3) for 45 minutes.

Remove from the oven and pour off the accumulated fat. Add the wine and *anis*, if using, bring to a simmer on top of the stove, cover and return the casserole to the oven for 45 minutes longer. Ten minutes before the duckling is cooked, add the chestnuts and enough chicken stock to make a sauce. Remove and discard the bouquet garni. Serve the duckling with the sauce poured over, surrounded by the vegetables and chestnuts. Serve with a salad and drink a light, fruity, dry red wine.

Codornices Estofadas
Braised Quail

Quail are plentiful in Spain as the little birds, weighing only about 125 g/ 4 ounces when ready to cook, migrate from their winter home in India to the Mediterranean in huge numbers in the spring. Many are caught, but many escape, which leaves cooks with a tranquil conscience. This is the simplest of all ways to cook quail, and is popular in Andalucía and other parts of Spain.

SERVES 4
2 tablespoons olive oil
8 oven-ready quail
1 medium onion, finely chopped
1 clove garlic, chopped
2 tablespoons brandy, preferably Spanish
salt and freshly ground pepper
1 bay leaf
250 ml/8 fl oz (1 cup) dry white wine

Heat the oil in a heavy flameproof casserole and sauté the quail over moderate heat until lightly browned all over. Lift out onto a dish and set aside. In the oil remaining in the casserole sauté the onion until it is soft, add the garlic and sauté for 2 minutes longer.

Return the quail to the casserole, pour in and light the brandy. When the flame dies down, season the quail with salt and pepper. Add the bay leaf, pour in the wine, bring to a simmer, cover tightly and cook over very low heat until the birds are tender, about 30 minutes. Serve with potatoes and drink a light red wine.

Codornices a la Riojana
Quail in Sweet Green (Bell) Peppers

This is a very pretty dish from Rioja with the little birds tucked neatly into the green peppers. Red peppers can also be used. Two quail is a usual serving per person.

SERVES 4
8 oven-ready quail
salt and freshly ground pepper
6 tablespoons olive oil
8 large sweet green (bell) peppers, peeled (see page 187)
1 medium onion, finely chopped
2 cloves garlic, chopped
250 g/8 oz (2 medium) tomatoes, peeled, seeded and chopped
125 g/4 ounces cured ham, chopped
50 ml/2 fl oz (¼ cup) dry white wine
125 ml/4 fl oz (½ cup) chicken stock

Season the quail inside and out with salt and pepper. Heat the oil in a frying pan (skillet) and sauté the quail until lightly browned all over. Lift out and set aside. In the oil remaining in the pan sauté the onion until soft. Add the garlic and sauté for 1–2 minutes longer. Add the tomatoes and cook until the mixture is well-blended, about 5 minutes. Stir in the ham. Place the mixture in a casserole.

Remove the stems from the peeled green peppers. Make a lengthwise slit and carefully scrape out the seeds. Stuff each pepper with a quail and arrange in the casserole, which should be large enough to hold the birds in a single layer. Pour in the wine and chicken stock and bake in a preheated 180°C/350°F-gas 4 oven for 30 minutes, or until the quail and peppers are both tender. Serve with the sauce poured over them. Some cooks like to serve the quail taken out of the peppers with the peppers at one side of the plate with the sauce and the quail in the centre of the plate. Others prefer to leave the quail in their pepper nest. Serve with crusty bread and a full-bodied dry red wine.

Codornices con Pochas
Quail with Beans

This dish from Rioja uses beans that have formed in the pod but have not yet been dried. They are not readily available anywhere else. An adequate substitute is small white haricot beans or Great Northern beans.

SERVES 2
175 g/6 oz (1 cup) small white haricot beans or Great Northern beans
4 tablespoons lard or olive oil
2 oven-ready quail
1 medium onion, finely chopped
2 cloves garlic, chopped
250 g/8 oz (2 medium) tomatoes, peeled, seeded and chopped
salt and freshly ground pepper
125 g/4 ounces cured ham, chopped
50 g/2 ounces *chorizo*, sliced (optional)

Soak the beans overnight in cold water to cover. Drain, rinse, put into a saucepan with fresh cold water to cover and simmer, covered, until almost tender, 1½–2 hours. The time for cooking the beans will vary, so test one from time to time.

Heat the oil in a frying pan (skillet) and sauté the quail until lightly browned all over. Lift out of the pan and set aside. In the oil remaining in the pan sauté the onion until soft. Add the garlic and sauté for 1–2 minutes longer. Add the tomatoes, season with salt and pepper and cook until the mixture is well-blended.

When the beans are almost tender and the cooking liquid somewhat reduced, stir in the tomato mixture, the ham, and the chorizo, if using. Add the quail, cover and simmer over very low heat for 30 minutes longer. Serve with a salad and drink a full-bodied dry red wine.

Pavo Adobado
Marinated Turkey

Turkeys were cultivated in Mexico in very remote times and it is recorded that Hermán Cortés, the Spanish conqueror of Mexico, was offered a turkey dish, the original version of the now famous *Mole Poblano de Guajolote* (Turkey in the Style of Puebla), at a banquet given him by Emperor Montezuma. The Spanish called the bird *pavo*, a sort of lesser form of the peacock, the *pavo real*, royal peacock, instead of the nahuatl *guajolote*. The original birds were undoubtedly much smaller than the modern American version that has become widely popular. Very small turkeys weighing no more than a 2.3 kg/5 pound capon, up to birds weighing 4 kg/9 pounds, are best for this dish. This recipe is from Old Castille.

SERVES 8–14
a 2.3–4 kg/5–9 pound turkey, cut into serving pieces

For the marinade
4 bay leaves
4 cloves garlic, coarsely chopped
1 teaspoon black peppercorns, crushed
1 medium onion, sliced
1 teaspoon salt
700 ml–1.4 litres/1¼–2½ pints (3–6 cups) dry white wine, or enough to cover

In a bowl large enough to hold the turkey pieces, combine the turkey with all the ingredients for the marinade. Refrigerate and marinate overnight, turning the pieces once or twice. Lift out and pat the turkey pieces dry with paper towels. Strain and reserve the marinade, discarding the solids.

For the turkey
4–6 tablespoons olive oil
2 medium onions, chopped
2 cloves garlic, chopped
250 g/8 ounces (about 2 medium) tomatoes, peeled, seeded and chopped
2.5 cm/1 inch piece stick cinnamon
2 cloves
salt and freshly ground pepper

Heat the oil in a large, heavy frying pan (skillet) and sauté the turkey pieces until lightly browned. Do this in batches, if necessary, adding a little more oil. Lift out the turkey pieces into a casserole. In the oil remaining in the pan sauté the onion and garlic until the onion is soft. Add the tomatoes and cook until the mixture is thick and well-blended. Add to the casserole with the cinnamon and cloves, and salt and pepper to taste. Pour in the reserved marinade, cover and cook in a preheated moderate oven (180°C/350°F/gas 4) for 1½ hours for a 2.3 kg/5 pound bird and up to 2½ hours for a 4 kg-9 pound bird. Serve with rice and drink a light dry red wine.

Faisão com Madeira
Pheasant with Madeira

Both Portugal and Spain have abundant game which are cooked with imagination and flair. Partridge can also be used for this Portuguese recipe.

SERVES 2
a 759 g/1½ pound pheasant
salt and freshly ground pepper
1 tablespoon Dijon mustard
25 g/1 oz (2 tablespoons) butter
125 ml/4 fl oz (½ cup) game or chicken stock
125 ml/4 fl oz (½ cup) dry Madeira

Season the pheasant with salt, pepper and mustard. Heat the butter in a casserole and brown the bird on both sides. Pour in the stock and Madeira, bring to a simmer, cover and cook over low heat for 1 hour. Serve the pheasant halved, with potatoes and a green salad. Drink a full-bodied dry red wine.

Conejo a la Asturiana
Rabbit, Asturian-style

This region in the north of Spain is noted for its cider which is used here to good effect. Rabbit is as much esteemed in Spain as in Portugal. A game animal caught in the wild, most are young and tender. Cooking times for our rabbits are usually longer. Domestic rabbit is a good substitute for households lacking a hunter.

SERVES 4
4 tablespoons olive oil
125 g/4 ounces (½ cup) butter
125 g/4 ounces, bacon, chopped
2 medium onions, finely chopped
2 cloves garlic, chopped
3 young turnips, peeled and sliced
3 medium carrots, scraped and sliced
3 medium potatoes, peeled and sliced
rabbit's liver, if available
25 g/1 ounce (¼ cup) pine nuts, ground
1 tablespoon plain (all-purpose) flour
250 ml/8 fl oz (1 cup) dry (hard) cider
a 1.1–1.4 kg/2½–3 pound rabbit, cut into serving pieces
salt and freshly ground pepper
1 tablespoon chopped parsley

In a casserole heat the oil and half the butter and sauté the bacon, onions, garlic, turnips, carrots and potatoes for about 5 minutes without letting them brown. In a food processor or blender purée the rabbit liver, if available, and mix it with the pine nuts. Add to the casserole. Stir in the flour, cook for 1–2 minutes, stirring, then add the cider and set aside.

Heat the rest of the butter in a frying pan (skillet) and sauté the rabbit pieces until lightly browned on both sides. Add them to the casserole. Season with salt and pepper. Cover and simmer until the rabbit is tender, about 1½ hours, adding a little more cider if necessary. Sprinkle with the parsley and serve with potatoes. Drink a light dry red wine, or cider.

Conejo en Salmorejo
Rabbit in Sauce

Salmorejo is a special sauce for cooking rabbit. The cooking method is simple yet brings out all the flavour of the rabbit.

SERVES 4

a 1.1–1.4 kg/2½–3 pound rabbit, cut into serving pieces
salt and freshly ground pepper
1 tablespoon white wine vinegar
475 ml/16 fl oz (2 cups) dry white wine
2 sprigs fresh thyme or ½ teaspoon dried
½ teaspoon oregano
1 bay leaf
50 ml/2 fl oz (¼ cup) olive oil
3 cloves garlic, crushed
2 teaspoons paprika
1 small hot dried red chilli pepper, seeded and soaked to soften, or ¼ teaspoon cayenne

Season the rabbit pieces with salt and pepper and put them into a bowl. Combine the vinegar, wine, thyme, oregano and bay leaf and pour this marinade over the rabbit. Cover and refrigerate overnight, or for several hours, turning the pieces once or twice.

Lift out the rabbit pieces and pat dry with paper towels. Reserve the marinade. Heat the oil in a flameproof casserole and sauté the rabbit pieces until browned all over. Pour in the reserved marinade, cover and simmer over low heat until the rabbit is tender, about 1½ hours.

Chop the hot chilli pepper as finely as possible or grind in a mortar. Mix to a paste with the garlic, paprika and a little salt. Halfway through the cooking, add to the casserole and continue cooking. If the sauce is very abundant, cook partially covered for the second half of cooking to reduce the sauce slightly. Serve with crusty bread and a full-bodied dry red wine.

Variation: Portuguese cooks have an even simpler recipe, which can be used for either rabbit or hare. It is from the province of Tras-Os-Montes. Do not marinate the rabbit or hare. Sauté it in a casserole with 25g/1oz (2 tablespoons) butter and 1 tablespoon olive oil and if liked, 125 g/4 ounces chopped bacon, and 2 onions, chopped. When the rabbit or hare pieces are browned and the onion is soft, sprinkle with 1 teaspoon plain (all-purpose) flour and stir to mix. Pour in 250 ml/8 fl oz (1 cup) each dry red wine and water or stock. Season with salt and pepper and cook, covered, over low heat until the rabbit or hare is tender. Sprinkle with 1 tablespoon chopped parsley and serve with rice. Drink dry red wine.

Conejo a la Bilbaina
Rabbit, Basque-style

Basques have a reputation for being lovers of good food with a strongly traditional approach, their recipes are handed down through the generations. This recipe has sixteenth-century overtones, since chocolate, indigenous to Mexico, was unknown in Spain until after the Conquest. The bitter chocolate used in the sauce lends a subtly distinctive flavour but does not overwhelm.

SERVES 3–4
a 1.1–1.4 kg/2½–3 pound rabbit, cut into serving pieces
salt
plain (all-purpose) flour for dredging
1 tablespoon lard
4 tablespoons olive oil
1 head garlic, peeled and crushed
1 tablespoon parsley, finely chopped
50 g/2 ounces (½ cup) ground hazelnuts (filberts)
rabbit liver, if available, puréed
1 teaspoon grated unsweetened dark chocolate
1 bay leaf
2 cloves
250 ml/8 fl oz (1 cup) dry red wine
250 ml/8 fl oz (1 cup) stock or water
125 g/4 ounces mushrooms, thinly sliced

Season the rabbit pieces with salt and dredge with flour, shaking to remove the excess. Heat the lard and oil in a flameproof casserole, preferably earthenware, and brown the rabbit pieces on both sides. Mix together the garlic, parsley, hazel nuts and rabbit liver. Add to the casserole with the chocolate, bay leaf, cloves, wine and stock. Season with salt, bring to a simmer, cover and cook over moderate heat until the rabbit is tender, 1½–2 hours. In the last 10 minutes of cooking add the mushrooms. Serve straight from the casserole with potatoes or rice and a green salad. Drink a full-bodied dry red wine.

Conejo a la Navarra
Rabbit, Navarre-style

This rabbit dish exemplifies the individuality of the Navarre kitchen. It has a deceptive simplicity as herbs, tomato and wine blend into subtle flavour.

SERVES 2–3
a 1.1–1.4 kg/2½–3 pound rabbit, cut into serving pieces
salt and freshly ground pepper
4 tablespoons lemon juice
3 tablespoons lard
12 small white onions, peeled, or 12 spring onions (scallions), trimmed, using some of the green part
2 cloves garlic, chopped
250 g/8 ounces (about 2 medium) tomatoes, peeled, seeded and finely chopped
1 bay leaf
½ teaspoon rosemary, crumbled
1 tablespoons chopped parsley
250 ml/8 fl oz (1 cup) dry white wine
500 g/1 pound potatoes, peeled and sliced

Season the rabbit pieces with salt, pepper and lemon juice. Let stand for 15 minutes, then pat the pieces dry with paper towels. Heat the lard in a casserole and brown the rabbit pieces on both sides. Add the onions and cook for 2–3 minutes longer. Add the garlic, tomatoes, bay leaf, rosemary, parsley and wine. Bring to a simmer, cover and cook for 1 hour, then add the potatoes, seasoned with salt, and continue cooking until the potatoes and rabbit are both tender, about 30 minutes. Taste for seasoning and add salt and pepper if necessary. Serve with a salad and drink a fruity light dry red wine.

Variation: Arrange the potatoes on top of the casserole, season with salt and pepper and pour 2 tablespoons melted lard over them. Put the casserole into a preheated moderate oven (180°C350°F/gas 4) and cook, uncovered, until the potatoes are tender and golden.

Liebre con Lentejas
Hare with Lentils

Hare is used in this recipe from Spain's Extremeña province. The dark, strongly flavoured meat makes for a very rich dish, but hare is not always available and rabbit makes an excellent substitute.

SERVES 4

275 g/9 oz (1½ cups) brown lentils
beef stock to cover, about 475 ml/16 fl oz (2 cups)
a 1.4 kg/3 pound young hare, cut up, or 1 1–1.4 kg/2½–3 pound rabbit, cut into serving pieces
1 bay leaf
2 tablespoons olive oil
1 medium onion, finely chopped
2 cloves garlic, chopped
1 sweet red (bell) pepper, seeded and chopped
1 small hot fresh red chilli pepper, seeded and chopped
250 g/8 ounces (about 2 medium) tomatoes, peeled, seeded and chopped
salt and freshly ground pepper

Soak the lentils in cold stock to cover for 3–4 hours. In a casserole combine the lentils, stock, rabbit or hare pieces and the bay leaf and simmer, covered, for 1 hour.

In a small frying pan (skillet) heat the oil and sauté the onion, garlic, pepper, hot pepper, tomatoes and salt and pepper to taste. Cook until the mixture is well-blended, about 5 minutes. Let the mixture cool slightly, then purée in a blender or food processor. Add to the rabbit or hare and cook for about 30 minutes longer, or until the meat is tender. Taste for seasoning and add salt and pepper if necessary. Serve with rice or potatoes and a salad. Drink a full-bodied dry red wine.

5

Meats
Carnes

Eating roast suckling pig in Portugal or Spain is an experience never to be forgotten, with roast baby lamb a close second. Because of a general lack of good grazing land, inevitable in mountainous areas, animals are slaughtered young, so that there is an abundance of suckling pig, young lamb, kid and veal. Cooks have made a virtue of necessity and most beef appears as stew, though some very fine beef is always available: Portugal has notable recipes for steak. Tripe is popular and so are liver and kidneys, especially veal kidney. No meat lover should feel deprived as there is a great deal of variety in meat dishes thanks to the ingenuity and imagination of the peninsula's cooks.

Bifes com Ovos
Fillet Steaks with Egg Garnish

This is a luxurious dish from Estremadura, the province that has Portugal's capital, Lisbon, at its southern tip. For such a luxurious dish it is singularly uncomplicated.

SERVES 2
salt and freshly ground pepper
1 tablespoon lemon juice
2 fillet steaks, each weighing about 100 g/4 ounces
1 large clove garlic, crushed
50g/2oz (4 tablespoons) butter
1 tablespoon chopped chives
2 large eggs, lightly beaten

In a bowl mix together the salt, pepper and lemon juice. Add the steaks, turning to coat on both sides with the mixture. Let stand for 15 minutes.

Mix the garlic with 2 tablespoons of the butter, melted. In a frying pan (skillet) heat the remaining 2 tablespoons of butter. Scrape off and reserve any marinade from the steaks. Sauté the steaks over moderate heat for 2 minutes, then dip into the garlic butter. Sauté for 1 minute longer, turn and repeat for rare steaks: cook longer if liked. Transfer to a warmed dish and keep warm.

Mix the reserved marinade and chives with the eggs. Add any remaining garlic butter to the pan and scramble the eggs, adding a little salt if necessary, until they are just set and still soft. Pile the eggs on to the steaks and serve immediately. Serve with potatoes and a good dry red wine.

Variation:
A popular variation is *Bife com Ovo a Cavalo* (Steak with Egg on Horseback). Season 4 fillet steaks with salt, pepper and 4 cloves minced garlic. Let stand for 30 minutes. Sauté in 2 tablespoons lard or oil for 4 minutes on each side for medium-rare, or to taste. Heat 2 tablespoons olive oil in a frying pan (skillet) and fry 4 eggs. Place an egg on top of each steak and serve immediately with fried potatoes. Drink a full-bodied dry red wine.

Bifes de Cebolada
Fillet Steaks with Onions

This is another of the simple yet imaginative steak dishes that are distinctively Portuguese, created by cooks in Estremadura.

SERVES 4
For the cebolada
3 tablespoons olive oil
2 large onions, very thinly sliced
2 cloves garlic, chopped
250/8 oz (2 medium) tomatoes, peeled, seeded and chopped
salt and freshly ground pepper
1 tablespoon chopped parsley

For the steak
1 tablespoon olive oil
25g/1oz (2 tablespoons) butter
4 fillet steaks, each weighing 100–175 g/4–6 ounces

To prepare the *cebolada*, heat the oil in a frying pan (skillet) and sauté the onions over moderate heat until soft. Add the garlic and saute for 1–2 minutes longer. Add the tomatoes, season with salt and pepper and simmer until the mixture is thick and well blended, about 10 minutes. Stir in the parsley and cook for 1 minute longer. Set aside and keep warm.

In another frying pan (skillet) heat the oil and butter. Season the steaks with salt and pepper and sauté over moderate heat for 4 minutes on each side for medium-rare, or cook to taste. Lift out on to a warmed dish, pour the sauce over the steaks and serve with mashed potatoes, or boiled potatoes sprinkled with parsley. Drink a full-bodied dry red wine.

Bifes na Frigideira
Sautéed Fillet Steaks

This is another of the excellent steak dishes to be enjoyed in Lisbon and wherever good beef is to be found throughout Portugal.

SERVES 4
1 tablespoon olive oil
25g/1oz (2 tablespoons) butter
4 cloves garlic, crushed
1 bay leaf
salt and freshly ground pepper
4 fillet steaks, each weighing 100–175 g/4–6 ounces
100 g/4 ounces *presunto* or any other smoked ham, chopped
2 tablespoons dry Port or dry Madeira
1 lemon, cut into 4 wedges, to garnish

In a heavy frying pan (skillet) heat the oil and butter. Add the garlic and bay leaf and cook over very low heat for 1–2 minutes. Season the steaks with salt and pepper and sauté over moderate heat for 4 minutes on each side for medium-rare, or cook to taste. Lift out and keep warm.

Add the ham, Port or Madeira to the pan and heat through. pour the sauce over the steaks and serve immediately, garnished with the lemon and accompanied by fried potatoes. Drink a full-bodied dry red wine.

Rabo de Toro
Oxtail Stew

I suppose this should really be translated as Tail of the Bull Stew and indeed it is credited to Andalucía, home of the fighting bulls. The dish turns up in Navarre, Old Castille and Léon, and in fact wherever there are male cattle with tails, which makes it pretty widespread. Few cold-weather dishes are as delightful as oxtail stew, cooked slowly to bring out its hearty flavour, and the nibbly delicious quality of the meat round the bones.

SERVES 6
1.8 kg/4 pounds oxtails, jointed
plain (all-purpose) flour for dredging
salt and freshly ground pepper
2 tablespoons beef dripping or lard
2 tablespoons olive oil
2 medium onions, chopped
2 cloves garlic, chopped
3 medium carrots, scraped and sliced
2 stalks celery, sliced
1 bay leaf
1 sprig fresh thyme or ¼ teaspoon dried
250 ml/8 fl oz (1 cup) dry white wine
beef stock or water

Pat the oxtail pieces dry with paper towels. Season the flour with salt and pepper and dredge the oxtail pieces, shaking to remove the excess. In a large frying pan (skillet) heat the dripping or lard and brown the oxtails on all sides. Lift out and transfer to a deep, heavy flameproof casserole.

Discard the fat in the pan and wipe it out with paper towels. Add the oil and sauté the onions until soft. Add the garlic and saute for 1–2 minutes longer. Add to the casserole with the carrots, celery, bay leaf and thyme. Pour in the wine and enough stock or water barely to cover. Bring to a simmer, cover and cook over low heat for about 3½ hours or until the oxtail pieces are tender. Lift the meat out on to a warmed platter and cover to keep warm.

Skim as much fat as possible from the sauce, taste for seasoning and add salt if necessary. If the sauce is very abundant reduce it over brisk heat. Return the meat to the casserole and cook just long enough to heat it thoroughly. Serve from the casserole with a green vegetable such as green beans, potatoes if liked, and a robust, full-bodied dry red wine, such as a Rioja.

Estofado de Vaca a la Aragonesa
Beef Stew, Aragon-style

Originally from Aragon, a landlocked province in north eastern Spain abounding in meat, poultry and game, this stew is popular wherever good beef is available in the country, even though Estofado de Vaca translates as Cow Stew, a less than appetizing title! On the stove it can be left to itself, requiring minimum attention, an ideal dish for family and friends. There are interesting variations on the basic recipe as well as regional variations that lift the dish out of the ordinary, including a Catalan version with a little unsweetened chocolate lending an exciting flavour to the sauce.

SERVES 4
900 g/2 pounds lean stewing beef, into 3.5 cm/1½ inch pieces
3 tablespoons olive oil
1 medium onion, chopped
4 large cloves garlic, chopped
1 teaspoon plain (all-purpose) flour
125 g/4 oz (1 medium) tomatoes, peeled and sliced
salt and freshly ground pepper
1 sprig fresh thyme or ¼ teaspoon dried
1 bay leaf
225 ml/8 fl oz (1 cup) dry white wine

Pat the beef pieces dry with paper towels. Heat the oil in a heavy frying pan (skillet) and brown the beef in batches over moderately high heat, using a slotted spoon to transfer the pieces to a flameproof casserole, earthenware if possible. In the oil remaining in the pan adding a little more oil if necessary, sauté the onion until soft. Add the garlic and sauté for 1–2 minutes longer. Stir in the flour, then add the tomatoes, salt, pepper, thyme, bay leaf and wine. Stir gently to mix, bring to a simmer and pour over the beef. Cook, covered, over low heat until the meat is tender, 1½–2 hours. Check from time to time to make sure the stew is not drying out and add a little beef stock or extra wine if necessary.

Variation: If liked, 500 g/1 pound potatoes, peeled and left whole if small, halved if larger, may be added to the casserole about 45 minutes before serving time.

Variation: Instead of the chopped garlic, add a whole head of garlic, peeled, with the cloves left whole. Long, slow cooking gentles the flavour of the garlic.

Variation: For a more exotic dish simmer 250 g/8 ounces halved pitted prunes until tender, about 10 minutes, and add them to the casserole with 50 g/2 oz (½ cup) pine nuts for just long enough to heat them through before serving.

Variation: Asturia, has its own version of beef stew, *Estofado de Buey*. The beef, shank or other stewing cut, should be in one piece. Brown the beef in 1 tablespoon lard in a large flameproof casserole, add 250 g/8 ounces chopped bacon, 6 medium onions, thinly sliced, 4 medium carrots, scraped and sliced, 4 small white turnips, peeled and sliced, and cook for 5 minutes over moderate heat. Add 125/8 fl oz (1 cup) dry red wine, 2 tablespoons red wine vinegar, a sprig each of thyme, mint and parsley and a bay leaf tied together with cotton thread, with salt and pepper to taste. Cover and cook over very low heat until the meat is tender, 2–2½ hours. Slice the meat and serve together with the vegetables and cooking liquid. Discard the herb bouquet.

Variation: *Estofado de Buey a la Catalana* (Beef Stew, Catalan-style), combine 2 tablespoons lard or olive oil with 125 g/4 ounces coarsely chopped lean bacon in a large flameproof casserole and sauté until the bacon has given up any fat. In the fat remaining in the casserole sauté 900 g/2 pounds stewing beef, such as chuck, cut into 3.5 cm/1½ inch pieces, over moderately high heat until lighly browned. Add 1 medium onion, finely chopped, and 4 cloves of garlic, chopped, and sauté for about 3 minutes longer. Add 1 tablespoon chopped parsley, 1 bay leaf, 1 sprig thyme or ¼ teaspoon dried thyme, ¼ teaspoon oregano, salt, freshly ground pepper, 250 g/8 oz (2 medium) tomatoes, peeled, seeded and chopped, 250 ml/8 fl oz (1 cup) dry white wine and 250 ml/ 8 fl oz (1 cup) beef stock. Cover and simmer over low heat until the beef is tender, 1½–2 hours. While the meat is cooking grind together in a food processor or blender, 2 cloves garlic, 1 slice white bread, fried in olive oil, 6 almonds and 15 g/½ oz (½ square) unsweetened dark chocolate. Stir the mixture into the stew 15 minutes before it is ready. Serve with potatoes. A full-bodied dry red wine is good with all these stews.

Cocido Madrileno
Boiled Dinner, Madrid-style

Every cuisine has its one-dish meals, rich with a variety of meat and vegetables. The Iberian Peninsula has the Spanish *cocido* and the Portuguese *cozido*, marvellous dishes whose simplicty and good flavour make them esteemed members of the universal culinary family of one-dish meals. Wherever such dishes occur they are basically the same, yet always different, ranging from the *pot-au-feu* of the French to the *sancochos* of the Dominican Republic to the New England Boiled Dinner. They are flexible dishes where it is possible to add a little more, or a little less, of this or that to suit seasonal availability or personal taste. All they need is careful and loving cooking to produce a great meal.

In Spain the most popular *cocido* is the *Cocido Madrileño*, (Madrid-style Boiled Dinner), the classic of this type. Traditionally a boiling fowl is used, but these are hard to find and a good substitute is a whole 1.4 kg/ 3 pound chicken, or 6 chicken thighs. If liked, tinned (canned) chickpeas can be used. These will need only to be rinsed and heated through.

SERVES 6
250 g/8 ounces chickpeas
salt
3 litres 5½ pints (12 cups) water
1 whole head garlic, unpeeled
250 g/8 ounces *chorizo* sausage
125 g/4 ounces *morcilla* (blood sausage, black pudding)
125 g/4 ounces bacon in one piece
750 g/1½ pounds beef chuck, in one piece
2 large onions, chopped
6 small carrots, trimmed and scraped
6 small white turnips, trimmed and peeled
freshly ground pepper
a 1.4 kg/3 pound chicken or 6 chicken thighs
6 small potatoes, peeled
125 ml/4 fl oz (1/2 cup) olive oil
a 900 g/2 pound cabbage, trimmed and coarsely chopped
125 g/4 ounces cooked vermicelli (very fine noodles) or croûtons (optional)
Salsa de Tomate (Tomato Sauce) (page 244)

Pick over and rinse the chickpeas. Put them to soak overnight in cold, salted water to cover. When ready to cook, drain them and put them into a large saucepan with fresh cold salted water to cover by about 2.5 cm/1 inch. Add the garlic, bring to a simmer and cook, covered, for about 1½ hours, or until the chickpeas are tender. Add more water during the cooking time if necessary. Five minutes before serving, add the *chorizo* and *morcilla* sausages. Remove and discard the garlic.

As soon as the chickpeas have been put on to cook, put the bacon and beef into another saucepan with 2.5 litres 4½ pints (10 cups) water, one of the onions, and the carrots and turnips. Season with salt and pepper and simmer gently for 1 hour. Add the whole chicken or the chicken thighs and the potatoes and cook for 1 hour longer, or until the meats and vegetables are all tender.

Meanwhile, heat the oil in a large frying pan (skillet), add the remaining onion and sauté until limp. Add the cabbage, season with salt and pepper and cook, stirring, over moderate heat for about 5 minutes. Add 475 ml/ 16 fl oz (2 cups) of the stock from the meats and vegetables, bring to a simmer, cover and cook until the cabbage is tender, about 5 minutes longer.

To assemble the dish, transfer the sausages from the chickpeas to the saucepan with the meats. Strain the liquid from the chickpeas into a large saucepan and add the cooked noodles, if using. Keep the chickpeas warm. Strain the liquid from the cabbage into the saucepan and keep the cabbage warm. Add all but 125 ml/4 fl oz (½ cup) of the liquid from the meats and vegetables to the saucepan and keep warm. Taste the stock in the saucepan and add salt and pepper if necessary. Heat it through, pour it into a large tureen and serve as the soup course of the meal. If serving croutons, have them ready in a bowl at the table.

Slice the sausages, beef and bacon on a warmed platter. Cut the chicken into serving pieces, or arrange the chicken thighs on the platter. Moisten the meats with the reserved stock.

Put the chickpeas in the centre of another warmed platter with the cabbage at one end and the carrots, turnips and potatoes at the other. Serve with Tomato Sauce separately in a bowl and drink a robust dry red wine.

Cozida a Portuguesa
Portuguese Boiled Dinner

This is a popular dish everywhere in Portugal, but more especially in the northern provinces of Tras-Os-Montes, Minho and Douro, where it is very welcome in cold winter weather. It is less complicated than the Spanish *cocido* and kinder to the cook who can put it on then forget it, though this does not diminish the attractiveness of the dish.

SERVES 6
500 g/1 pound beef chuck, or similar cut, in one pice
500 g/1 pound boneless pork loin, in one piece
a 1.4 kg/3 pound chicken
250 g/8 ounces bacon, in one piece
250 g/8 ounces *chourico* or *chorizo*
250 g/8 ounces *farinheira* (Portuguese pork-fat sausage) or any garlic-flavoured smoked pork sausage
1 bay leaf
3 large sprigs parsley
1 large sprig mint
2 litres/3½ pints (8 cups) water
3 large potatoes, peeled and quartered
3 large carrots, scraped and thickly sliced
3 large white turnips, peeled and sliced
1 cabbage, preferably Savoy, cut into 6 wedges
250 g/8 ounces *morcilla* (black pudding, blood sausage)
salt, and freshly ground pepper
1 recipe Arroz à Tomate (Tomato Rice) (page 220)

Combine the beef, pork loin, chicken, bacon, *chouriço or chorizo, farinheira* or smoked pork sausage, bay leaf, parsley, mint and water in a large saucepan. Bring to a simmer and cook, covered, at a bare simmer for 1½ hours or until the meats are tender. Lift out all the meats, including the chicken, to a large dish, cover and set aside. Remove and discard the bay leaf, parsley and mint. Add the potatoes, carrots, and turnips to the pan. Season to taste with salt and pepper, bring back to a simmer, cover and cook until the vegetables are tender, about 20 minutes. Add the cabbage and *morcilla* and simmer 10 minutes longer, or until the cabbage is done.

While the vegetables are cooking, cut the bacon into small cubes and sauté them in a small, heavy frying-pan (skillet) with a little oil until they have given up all their fat and are crisp and brown. Set them aside.
Slice the beef and pork and cut the chicken into serving pieces. Halve the sausages. Add the sliced meats and chicken to the saucepan for just long enough to heat them through, a few minutes before the vegetables are done.

To serve, strain the stock into a large warmed soup tureen and serve it as a first course with a Portuguese bread such as *Pão* or *Broa*. Arrange the meats and vegetables on a platter and put the rice onto another platter. Sprinkle the rice with the reserved bacon bits and pan drippings and, if liked a few slices of sausage. Serve hot.

Fritada de Ternera
Sautéed Veal Strips

Galicia is famous for the excellence of its fish and shellfish from the cold waters of the Atlantic. It is also esteemed for other dishes, including simple ones like this *fritada*, which present veal in an interesting way.

SERVES 4
50 ml/2 fl oz (¼) cup olive oil
50 g/2 oz (4 slices) bacon, chopped
2 medium onions, sliced
2 cloves garlic, chopped
250g/8oz (2 medium) tomatoes, seeded and coarsely chopped
2 sweet red (bell) peppers, peeled, seeded and cut into strips (page 187)
salt and freshly ground pepper
750 g/1½ pounds lean boneless veal, cut into 1cm/½ inch strips

Heat 2 tablespoons of the oil in a frying pan (skillet) and sauté the bacon until it has given up its fat. Add the onions, garlic and peppers and sauté until the onion is soft. Add the tomatoes and cook until the mixture is thick and well blended, about 5 minutes. Season with salt and pepper.

Heat 2 more tablespoons of oil in a shallow flameproof casserole and sauté the veal strips until they are lightly browned. Add the onion, pepper and tomato mixture to the veal and cook until the meat is tender, about 15 minutes. Serve straight from the casserole, with potatoes or a salad. Drink a light red wine.

Variation: *Guisado de Ternera a la Catalana* (Veal Stew, Catalan-style) is a variation of this Galician dish in which the sauce is enriched wih ground almonds and saffron. Cut 750 g/1½ pounds boneless veal into 2.5 cm/1 inch pieces, season with salt, dredge with flour and sauté in a casserole in 2 tablespoons olive oil. Lift out and set aside. Sauté 1 finely chopped onion in the oil remaining in the casserole, until the onion is soft, adding a little more oil if necessary. Add 250 g/8 oz (2 medium) tomatoes, peeled, seeded and chopped, 1 bay leaf, 1 sprig parsley, chopped, ¼ teaspoon thyme, and cook until well-blended, about 5 minutes. Pour in 250 ml/8 fl oz (1 cup) each dry white wine and veal or chicken stock, and add the veal and any liquid that may have accumulated. Season with salt and pepper, bring to a simmer, cover and cook over low heat until the veal is tender, about 1 hour. While the veal is cooking grind 25 g/1 oz (⅛ cup) blanched almonds to a paste with 2 cloves garlic, 1 tablespoon chopped parsley and ⅛ teaspoon saffron threads. Stir the mixture into the veal and simmer for 5 minutes longer. Drink a light red wine.

Ternera a la Catalana
Veal, Catalan-style

The province of Catalonia is known for the excellence of its veal and also for the complex influences that have played a role in the creation of its richly varied kitchen, not the least of which is having once been part of France with its incomparable cuisine.

SERVES 6
900 g/2 pounds boneless veal, in one piece
1 large onion, chopped
1 head garlic, left whole
1 sweet red (bell) pepper, peeled, seeded and sliced (page 187)
250 g/8oz (2 medium) tomatoes, peeled, seeded and chopped
1 tablespoon chopped parsley
salt and freshly ground pepper
¼ teaspoon ground cinnamon, or to taste
2 tablespoons lard or olive oil
475 ml/16 fl oz (2 cups) dry white wine
grated rind of 1 lemon
50 ml/2 fl oz (¼ cup) veal or beef stock

Put the veal into a heavy flameproof casserole with the onion, garlic, pepper, tomatoes, parsley, salt, pepper, cinnamon, lard and wine. Bring to a simmer, cover and cook over very low heat until the veal is tender. 1½–2 hours.
    Lift out and discard the garlic. Add the lemon rind and stock and heat through. Transfer the veal to a warmed platter and slice. Pour the sauce over it. Serve with potatoes and a green salad. Drink a full bodied dry red wine.

Ternera con Alcachofas
Veal with Artichoke Hearts

Artichokes originated in the Mediterranean region and were introduced into Spain by the Arabs, as their name in Spanish with its prefix of 'al' implies. They are used in this Andalucian dish to give the sauce a special flavour.

SERVES 4
2 tablespoons olive oil
750 g/1½ pounds boneless veal, cut into 4 slices
1 large onion, thinly sliced
salt and freshly ground pepper
250 ml/8 fl oz (1 cup) dry white wine
2 tablespoons brandy
250 ml/8 fl oz (1 cup) beef or veal stock
8 cooked artichoke hearts (see page 194)
500 g/1 lb (about 4 medium) tomatoes, peeled, seeded and chopped

Heat the oil in a flameproof casserole and brown the veal slices lightly on both sides. Remove from the casserole and set aside. In the oil remaining in the casserole, sauté the onion until it is soft, adding a little more oil if necessary. Return the veal to the casserole, season with salt and pepper, add the wine, brandy and stock, cover and simmer over low heat until the veal is tender, about 1–1½ hours. During the last 15 minutes of cooking add the artichoke hearts and tomatoes.

Lift the veal out on to a warmed platter and pour the sauce over it. If the sauce is very abundant, reduce it over brisk heat for a few minutes.

Ternera al Jerez
Veal with Sherry

This Andalucian dish shows its Arab influence in the use of almonds. It also uses sherry for which the province is famous, to produce a dish of great elegance.

SERVES 4
8 thin veal escalopes (scallops), each weighing about 50g/2 ounces
6 tablespoons olive oil
4 tablespoons lemon juice
4 cloves garlic
25 g/1 oz (scant ¼ cup) blanched toasted almonds, finely ground
50 ml/2 fl oz (¼ cup) dry sherry
300 ml/½ pint (1¼ cups) beef stock
salt and freshly ground pepper
1 egg, lightly beaten
plain (all-purpose) flour for dredging

Combine the veal, 3 tablespoons of the olive oil and the lemon juice in a bowl and set aside.

Heat 1 tablespoon of the oil in a small frying pan (skillet) and sauté the garlic until lightly browned. Lift out the garlic and crush it into the almonds. Reserve the oil. Scrape the almond–garlic mixture into a medium bowl, add the sherry and stock, season to taste with salt and pepper and set aside.

Lift the veal escalopes (scallops) out of the marinade and pat them dry with paper towels. Dip them in the beaten egg, then in flour, and sauté them in a frying pan (skillet) in the remaining oil plus the oil in which the garlic was fried, until lightly browned on both sides. Lift them out in to a shallow casserole, preferably earthenware, as they are cooked.

Pour the reserved sauce over the veal, bring to a simmer and cook, uncovered, for about 10 minutes, or until the sauce is thickened. If liked, the dish may be garnished with triangles of bread fried in olive oil. Serve accompanied by a green salad. Drink a light red wine.

Ternera Mechada
Cinnamon-stuffed Veal

This dish from Extremadura reflects the passion of the fifteenth century for spices. The veal is larded or stuffed with slivers of stick cinnamon which gives it a delicately exotic taste.

SERVES 6
5 cm/2 inch pieces stick cinnamon
900 g/2 pounds boneless veal, in one piece
2 tablespoons lard or olive oil
2 medium onions, finely chopped
1 clove garlic, chopped
500 g/1 lb (4 medium) tomatoes, peeled, seeded and chopped
125 ml/4 fl oz (½ cup) dry sherry
250 ml/8 fl oz (1 cup) beef stock
salt and freshly ground pepper

Break or cut the cinnamon stick into slivers. Using a skewer or small sharp knife, make holes all over the piece of veal and push in the slivers of cinnamon. Heat 1 tablespoon of the lard in a frying pan (skillet) and brown the meat on both sides. Lift it out in to a flameproof casserole.

Add the remaining tablespoon of lard or oil to the pan and sauté the onions until soft. Add the garlic and sauté for 1 minute longer. Add the tomatoes and cook until the mixture is thick and well-blended, about 5 minutes. Stir in the sherry and stock, season with salt and pepper and pour over the veal. Bring to a simmer, cover and cook over very low heat, turning the meat halfway through the cooking, for about 2 hours, or until tender. Serve sliced with the sauce poured over. Serve with fried potatoes or *Patatas a lo Pobre* (Poor Man's Potatoes) (page 191) and a green salad. Drink a light red wine.

Ternera a la Manchega
Veal, Manchega-style

This veal dish is from New Castille and is named after the region which Cervantes chose as the setting for *Don Quixote de la Mancha*. The cuisine is not very different from that of Old Castille, but since it is the home of the capital, Madrid, it has attracted dishes from the cuisines of the whole nation while keeping its own specialities. This simple dish is typical of the region.

SERVES 4
750 g/1½ pounds boneless veal, cut into 4 pieces lengthwise
4 tablespoons lemon juice
salt
1 medium onion, finely chopped
250 g/8 oz (2 medium) tomatoes, peeled, seeded and chopped
2 sweet red (bell) peppers, peeled, seeded and chopped
125 ml/4 fl oz (½ cup) olive oil

Season the veal pieces with lemon juice and salt and put into a casserole large enough to hold the meat in a single layer. Add the onion, tomatoes and peppers. Pour the oil over the dish and simmer, covered, until the meat is tender, about 1 hour. Taste for seasoning and add salt if necessary.

Variation: *Ternera a la Asturiana* (Veal, Asturian-style), from the Celtic north of Spain, is an interesting variation of its New Castille culinary neighbour. Famed for its *fabada* (bean stew), the cooking has links with Normandy and Brittany in France, and cider, not wine, is the preferred drink. Sauté 900 g/2 pounds boneless veal, in one piece, dredged with flour seasoned with salt, in a frying pan (skillet) in 2 tablespoons lard. Transfer the veal to a casserole. Add 2 more tablespoons lard to the lard remaining in the pan. Sauté a finely chopped onion until golden. Add 250g/8 oz (2 medium) tomatoes, peeled, seeded and chopped, and cook until the mixture is thick and well-blended. Stir in 250 ml/8 fl oz (1 cup) beef or veal stock and pour over the veal. Cover and simmer over low heat until the veal is tender, turning the meat once or twice during cooking. It will take about 1½–2 hours. Drink cider or a dry white wine.

Cochinillo Asado
Roast Suckling Pig

Roast suckling pig is a favourite dish in Castille, and I have enjoyed it in Madrid where visitors and locals alike save up their appetites for it. I did not think it possible to have better suckling pig anywhere in the world until I enjoyed it in a small restaurant in a mountain village not far from Coimbra in Beira in Portugal. It was the season for weddings and the village was celebrating the happy time of year with the most delicate, delicious suckling pig I've ever had the pleasure to eat. The crackling was both tender and crisp at the same time, the meat juicily succulent. Ideally in Castille the piglet is roasted in a woodburning butcher's oven, but a domestic oven gives very good results, making it possible to enjoy this delight at home.

SERVES 4–6
a 3.2 kg/7 pound suckling pig
salt and freshly ground pepper
125 ml/4 fl oz (½ cup) dry white wine
125 ml/4 fl oz (½ cup) water
1 clove garlic, crushed
4 tablespoons lard, melted
olive oil or extra melted lard

Have the butcher open the pig through the underside, and flatten it slightly, or do it yourself. Season both sides with salt and pepper. Pour the wine and water into the bottom of a large, shallow, flameproof baking dish, preferably earthenware. Add the garlic and the lard. Arrange the pig, skin side down, in the dish. Cover the pig's ears and tail with little cones of aluminium foil. Roast the pig in a preheated moderate oven (180°C/350°F gas 4), for 1 hour. Turn the pig over so that it is skin side up, pour off the liquid from the pan and keep it for basting. Brush the pig with olive oil or melted lard and continue roasting, basting with the reserved liquid, until the skin is golden-brown and crusty. Cooking time will be between 2½ and 3 hours.

Remove the foil from the ears and tail. Transfer the pig to a large platter. Brush it with a little olive oil or melted lard and sprinkle lightly with salt. Pour any basting liquid back into the dish and mix with the juices there. If they are scanty, add a little more wine. Taste and add salt and pepper if needed. Warm through and pour into a sauceboat.

To serve, remove the pig's head and quarter the pig. Serve with the pan juices, potatoes and a green salad. Drink a light dry red wine.

Variation: For *Leitão Assado* (Roast Suckling Pig) from Portugal the method is almost exactly the same. Mix together 8 tablespoons melted lard, or olive oil with 1 tablespoon salt, a generous amount of freshly ground pepper, 2 cloves crushed garlic, 50 g/2 ounces very finely chopped bacon, 4 tablespoons chopped parsley and 250 ml/8 fl oz (1 cup) dry white wine. Rub this mixture into the pig, inside and out, and let it marinate for 2 hours. Roast as in the main recipe, basting every 30 minutes with dry white wine. Serve with fried potatoes, green salad and, if liked, quartered oranges. Drink a light dry red wine.

Lombo de Porco com Ameijoas
Pork with Clams, Alentejo-style

This is a classic dish in the Alentejo. The unlikely combination of pork and clams produces a delicious dish full of subtle flavour. The clams used in Portugal, *ameijoas*, are the *palourdes* of France, and widely available in Europe. Small littleneck clams are the best substitute in the United States, though any small, delicate clam will do.

SERVES 4

2 tablespoons *Massa de Pimentão* (Sweet Red (Bell) Pepper Paste) (page 242) or 1 tablespoon paprika, 1 teaspoon salt and 1 teaspoon olive oil
3 cloves garlic, crushed
900 g/2 pounds boneless pork loin, cut into 2.5 cm/1 inch pieces
250 ml/8 fl oz (1 cup) dry white wine
2 teaspoons white wine vinegar
1 bay leaf
1 large sprig parsley
salt and freshly ground pepper
2 tablespoons lard
2 tablespoons olive oil
1 large onion, coarsely chopped
900 g/2 pounds clams, *palourde*-type, or 24 small, littleneck clams, both in the shell

Mix together the pepper paste and garlic, or mix the garlic, paprika, teaspoon of salt and olive oil together to make a paste. Add to the pork in a large bowl and mix well. Add the wine, vinegar, bay leaf, parsley and salt and pepper to taste, cover and marinate for 24 hours, preferably in the refrigerator, turning the pork pieces from time to time.

When ready to cook, take the pork pieces out of the marinade and pat them dry with paper towels. Reserve the marinade. Heat the lard and oil in a casserole and sauté the pork pieces until they are browned. Add the onion and sauté until soft. Add the marinade to the casserole and cook, covered, over very low heat until the pork is tender. Check during cooking to make sure the pork is not burning. Add a little more wine if necessary.

While the pork is cooking, prepare the clams. Wash them thoroughly. To rid them of any sand, put them into a large bowl of cold water to cover with 1 tablespoon of maize meal (cornmeal) and let them stand for 45 minutes. Drain and rinse well. Add them to the casserole, cover and cook just until the clams open, about 15–20 minutes. Discard any that do not open. Serve with Portuguese bread, a green salad, and a full-bodied dry red wine.

Chuletas de Cerdo a la Riojana
Pork Chops with Sweet Red Peppers

The region of Rioja is famous for the flavour of its sweet red peppers which are used in many meat and poultry dishes. This pork and pepper combination is a general favourite all over Spain.

SERVES 4
2 tablespoons olive oil
4 pork loin chops, about 2.5 cm/1 inch thick
1 medium onion, finely chopped
1 clove garlic, chopped
4 sweet red (bell) peppers, peeled, seeded and cut into strips
250 g/8 ounces (2 medium) tomatoes, peeled, seeded and chopped
salt and freshly ground pepper

Heat the oil in a heavy frying pan (skillet) with a lid. Sear the chops quickly on both sides over moderately high heat. Reduce the heat and sauté the onion until soft. Add the garlic and cook for 1 minute longer. Add the peppers and tomatoes, season with salt and pepper, cover and simmer until the chops are tender, about 30 minutes. Serve with rice or potatoes and a dry red wine, preferably a Rioja.

Variation: For a simpler version grill (broil) the chops for about 12 minutes in all and serve garnished with the peppers cut into strips or quarters and drizzled with a little olive oil. Serve with fried potatoes.

Rojões à Modo do Minho
Pork Stew, Minho-style

Pork stew is known as *rojões* in Minho Province in Northern Portugal where it is a favourite dish.

SERVES 4
125 ml/4 fl oz (½ cup) dry white wine
1 tablespoon lemon juice
2 teaspoons ground cumin
4 cloves garlic, crushed
1 bay leaf
salt and freshly ground pepper
900 g/2 pounds boneless pork, cut into 2.5 cm/1 inch pieces
2 tablespoons olive oil
1 tablespoon lard
black olives
1 lemon, cut into 8 wedges

In a bowl mix together the wine, lemon juice, cumin, garlic, bay leaf, salt and pepper. Add the pork pieces, mixing thoroughly. Cover and refrigerate overnight, turning once or twice.

When ready to cook, drain and reserve the marinade. Heat the oil and lard in a heavy flameproof casserole and sauté the pork until the pieces are lightly browned all over. Pour in the reserved marinade, cover and cook over very low heat until the meat is tender, about 1–1½ hours. Serve garnished with the olives and lemon wedges. Accompany the stew with fried potatoes. Drink a dry red wine such as Dão.

Lomo de Cerdo al Estilo Vasco
Loin of Pork, Basque-style

The Basques are famed for their devotion to fine food with private, men only, gastronomic societies dedicated to serving memorable meals. There are also fine women cooks often using recipes that have been handed down for generations, many of which have migrated to the New World. Argentina has a version of this pork cooked in milk, and so does Chile, both subtly different from the Basque original. Italians also cooked in milk, and there is no sure way of finding out who thought of this method first. Perhaps Basque and Italian cooks were inspired simultaneously.

SERVES 4
½ teaspoon salt or to taste
2 cloves garlic, crushed
750 g/1½ pounds pork loin, rind removed
2 tablespoons lard or olive oil
1 onion, finely chopped (optional)
600 ml/20 fl oz (2½ cups) warm milk
freshly ground white pepper

Mix the salt and garlic together and rub into the pork. In a casserole heat the lard or oil and sauté the pork until lightly browned all over. Lift out and add the onion, if using, and sauté until soft. Return the pork to the casserole and pour in the warm milk, adding a little more if necessary to cover the pork. Bring to a simmer, season with white pepper, cover and cook over low heat until the pork is tender, 2–2½ hours.

Lift out the pork on to a warmed platter and slice it. Pour the milk sauce, which will be grainy, over the meat and serve with potatoes, a salad and light red wine.

Lomo de Porco à Alentejana
Pork Loin, Alentejo-style

Pork is the favourite meat in Alentejo province. The Portuguese say the excellence of the meat is the result of the pigs' diet of chestnuts and acorns from the cork oaks that abound in the region. Start the recipe a day ahead as the pork loin marinates overnight.

SERVES 6
900 g/2 pounds boneless pork loin
2 tablespoons *Massa de pimentão* (Sweet Red (Bell) Pepper Paste) (page 242) or 2 tablespoons paprika
4 cloves garlic, crushed
salt and freshly ground pepper
475 ml/16 fl oz (2 cups) dry white wine
1 tablespoon lard
1 tablespoon olive oil

In a bowl mix together the pepper paste or paprika, garlic, salt and a generous amount of pepper, 1/4–1/2 teaspoon. Rub the mixture into the pork loin and put the meat into a bowl or other container that will hold it comfortably, and pour in the wine. Cover and refrigerate overnight, turning 2–3 times.

When ready to cook, lift out the pork and pat it dry with paper towels. Cut the meat into 6 even slices. Heat the lard and oil in a large, heavy frying pan (skillet) over fairly high heat and brown the meat quickly on both sides. Lower the heat and cook the pork slices for 6–8 minutes on each side. While the pork is cooking, pour the marinade into a small saucepan and reduce it over moderate heat to about one-quarter of its volume, or until it is lightly thickened. Pour it over the pork and serve with rice or fried potatoes. Drink a fairly robust dry red wine.

Variation: For *Costeletas de Porco à Alentejana* (Pork Chops, Altentejo-style), have 4 pork loin chops, cut 2.5 cm/1 inch thick. Make a marinade of 2 cloves of crushed garlic, 1 bay leaf, salt, 1 tablespoon *Massa de Pimentão* (Sweet Red (Bell) Pepper Paste) or 1 tablespoon paprika, and 125 ml/4 fl oz (1/2 cup) each orange juice and dry white wine. Put the chops into a bowl, pour the marinade over them and leave for 24 hours in the refrigerator, turning 2–3 times. When ready to cook, transfer the chops and the marinade to a casserole, bring to a simmer on top of the stove, cover and cook in a 180°C/350°F/gas 4 oven for 1 hour, or until tender. Serve garnished with orange slices or a quartered orange, accompanied by fried potatoes and rice. Drink a light red wine. Serves 4.

Chuletas de Cerdo a la Naranja
Pork Chops with Orange

This dish is from Valencia's great orange country. Cooks have used the oranges and their own imaginations to create some wonderful dishes.

SERVES 4

4 pork loin chops, cut about 2.5 cm/1 inch thick
salt and freshly ground pepper
2 tablespoons olive oil
grated rind of 4 oranges
125 ml/4 fl oz (½ cup) dry sherry
¼ teaspoon ground ginger
50 ml/2 fl oz (¼ cup) chicken stock
2 teaspoons cornflour (cornstarch) (optional)

Season the chops with salt and pepper. Heat the oil in a frying pan (skillet) and sear the chops quickly on both sides over fairly high heat. Transfer the chops to a flameproof casserole and add the orange rind, sherry, ginger and stock. Bring to a simmer, cover and cook over low heat until the chops are tender, about 20 minutes. If using the cornflour (cornstarch), mix it with a little water, stir into the casserole and cook, stirring, just long enough to lightly thicken the sauce. Serve with plain rice and drink a light red wine.

Chuletas de Cerdo a la Madrileña
Pork Chops, Madrid-style

Madrid-style dishes are from the province of New Castille where the capital is located. They are often very sophisticated, innovative dishes.

SERVES 4

3 cloves garlic, finely chopped
1 tablespoon chopped parsley
1 teaspoon paprika
1 bay leaf, crumbled
½ teaspoon dried thyme or 1 teaspoon fresh, chopped
salt and freshly ground pepper
3 tablespoons olive oil
4 pork loin chops, cut about 2.5 cm/1 inch thick

In a bowl mix together all the ingredients except the chops and using only one tablespoon of the oil. Add the chops, mix well with the marinade and let stand for 1 hour, turning from time to time so that each chop is well coated. In a frying pan (skillet) heat the remaining 2 tablespoons of oil, and sauté the chops without removing any of the marinade, over fairly high heat for one minute each side. Then reduce the heat to low and cook for about 10 minutes on each side, or until tender. Serve with fried potatoes and a green vegetable or a salad Drink a light red wine.

Cochifrito
Lamb with Lemon and Garlic

This very easy-to-cook lamb dish is from Aragon. It is deceptively simple and there is a temptation to add stock or wine to it, but this is seldom needed as the meat cooks in its own juices. The cooking method brings out the full flavour of the lamb enhanced by the slight sharpness of the lemon, garlic and parsley sauce.

SERVES 4

900 g/2 pounds lean boneless lamb, cut into 2.5 cm/1 inch pieces
salt and freshly ground black pepper
3 tablespoons olive oil
1 large onion, finely chopped
3 cloves garlic, finely chopped
1 tablespoon paprika
3 tablespoons lemon juice
3 tablespoons finely chopped parsley
4 tablespoons lamb stock or dry white wine, if necessary

Season the lamb pieces with salt and pepper. In a frying pan (skillet) heat the oil and sauté the lamb pieces until lightly browned all over. Lift out the lamb into a heavy flameproof casserole and set it aside. In the oil remaining in the pan sauté the onion until soft, adding a little more oil if necessary. Add the garlic and sauté for 1–2 minutes longer. Stir in the paprika and add the mixture to the casserole. Stir in the lemon juice and the parsley, cover and cook over low heat until the lamb is tender, about 1–1½ hours. If the lamb seems to be drying out during cooking add up to 4 tablespoons stock or wine but this is seldom needed.

Chanfana à Moda de Coimbra
Braised Kid, or Lamb

The first time I ordered *Chanfana* in a restaurant in a tiny village in the mountains above Coimbra in the province of Beira Litoral I had no idea of the delight in store. The kid (baby goat) was cut in very nearly boneless slices and there was enough for 2, as portions in Portugal are more than generous. *Chanfana* is greater than the sum of its parts. The meat is cooked in wine with onion, garlic, oil and seasonings in the oven until it is very tender, then served from the casserole with plainly boiled potatoes. It has an exquisite flavour from the combined wine and oil. It is a favourite dish in the region for weddings and baptisms. Lamb or kid may be used.

SERVES 4
900 g/2 pounds boneless kid or lamb, cut into large pieces, about 5 cm/2 inches
2 tablespoons olive oil
1 tablespoon lard
1 onion, halved and sliced
2 cloves garlic, chopped
1 bay leaf
3 cloves
salt and freshly ground pepper
about 700 ml/1½ pint (3 cups) full-bodied dry red wine

Combine all the ingredients in a flameproof casserole, preferably earthenware, with enough wine to cover the meat. Bring to a simmer on top of the stove, then cover and cook in a preheated moderate oven (180°C/350°F/gas 4) for 2 hours, or until the meat is very tender. The time will depend on the tenderness of the meat and may take 3 hours or even longer. Check during cooking and add more wine if necessary. Serve from the casserole with potatoes boiled in their skins, then peeled and halved.

Variation: In other parts of Beira Litoral cooks add 1 tablespoon chopped flat-leaved parsley, 1 teaspoon paprika, 125 g/4 ounces chopped bacon and ½ teaspoon grated nutmeg to the casserole.

Ensopado de Borrego
Lamb Stew, Alentejo-style

This lamb stew is from Alentejo where sheep feed on acorns from the cork oaks and are sweetly flavoured. Sliced day-old bread is put in the bottom of the serving dish and the stew is poured over it. The bread used is always a firm, chewy bread which absorbs the rich sauce of the stew and thickens it at the same time. *Ensopada* translates as 'soaked in', providing a splendid way of mopping up the good liquid of the stew.

SERVES 4
500 g/1 pound lean boneless lamb cut into 2.5 cm/1 inch pieces
salt and freshly ground pepper
2 tablespoons cider vinegar or white wine vinegar
25 g/1 oz (½ cup) chopped flat-leaved parsley
25 g/1 oz (½ cup) chopped fresh coriander
2 cloves
1 bay leaf
2 medium onions, chopped
2 cloves garlic, chopped
1 tablespoon plain (all-purpose) flour
2 tablespoons olive oil
½ tablespoon lard
475 ml/16 fl oz (2 cups) lamb or beef stock, or water
500 g/1 pound potatoes, peeled and cubed
½ teaspoon, or to taste, Piri-piri sauce or Tabasco or other hot red chilli pepper sauce
4 slices stale firm white or French-type bread

In a bowl combine the lamb, salt, pepper, vinegar, parsley, coriander, cloves, bay leaf, onions and garlic. Mix thoroughly, cover and refrigerate for 3–4 hours. Remove from the refrigerator and bring to room temperature. Strain through a sieve, reserving the liquid. Sprinkle the meat and vegetables with the flour and mix.

In a flameproof casserole heat the oil and lard and sauté the lamb mixture until the meat is lightly browned. Add the reserved liquid from the marinade and the stock or water, the potatoes and the *Piri-piri*. Bring to a simmer, cover and cook over low heat until the lamb is tender, about 1½ hours. Put the bread in the bottom of a deep serving dish and pour the stew over it. Serve with a salad and drink a full-bodied dry red wine.

Variation: For *Carneiro com Feijão Branco* (Lamb with Dried White Beans), omit the potatoes. Soak 275 g/9 oz (1½ cups) dried white haricot (navy) beans in cold water to cover overnight or for several hours. Drain the beans and put them on to cook in a large saucepan with fresh cold water to cover. Cook for 30 minutes. Drain, reserving the cooking liquid. Add the beans to the lamb at the same point as the potatoes were added. Measure the reserved liquid and, if necessary, make up the quantity with water or stock to 475 ml/16 fl oz (2 cups) and add it to the casserole instead of the stock or water in the main recipe. Cook in the same way but do not put bread in the bottom of the serving dish.

Carneiro à Alentejana
Lamb Stew, Alentejo-style

This is from Alentejo, the Portuguese province to the east and south of Lisbon. There is an interesting use of both paprika and cayenne in the same dish.

SERVES 4–6
4 cloves garlic, crushed
1 tablespoon finely chopped parsley
salt and freshly ground pepper
900 g/2 pounds, lean, boneless lamb, cut into 3.5 cm/1½ inch pieces
6 tablespoons olive oil or lard
2 medium onions, finely chopped
1 tablespoon paprika
⅛ teaspoon cayenne
⅛ teaspoon ground cloves
175 ml/6 fl oz (¾ cup) dry white wine

Mix the garlic, parsley, salt and pepper to taste to a paste. Put the lamb into a bowl, add the garlic mixture and leave to marinate for about 2 hours. In a large frying pan (skillet) heat the oil or lard and brown the lamb pieces all over. Transfer the lamb to a flameproof casserole. In the oil remaining in the pan, sauté the onions until soft and transfer them to the casserole together with the paprika, cayenne, cloves and wine. Add a little water if necessary. Bring to a simmer on top of the stove, then transfer to a preheated moderate oven (180°C/350°F/gas 4) and cook, covered, until the lamb is tender, about 1½ hours. The dish may be cooked on top of the stove if preferred. Serve with a light red wine such as a red Vinho Verde, or Dão. In Portugal meats are usually served with both potatoes and rice.

Carneiro Estufado com Pimentas Vermelhos Doces
Lamb Stew with Sweet Red Peppers

This Portuguese lamb dish is from northern Portugal from the provinces of Minho and Douro Litoral. Like all Portuguese cooking it is simple, relying on the natural taste of the ingredients to give it distinction. There are not a great many lamb dishes as kid (*cabrito*) is preferred, sheep being used to provide wool and ewe's milk for cheese.

SERVES 4
750 g/1½ pounds lean boneless lamb, cut into 2.5 cm/1 inch pieces
3 large cloves garlic, crushed
salt and freshly ground pepper
4 tablespoons olive oil
4 medium sweet red (bell) peppers, seeded and cut into 1 cm/½ inch strips lengthwise
250 ml/8 fl oz (1 cup) dry white wine
125 ml/4 fl oz (½ cup) lamb or chicken stock

Put the lamb into a bowl. Mix the garlic, salt and pepper together and add to the lamb, tossing to mix thoroughly. Cover and marinate in a cool place, or in the refrigerator for 3–4 hours, stirring with a wooden spoon from time to time.

Heat the oil in a large frying pan (skillet) with a lid and brown the lamb all over. Do this in batches so as not to overcrowd the pan. Transfer the lamb to a bowl. Add the peppers to the oil remaining in the pan and sauté over moderate heat, turning frequently, for 5 minutes. Add to the lamb.

If there is a great deal of oil in the pan pour off all but 1 tablespoon. Pour in the wine, bring to a simmer and stir with a wooden spoon to scrape up any brown bits. Pour in the stock and add the lamb and peppers.

Simmer, covered, for about 1 hour or until the lamb is tender. Transfer the lamb to a warmed platter and arrange the peppers on top of the meat. Pour the sauce over the dish. If the sauce is very abundant, reduce it over high heat. Serve with *Patatas com Coentro* (Potatoes with Coriander). In Portugal rice would also be served. Drink a light red wine like a red Vinho Verde.

Cordero a la Levantina
Lamb, Valencia-style

Cooking in Spain's Levante, as Valencia on the east coast is known, is lively and full of surprises. This lamb dish with its simple list of ingredients gains unexpected flavour from the lemon juice and egg yolk, which greatly enhance the sweetness of the young lamb.

SERVES 4
900 g/2 pounds lean boneless lamb, cut into 3.5 cm/1½ inch pieces
salt and freshly ground pepper
2 tablespoons lard or olive oil
1 medium onion, finely chopped
1 clove garlic
750 g/1½ pounds (6 medium) tomatoes, peeled, seeded and chopped
1 sprig thyme or ¼ teaspoon dried
1 bay leaf
1 large egg yolk
4 tablespoons lemon juice

Season the lamb with salt and pepper. Heat the lard or oil in a casserole and brown the meat all over. Lift out into a bowl and set aside. In the fat remaining in the casserole sauté the onion until soft. Add the garlic, tomatoes, thyme and bay leaf and cook over moderate heat for 5 minutes.

Return the lamb, and any juices that have collected, to the casserole, cover and simmer gently until the lamb is tender, about 1½ hours. Beat the egg yolk with the lemon juice and stir into the lamb stew. Cook, stirring for 3–4 minutes, or until the liquid is lightly thickened. Serve with potatoes and a green salad. Drink a light red wine.

Cordero en Chilindrón
Lamb with Sweet Red Peppers

This is a popular way of cooking lamb in Navarre. Chicken, pork, lamb and rabbit are also cooked in this way in Arágon, not surprising since both provinces are near to Rioja, famed for the excellence of its sweet red peppers which give richness as well as colour to the sauce.

SERVES 4–6
900 g/2 pounds lean boneless lamb, cut into 5 cm/2 inch pieces
salt and freshly ground pepper
4 tablespoons olive oil, or a mixture of oil and lard
1 medium onion, finely chopped
1 clove garlic, chopped
3 medium sweet red (bell) peppers, peeled, seeded and cut into
5 mm/¼ inch strips
250 g/8 oz tomatoes, (about 2 medium) peeled, seeded and chopped

Pat the lamb pieces dry with paper towels and season them with salt and pepper. Heat the oil in a casserole and sauté the lamb until lightly browned all over. Lift out into a dish. Add the onion, garlic and peppers to the casserole and sauté over moderate heat until the vegetables are soft. Add the tomatoes and cook until the mixture is well blended, about 5 minutes. Add the lamb and any juices that may have collected in the dish. Cover and simmer over low heat until the lamb is tender, about 1½ hours. Serve with potatoes and a green salad. Drink a full-bodied dry red wine.

Variation: In nearby Aragón the dish is cooked slightly differently. Lard by itself is used instead of oil or a mixture of oil and lard. Sauté 2 onions, finely chopped, in 2 tablespoons lard until golden. Add the lamb pieces and sauté until the lamb is lightly browned all over. Stir in 1 tablespoon plain (all-purpose) flour, mixing well. Set aside. In a small saucepan mix together 1 tablespoon paprika, salt, 4 tablespoons brandy, 1 clove garlic, finely chopped, and 1 tablespoon red wine vinegar. Simmer over low heat for 1–2 minutes, then pour over the lamb. Cover and cook the lamb over low heat until tender. If the lamb seems to be drying out, add a little stock or white wine. Serve with *Ensalada de Lechuga* (Lettuce Salad) (page 196) and potatoes. Drink a full-bodied dry red wine.

Estofado de Cordero a la Andaluza
Lamb Stew, Andalucía-style

Finely chopped fresh mint gives this stew a refreshing and unusual flavour. It clearly echoes the Moorish influence on this province, the first to be invaded by the Moors and the last to be liberated in the *reconquista*.

SERVES 4–6
4 tablespoons olive oil
4 large cloves garlic, peeled and left whole
900 g/2 pounds lean boneless lamb, cut into 3.5 cm/1½ inch pieces
2 medium onions, finely chopped
2 medium onions, finely chopped
salt and freshly ground pepper
1 tablespoon plain (all-purpose) flour
250 ml/8 fl oz (1 cup) lamb stock or water
2 tablespoons finely chopped mint

Heat the oil in a large frying pan (skillet). Add the garlic and sauté over moderate heat until the garlic is lightly browned. Lift out and reserve the garlic. Pat the lamb pieces dry with paper towels and sauté in the oil until lightly browned all over. Do this in batches so as not to overcrowd the pan. Transfer the lamb pieces to a casserole. In the oil remaining in the pan sauté the onions until soft. Stir in the flour and cook, stirring, for 1 minute. Add the stock or water and cook, stirring, until the liquid is smooth and slightly thickened. Pour the contents of the pan into the casserole. Season with salt, cover and cook over low heat until the lamb is tender, 1½–2 hours.

While the meat is cooking pound the reserved garlic cloves to a paste. Add ⅛ teaspoons freshly ground pepper and the mint and pound to mix. Stir in a little of the cooking stock, about 50 ml/2 fl oz (¼ cup), and pour the mixture into the casserole. Simmer for 1–2 minutes. Serve with rice and a green salad. Drink a full-bodied dry red wine.

Cordero con Cebollas a la Vasca
Lamb with Onions, Basque-style

As the northern provinces of Spain rejoice in excellent and abundant lamb, cooks have created a multitude of recipes using the meat. The dishes are all characterized by simplicity, making them ideal family recipes which is, after all, how they began.

SERVES 4
750 g/1½ pounds lean boneless lamb, cut into 3.5 cm/1½ inch pieces
salt and freshly ground pepper
plain (all-purpose) flour for dredging
2 tablespoons olive oil
2 large onions, finely chopped
250 ml/8 fl oz (1 cup) dry white wine or lamb stock, or a mixture

Pat the lamb pieces dry with paper towels. Season to taste with salt and pepper and dredge with flour, shaking to remove the excess. Heat the oil in a casserole and sauté the lamb pieces until browned all over. Lift out into a dish and set aside.

In the oil remaining in the casserole sauté the onions until they are soft, adding a little more oil if necessary. Return the lamb pieces and any juice that has collected to the casserole, add the wine or stock, bring to a simmer, cover and cook over low heat until the lamb is tender, about 1½ hours. If the lamb seems to be drying out add a little wine or stock sparingly. Serve with potatoes and a green salad. Drink a light red wine.

Variation: Sauté the lamb in the same way and set it aside. Add 1 medium onion, finely chopped, and 1 clove garlic, chopped, to the casserole and sauté until the onion is soft. Return the lamb to the casserole and add 1 tablespoon chopped parsley, 1 bay leaf and ⅛ teaspoon saffron threads ground in a mortar. Pour in 125 ml/4 fl oz (½ cup) each brandy and lamb stock. Bring to a simmer, cover and cook over low heat until the lamb is tender, about 1½ hours. Serve with fried potatoes and a salad. Drink a light red wine.

Cordero Asado a la Riojana
Roast Lamb, Rioja-style

There are innumerable recipes for roast lamb throughout Spain, especially in the north where the lamb is exceptionally good. Baby lamb weighing only 750–900 g/1½–2 pounds is popular but not generally available outside Spain. The same cooking method can be used for our larger young spring lambs.

SERVES 6
1.4–1.8 kg/3–4 pound leg of baby lamb
salt and freshly ground pepper
2 tablespoons lard, softened
½ medium onion, chopped
1 bay leaf
250 ml/8 fl oz (1 cup) dry white wine
2 cloves garlic, finely chopped
1 tablespoon finely chopped parsley
1 tablespoon red wine vinegar
250 ml/8 fl oz (1 cup) lamb or chicken stock, or water

Season the lamb generously with salt and pepper and rub with the lard.
Put the onion and bay leaf into a roasting pan. Put the lamb on top and
roast in a preheated moderate oven (180°C/350°F/gas 4) for 30 minutes.
Pour a little wine over the lamb, then baste with the wine every 10 minutes
or until the wine is used up and the lamb is cooked. The lamb is roasted
12–20 minutes to the 500 g/1 pound according to the degree of doneness
desired. 12 minutes will be rare, 20 well done. Lift out the lamb on to a
warmed platter and keep warm while making the sauce.

Pour off and discard all but 1 tablespoon of the fat in the roasting pan.
Pour the fat into a small saucepan, heat and sauté the garlic and parsley.
Add the vinegar and stock or water as well as any residue in the roasting
pan, discarding the bay leaf. Bring to a boil and simmer for a few minutes.
Serve as a sauce with the lamb. Serve with *Ensalada de Lechuga* (Lettuce
Salad) (page 196), fried potatoes and a full-bodied dry red wine, preferably
Rioja.

Pierna de Cordero a la Extremeña
Leg of Lamb, Extremeña-style

South of Old Castille and next door to New Castille, Extremadura on the
west coast of Spain has an interesting kitchen based, it is said, on recipes
developed in the monasteries of Alcántara, Yuste, Tentudia and Guad-
alupe. Lamb recipes are expecially good as the region is famed for the
quality of its lamb. I find this recipe of inspired simplicity. As it is not
often easy to get really small young legs of lamb, I have found the dish
works equally well using an equivalent amount of lean, boneless lamb.

SERVES 4
900 g/2 pound leg baby lamb or 750 g/1½ pounds lean, boneless lamb,
cut into 5 cm/2 inch pieces
salt and freshly ground pepper
2 tablespoons olive oil
475 ml/16 fl oz (2 cups) dry red wine
250 ml/8 fl oz (1 cup) lamb stock or water)
1 tablespoon plain (all-purpose) flour

Ask the butcher to bone and tie the lamb, or do it yourself. Season the
lamb with salt and pepper and put into a flameproof casserole with the
oil and wine. Let marinate for 1 hour. Pour in the lamb stock or water,
bring the liquid to a simmer, cover and cook over very low heat until the
lamb is tender, about 1½ hours. Lift out the lamb on to a warmed dish,
cover and keep warm.

Skim off the excess fat from the liquid in the casserole. Mix the flour
with a little of the liquid and stir it into the casserole. Bring to a simmer
and cook, stirring, until the sauce is lightly thickened. Add a little salt and
pepper if necessary. If using the leg of lamb, remove the string from the
meat and slice it. Pour the sauce over the lamb and serve. Serve with
boiled potatoes, preferably new, a green vegetable or salad and drink a
full-bodied dry red wine.

Cordero con Ajo
Lamb with Garlic, Basque-style

This is a Catalan dish and first cousin to the Provençal *Poulet aux Quatre
Clous d'Ail* (Chicken with Forty Cloves of Garlic). The robust flavour of
lamb is much enhanced by the garlic which cooks to a gentle mildness.

SERVES 4
3 tablespoons olive oil
900 g/2 pounds lean, boneless lamb, cut into 5 cm/2 inch cubes
1 medium onion, finely chopped
1 head garlic, peeled
1 bay leaf
2 teaspoons paprika
2 tablespoons red wine vinegar
salt and freshly ground pepper
about 125 ml/4 fl oz (½ cup) lamb stock or water

Heat the oil in a frying pan (skillet) and brown the lamb pieces all over. Transfer them to a casserole. In the oil remaining in the pan sauté the onion until soft. Add the onion to the lamb in the casserole. Drop the garlic cloves into a saucepan of briskly boiling water and blanch for 30 seconds. Lift out and peel. Blanching makes them very easy to peel.

Add the garlic to the casserole with the bay leaf, paprika, vinegar, salt, pepper and stock or water, adding a little more stock if necessary barely to cover the lamb. Cover and cook over very low heat for about 1½ hours or until the lamb is tender. Check during cooking to make sure the lamb is not drying out. The sauce should not be abundant. Serve with a green vegetable or a salad. Drink a light red wine.

Cordero con Ajillo
Lamb with Garlic, Andalucian-style

This is another of the uncomplicated, well-flavoured dishes characteristic of the Andalucian kitchen. In Spain a suckling lamb would be used. Tender young boneless lamb is a more than adequate substitute as well as being a practical one. The garlic will not be overpowering as cooking tames it.

SERVES 4
900 g/2 pounds lean, boneless lamb, cut into 3.5 cm/1½ inch pieces
salt and freshly ground pepper
2 tablespoons olive oil
1 tablespoon paprika
6 large cloves garlic, crushed
⅛ teaspoon saffron threads, ground
2 teaspoons plain (all-purpose) flour
250 ml/8 fl oz (1 cup) dry white wine

Pat the lamb pieces dry with paper towels and season with salt and pepper. Heat the oil in a flameproof casserole and sauté the lamb pieces over moderate heat until browned all over. Stir in the paprika, then add the garlic, saffron and flour. Cook for 1 minute, then stir in the wine, mixing well. Bring to a simmer, cover and cook over low heat until the lamb is tender, about 1½ hours. Serve with a green vegetable or a salad and drink a light red wine.

Calderete de Cordero a la Navarra
Lamb Stew, Navarre-style

The subtle variety of lamb stews in Spain seems almost endless. Minor variations in ingredients produce major variations in flavour so that no Spanish lamb stew is ever dull or boring. This one from Navarre, where the lamb is very splendid, is no exception. It has the merit of being easy to cook and in no way time-consuming, a feature of much of the cooking of the north of the country.

SERVES 4–6
750g/1½ pounds lean, boneless lamb, cut into 5cm/2 inch pieces
2 tablespoons olive oil
2 medium onions, chopped
4 cloves garlic, chopped
2 sweet green (bell) peppers, seeded and cut into 1 cm/½ inch strips
750 g/1½ pounds potatoes, peeled and cubed or sliced
salt and freshly ground pepper
475 ml/16 fl oz (2 cups) lamb stock or water

In a deep casserole sauté the lamb in the olive oil until the lamb pieces are browned all over. Lift out to a bowl. In the oil remaining in the casserole, sauté the onions, garlic and green peppers until the onion is soft, adding a little more oil if necessary. Return the lamb to the casserole with any juices that may have collected, season with salt and pepper, add the potatoes, pour in the stock, cover and cook over low heat until the lamb is tender, 1–1½ hours. Serve with a green salad and drink a light, dry red wine.

Tripas
Tripe

All the innards (offal) are esteemed in Spain and tripe dishes are among the favourites. There are many provincial recipes which may be called *tripas*, *callos* or *mondongo*. All the dishes are delicious, hearty, down-to-earth, easy to cook and inexpensive. Perhaps the most hearty of all is Portugal's version, from Porto.

Tripe, which comes from the first and second stomachs of beef, is always sold precooked, but as it is very tough it can need up to 2 hours' more cooking. Some packing houses precook the tripe longer than others, so a wise plan before starting to cook is to nibble a little piece to test how tough it is, and to check again during cooking. It must be tender but still firm as overcooked tripe is listless and without character. Spanish tripe is usually cooked for a very long time, much like *Tripes à la Mode de Caen*, as in the past tripe was not precooked. Cooking times need to be adjusted, especially when a pig's or calf's foot is used. These should be parboiled separately for about 2 hours before being added to the tripe. Calf's feet are seldom available and pig's feet, readily available, are a good substitute.

The Spanish and Portuguese love of tripe migrated to the New World and throughout Latin America there are great recipes evolved from the Iberian originals. Probably the most famous of them all is Mexico's *Menudo* from the State of Sonora, said to be an effective hangover cure when taken for breakfast and a respectable family dish for other meals.

Tripas à Moda do Porto
Tripe, Porto-style

Besides being famous for its port, Porto is also famous for its tripe. There is even a story that Henry the Navigator provisioned his ships with all the meat he could find in Porto before going off to fight the Moors at Ceuta. He left only tripe, so making the best of a bad situation, the cooks of Porto created this splendid dish. The story is unlikely, but the tripe dish of Porto is worth a journey to that city.

SERVES 4
250 g/8 oz (1 cup) dried haricot or Great Northern beans
1 calf's foot or pig's foot
salt and freshly ground pepper
4 tablespoons olive oil or lard
2 medium onions, finely chopped
1 medium carrot, scraped and sliced
500 g/1 pound tripe, cut into 2.5 cm/1 inch squares
1 clove garlic, chopped
½ teaspoon ground cumin
1 bay leaf
2 teaspoons paprika
1 tablespoon finely chopped parsley
125 g/4 ounces *chouriço* or *chorizo* sausage, sliced
125 g/4 ounces *presunto* or *smoked* ham, chopped

Soak the beans in cold water overnight. Drain and put into a large saucepan with water to cover by about 5 cm/2 inches and simmer, covered, until they are tender, 1–2 hours. Set aside.

Into another saucepan put the calf's or pig's foot to cook in salted water for 2 hours. Add the tripe and cook until both the tripe and pig's foot are tender. Lift out the calf's or pig's foot and remove the bones. Cut the meat into pieces and return it to the pot. Drain and add the beans.

In a frying pan (skillet) heat the oil or lard and sauté the onion and carrot until the onion is soft. Add the garlic und sauté for 1 minute longer. Add the cumin, bay leaf, paprika, parsley, sausage and ham and cook for 2–3 minutes longer. Add to the pot with the tripe and beans. Season to taste with salt and pepper: salt will probably not be needed. Cook, uncovered, for 30 minutes to blend the flavours. There should not be a great deal of liquid. If necessary pour off some of the liquid from the cooked tripe. Use only about 350 ml/12 fl oz (1½ cups). More can be added if the mixture seems to be drying out.

If liked, 500 g/1 pound (about 4 medium) tomatoes, peeled, seeded and chopped can be added to the onion and carrot mixture.

Serve with rice, a green salad, crusty bread and a robust dry red wine.

Tripas con Grão-de-Bico
Tripe with Chickpeas

This is a less elaborate dish than *Tripas à Moda do Porto* (Tripe, Porto-style). Dishes combining chickpeas and tripe are popular throughout Latin America, especially in Mexico. They all differ but clearly have the same original inspiration from Portuguese cooks.

SERVES 4
250 g/8 oz (1 cup) raw chickpeas, or a 500 g/1 pound tin (can) cooked chickpeas, rinsed and drained
salt and freshly ground pepper
500 g/1 pound tripe, cut into 2.5 cm/1 inch squares
2–3 sprigs parsley
1 clove
4 tablespoons lard or olive oil
1 medium onion, thinly sliced
1 stalk celery, thinly sliced
250 g/8 ounces (2 medium) tomatoes, peeled, seeded and sliced
2 cloves garlic, chopped
125 g/4 ounces *linguiça* sausage or *longaniza* or garlic-flavoured smoked sausage sliced

Soak the chickpeas overnight in cold water, then cook in salted water until tender, about 2 hours. The time will vary. Drain and set aside. If using tinned (canned) chickpeas, simply rinse, drain and set aside.

Rinse out and dry the saucepan in which the chickpeas were cooked and add the tripe, salt, pepper, parsley and clove. Cover with cold water, bring to a simmer and cook until tender. The time will vary as tripe is sold partially cooked and some needs little cooking. It is wise to nibble a bit before cooking. An hour's cooking is usually long enough: check from time to time. Strain the tripe and set aside.

Heat 3 tablespoons of the lard or olive oil in a casserole and sauté the onion and celery until soft. Add the tomatoes and garlic and cook until the mixture is well-blended, about 5 minutes. Add the tripe and chickpeas, cover and simmer over very low heat for 10 minutes. Meanwhile in a small frying pan (skillet) heat the remaining tablespoon of lard or oil and sauté the sliced sausage until lightly browned on both sides. Add to the tripe and simmer for 5 minutes longer. Serve with boiled potatoes and boiled, sliced carrots. Drink a light dry red wine.

Mondongo Gitano
Tripe, Gypsy-style

This tripe dish from Andalucía is especially interesting as it uses a sweet dried red pepper called *choricero*, which came originally from Mexico and has been developed and cultivated in New Mexico and other states in the United States. The nearest equivalent is probably the dried red Anaheim, or the New Mexican pepper, or the Mexican *chile colorado*. If none of these is available, use paprika in the proportion of 1 tablespoon paprika to 1 pepper. *Choriceros* add a very beautiful red colour and a subtle, hard-to-define flavour to the dish.

SERVES 4
250 g/8 oz (1 cup) raw chickpeas
salt
500 g/1 pound tripe, cut into 2.5 cm/1 inch squares
3 tablespoons lard
3 tablespoons olive oil
1 slice firm white bread
1 chorizo sausage, sliced
2 medium onions, chopped
2 cloves garlic, chopped
500 g/1 pound (4 medium) tomatoes, peeled, seeded and chopped
25 g/1 ounce (¼ cup) shelled walnuts, ground
⅛ teaspoon ground cloves
4 *pimientos secos choriceros*, seeded and soaked in warm water for 20 minutes
or 4 tablespoons paprika

Soak the chickpeas overnight in cold water, then cook in salted water until tender, about 2 hours. The time will vary. Drain and set aside.

In another saucepan cook the tripe in salted water until it is tender.

In a frying pan (skillet) heat 1 tablespoon each of the lard and oil and fry the bread until golden-brown on both sides. Lift out and drain on paper towels. In the fat remaining in the pan fry the sausage. Lift out and set aside. Add another tablespoon each of lard and oil and sauté the onion until soft. Add the garlic and cook for 1–2 minutes longer. Add the tomatoes and cook until the mixture is thick and well-blended, about 5 minutes. Break up the fried bread and process it in a food processor or blender with the walnuts and the peppers, drained and chopped, and salt and pepper to taste. Reduce the mixture to a paste. Add another tablespoon each of lard and oil to the frying pan (skillet) and sauté the paste for 2–3 minutes.

Drain the tripe and reserve the liquid. In a casserole combine the tripe, chickpeas, sausage and pepper mixture. Pour in 250 ml/8 fl oz (1 cup) of the reserved cooking liquid, stir to mix and simmer over very low heat, covered, for 15 minutes to blend the flavours and heat the tripe through. The sauce should be thick. The flavour of the dish is improved if made a day ahead and reheated. Serve with a salad and a full-bodied dry red wine.

Callos a la Extremeña
Tripe, Extremeña-style

Morcilla (black pudding or blood sausage) lends a distinctive flavour to this dish. In Extremeña lamb's feet would be used but pig's feet are an acceptable substitute.

SERVES 4–6

900 g/2 pounds tripe, cut into 2.5 cm/1 inch squares
2 pig's feet
1 onion, finely chopped
3 tablespoons olive oil
250 g/8 ounces *morcilla* (black pudding or blood sausage), cut into 1 cm/ ½ inch slices
1 tablespoon plain (all-purpose) flour
⅛ teaspoon cayenne pepper
salt and freshly ground pepper
2 cloves garlic, crushed
1 tablespoon finely chopped parsley

Nibble a piece of tripe before cooking and if it is fairly tender cook the pig's feet in salted water for 2 hours before adding the tripe. If the tripe is very tough, cook the two meats together until both are tender. Lift out the pig's feet, remove the bones and cut the meat into pieces. Set aside with the tripe. Pour out the liquid and reserve it. Rinse out and dry the saucepan or casserole in which the tripe was cooked.

Heat the oil in the casserole or saucepan and sauté the onion until soft. Add the sausage slices and sauté for 2–3 minutes. Stir in the flour, cayenne, salt, pepper, garlic and parsley mixed together and cook, stirring, for 2 minutes. Return the tripe and meat from the pig's feet to the casserole with 475 ml/16 fl oz (2 cups) of the reserved cooking liquid. Bring to a simmer and cook, uncovered, for 5 minutes to heat the tripe through and blend the flavours. Serve with a green salad, crusty bread and a full-bodied dry red wine.

Callos a la Madrileña
Tripe, Madrid-style

This is a popular way of cooking tripe in New Castille. The spicy dish is sometimes served in small quantities as a first course but is better appreciated by tripe lovers as the main dish in a meal. It can be made a day ahead and gently reheated before serving.

SERVES 6
1 pig's foot
1 bay leaf
1 onion, coarsely chopped
4 cloves garlic
salt and freshly ground pepper
900 g/2 pounds tripe, cut into 2.5 cm/1 inch squares
125 ml/4 fl oz (½ cup) dry white wine
2 teaspoons tomato purée or 1 small tomato, peeled, seeded and chopped
1 tablespoon chopped parsley
½ teaspoon thyme
2 tablespoons olive oil or lard
1 medium onion, finely chopped
50 g/2 ounces (¼ cup) diced cured ham
1 *morcilla* (black pudding or blood sausage), cut into 1 cm/½ inch slices (optional)
1 *chorizo*, about 125 g/4 ounces, cut into 5 mm/¼ inch slices
1 tablespoon paprika
1 dried hot chilli pepper, seeded and chopped

In a large saucepan or casserole simmer the pig's foot, bay leaf, coarsely chopped onion, one of the garlic cloves, left whole, salt and pepper with water to cover, covered, for 2 hours. At the end of that time lift out the pig's foot and measure the water. There should be 700 ml/1¼ pints (3 cups). Add or discard water as necessary. Add the tripe, wine, tomato purée or tomato, parsley and thyme together with the pig's foot to the liquid in the casserole and simmer, covered, for 1½ hours, or longer if the tripe is still very tough. Lift out the pig's foot, cool, remove the bones and cut the meat into pieces. Return to the casserole or saucepan.

In a frying pan (skillet) heat the olive oil or lard and sauté the finely chopped onion until soft. Add the remaining 3 cloves garlic, finely chopped, and sauté for 1–2 minutes longer. Add the ham, *morcilla*, if using, *chorizo*, paprika and dried hot chilli and sauté for 5 minutes longer. Stir the mixture into the tripe and cook, uncovered, at a gentle simmer for 30 minutes or until the tripe is tender and the sauce slightly thickened. Serve in warmed deep soup bowls with crusty bread. A green salad is the only accompaniment necessary. Serve a hearty dry red wine.

Tripa a la Catalana
Tripe, Catalan-style

This Catalan tripe dish is much simpler than the Madrid version but no less delicious for that.

SERVES 4
4 tablespoons olive oil or lard
750 g/1½ pounds tripe, cut into 3.5 × 1 cm/1½ by ½ inch strips
2 medium onions, finely chopped
375 g/12 oz (3 medium) tomatoes, peeled, seeded and chopped
1 sweet red (bell) pepper, seeded and coarsely chopped
1 aubergine, about 375 g/12 ounces, quartered lengthwise and cut into 1 cm/½ inch slices
salt
about 475 ml/16 fl oz (2 cups) beef stock

Heat the oil or lard in a flameproof casserole and sauté the tripe until golden. Lift out with a slotted spoon and set aside. Add the onions to the casserole, adding a little more oil or lard if necessary, and sauté until soft. Add the tomatoes, sweet pepper and aubergine, stir to mix, season with salt and cook for 5 minutes. Add the tripe to the casserole, stir in the stock and simmer gently, covered, for about 2 hours or until the tripe is tender. If necessary, add more stock if the mixture seems to be drying out. Serve with a green salad, crusty bread and a robust dry red wine.

Higado de Cordero Guisado
Lamb's Liver Ragoût

This unusual lamb's liver dish is from the extensive kitchen of Old Castille, home of many of Spain's most delicious dishes.

SERVES 4
4 tablespoons lard or olive oil
1 slice firm white bread
2 medium onions, finely chopped
1 clove garlic, chopped
500 g/1 lb (4 medium) tomatoes, peeled, seeded and cut into eighths
2 tablespoons finely chopped parsley
625 g/1 pound (4 medium) potatoes, sliced
500 g/1 pound lamb's liver, in one piece
salt and freshly ground pepper
about 475 ml/16 fl oz (2 cups, lamb or beef stock

Heat 2 tablespoons of the lard or oil in a frying pan and fry the bread until golden on both sides. Lift out and drain on paper towels, then grind in a food processor or blender. Set aside.

Heat the remaining lard or oil in the pan and sauté the onions until soft. Add the garlic and sauté for 10 minutes longer. Add the tomatoes and parsley and sauté for 5 minutes longer. Add the potatoes and cook for 5 minutes, then add the liver, season with salt and pepper and pour in enough stock barely to cover. Cover and cook over very low heat until the potatoes are tender and the liver cooked through. Lift out the liver onto a warmed dish and slice. Stir the fried breadcrumbs into the pan and cook for about 1 minute. Pour the sauce over the liver and serve with a green salad. Drink a light red wine.

Iscas
Pork Liver, Lisbon-style

This marinated pork liver is a great Portuguese favourite and a classic dish in Lisbon. Calf's or lamb's liver can be used if preferred.

SERVES 4
175 ml/6 fl oz (¾ cup) dry white wine
1 tablespoon white wine vinegar
4 cloves garlic, chopped
1 bay leaf
salt and freshly ground pepper
500 g/1 pound pork, calf's or lamb's liver, thinly sliced
50 g/2 oz (4 slices) bacon, chopped
3 tablespoons lard or oil

In a bowl combine the wine, vinegar, garlic, bay leaf and salt and pepper to taste. Add the liver and marinate in the refrigerator overnight.

When ready to cook, lift out and dry the liver. Heat the lard or oil in a frying pan (skillet) and sauté the bacon until crisp. Add the liver and cook over moderate heat for 1 minute on each side, if using pork liver, or 30 seconds on each side for calf's or lamb's liver. Lift out the liver and bacon onto a warmed serving dish, cover and keep warm.

Remove and discard the bay leaf from the marinade. Pour the marinade into the pan, bring to a boil over high heat and reduce it to about half. Pour over the liver and serve with sliced boiled potatoes sprinkled with chopped parsley, or sliced fried potatoes arranged round the liver. Drink a light white wine.

Figado de Porco de Cebolada
Pork Liver with Onions

This pork liver dish comes from the province of Ribatejo, next door to Estremadura, home of the classic liver dish, *Iscas*. It can be made with calf's or lamb's liver if preferred.

SERVES 4
500 g/1 pound pork, calf's or lamb's liver, thinly sliced
salt and freshly ground pepper
⅛ teaspoon paprika
125 ml/4 fl oz (½ cup) dry white wine
2 tablespoons each olive oil and lard
2 medium onions or 1 large onion, thinly sliced
2 cloves garlic, chopped
2 tablespoons white wine vinegar

Season the liver with salt, pepper, cumin and paprika and put into a bowl with the wine. Marinate the liver for at least 2 hours.

In a frying pan (skillet) heat 1 tablespoon each of the oil and lard and sauté the onion and garlic until the onion is lightly browned. In another pan heat the rest of the oil and lard. Pat the liver dry with paper towels and sauté in the pan for 1 minute on each side for pork liver, 30 seconds on each side for calf's or lamb's liver. Add to the pan with the onions, stir in the wine vinegar and serve with *Arroz de Manteiga* (Buttered Rice) (page 219). Drink a light dry red wine.

Higado con Ajillo
Calf's Liver with Garlic Sauce

Mallorcan cuisine is best known for its fish and shellfish but there are other very attractive dishes, such as this unusual liver one.

SERVES 4
500 g/1 pound calf's liver, in one piece
50 ml/2 fl oz]¼ cup) water
50 ml/2 fl oz (¼ cup) olive oil plus 25 ml/1 fl oz (⅛ cup)
1 slice white bread
2 cloves garlic, crushed
salt and freshly ground pepper
1 tablespoon red wine vinegar

In a frying pan (skillet) simmer the liver for 2 minutes in the water with 50 ml/2 fl oz (¼ cup) of the olive oil. Set aside.

In a small frying pan (skillet) heat the remaining oil and fry the bread until golden-brown on both sides. In a food processor or blender grind the bread with the garlic, salt and pepper. Lift the liver from the pan and slice it thinly. Add the fried bread mixture to the liquid in the pan. Stir in the vinegar and simmer for 2–3 minutes to blend the flavours. Add the liver and cook just long enough to heat it through. Serve with potatoes and a salad. Drink a full-bodied dry red wine.

Sesos a la Catalana
Brains, Catalan-style

This simple Catalan dish is made into something special by its puréed artichoke heart and potato garnish.

SERVES 4
500 g/1 pound calf's or lamb's brains
salt
plain (all-purpose) flour for dredging
1 large egg, lightly beaten
3 tablespoons olive oil
Alcachofas y Patatas (Artichoke Hearts and Potatoes) (page 191)

Put the brains into a bowl and soak in several changes of cold water to soften the filaments and get rid of bloody patches. Gently pull away the filament, taking care not to tear the brains. Soak again if necessary and remove as much of the filament as possible. Drain and put into a saucepan with fresh water and salt and simmer gently for 20 minutes. Drain and pat dry with paper towels.

Slice the brains, dredge with flour seasoned with salt and dip in the beaten egg. Heat the oil in a frying pan (skillet) and sauté the brains until golden all over. Pile into the centre of a warmed serving dish and surround with the vegetable purée.

Riñones al Jerez
Veal Kidneys with Sherry

This is the most popular way of cooking kidneys in Spain, so much so that it has spread to the New World and is also the favourite way of cooking kidneys throughout Latin America. The kidneys are sometimes served in smaller quantities as a first course.

SERVES 4
750 g/1½ pounds veal kidneys
salt
2 cloves garlic, crushed
4 tablespoons olive oil
125 ml/4 fl oz (½ cup) dry sherry
2 tablespoons chopped parsley

Wash and dry the kidneys and cut away any fat. Cut the kidneys into 2 cm/¾ inch cubes. Season with salt and garlic.

Heat the oil in a heavy frying pan (skillet), add the kidneys and sauté over moderately high heat for 1 minute, turning the pieces over once. Pour in the sherry, sprinkle with parsley and cook for 1 minute longer. Serve immediately, with rice and a green salad, and drink a light dry red wine.

Riñones a la Vasca
Veal Kidneys, Basque-style

This is another of the simple, good ways of cooking veal kidney popular in Spain.

Serves 4–6
1.4 kg/3 pounds veal kidney
2 tablespoons olive oil
1 medium onion, finely chopped
1 tablespoon chopped parsley
25 g/1 ounce (½ cup) fresh white breadcrumbs
125 ml/4 fl oz (½ cup) beef stock
salt and freshly ground pepper
50 ml/2 fl oz (¼ cup) dry white wine

Wash and dry the kidneys and cut away any fat. Cut the kidneys into 2 cm/¾ inch cubes. Heat 1 tablespoon of the oil in a heavy frying pan and toss the kidneys in the oil over moderately high heat for 1 minute. Transfer to a bowl and set aside.

Add the remaining oil to the pan and sauté the onion until soft, add the parsley and sauté for 1 minute longer. Add the pan contents to the reserved kidneys.

Add the breadcrumbs to the pan, stir in the beef stock, season with salt and pepper and cook, stirring, for 2–3 minutes. Add the wine, simmer for 1 minute to blend the flavours, then return the kidney and onion mixture to the pan with any juices that have collected and cook over moderately high heat to finish cooking the kidneys and heat them through. Serve immediately with a salad and drink a full-bodied dry red wine.

Variation: For the Catalan dish *Riñones Salteados* (Tossed Kidneys) prepare the kidneys in the same way and put them into a bowl with 250 ml/8 fl oz (1 cup) red wine vinegar, 2 tablespoons olive oil, salt and freshly ground pepper. Marinate the kidneys for 20 minutes, then drain and pat dry with paper towels. Heat 2 tablespoons lard or olive oil in a frying pan (skillet) and sauté the kidneys over high heat for 1 minute. Remove to a bowl and set aside. Add 2 cloves chopped garlic and 2 tablespoons chopped parsley to the pan with 250 ml/8 fl oz (1 cup) dry white wine and 1 tablespoon of the marinade. Stir and simmer over low heat for about 3 minutes. Add the kidneys and any liquid that has collected, season with salt and pepper and cook over moderately heat for 1 minute longer to finish cooking the kidneys and heat them through. Serve with a salad and drink a dry red wine.

Variation: For *Riñones Salteados a la Española* (Tossed Kidneys, Spanish-style), cut the kidneys into strips and toss in a frying pan (skillet) in 2 tablespoons lard for 1 minute over high heat. Heat 250 ml/8 fl oz (1 cup) tomato sauce and 1 tablespoon pine nuts chopped and mixed with the yolk of 1 large egg, in a small saucepan and pour into the pan. Stir to mix and cook over high heat for 1 minute. Serve with bread triangles fried in olive oil. Drink a dry red wine.

Rim Solteado à Moda do Porto
Pork Kidneys, Porto-style

In this dish from Porto pig's kidneys are transformed into a rare treat. The secret is the flavour of dry white Port which is worth searching for, both to cook with and to drink as an aperitif. A very dry Madeira is probably the best substitute.

SERVES 2
4 pork kidneys
salt and freshly ground pepper
4 tablespoons butter
1 tablespoon olive oil
1 medium onion, finely chopped
1 clove garlic, chopped
500 g/8 ounces (2 medium) tomatoes, peeled, seeded and chopped
125 ml/4 fl oz (½ cup) dry Port wine, or very dry Madeira
1 tablespoon chopped parsley
2 teaspoons plain (all-purpose) flour

Soak the kidneys for 10 minutes in cold, salted water. Lift the kidneys out and pat dry with paper towels, remove any fat and cut them into slices.

Heat the butter and oil in a casserole. Add the onion and garlic and sauté until the onion is soft. Add the kidneys and sauté over moderate heat, turning the slices once, for about 3 minutes. Add the tomatoes, pour in the wine, stir to mix, then add the parsley and season with salt and pepper. Mix the flour with a little water and stir it into the casserole. Bring to a simmer, cover and cook over very low heat for 2 hours, or until the kidneys are tender. Serve with potatoes, green salad and a full-bodied dry red wine.

6

Vegetables and Salads
Verduras y Ensaladas/Legumes e Saladas

The people of Spain and Portugal do not like their green vegetables plain, and they do not serve them two or three at a time to accompany meats, fish and poultry. Instead, they are usually served as a separate course before the main dish and are not simply cooked in boiling salted water but in combinations of vegetables and meat, or poultry or seafood, cured ham or sausage. Vegetables are more often than not cooked in olive oil. Many could be served as the main course of a light lunch or supper. One of the vegetable dishes I most enjoy is Catalan, *Acelgas a la Catalana* Swiss Chard with Raisins, Pine nuts and Salted Anchovies which makes a fine first course. This vegetable is sometimes sold as silver beet, or even as spinach. My favourite version of it was at the Ritz in Barcelona where it was made with spinach. The dish can be made successfully with collards or kale, which makes it accessible year round.

The Basques have a special approach to vegetables with *menestra*, young spring vegetables, *primeurs*, tiny carrots, potatoes, peas, green and broad beans, as well as asparagus and artichokes cooked and served with eggs. There are many versions of *menestra* which are really variations on a theme. They are hearty enough to be a main course.

There are other vegetable medleys like *pisto* which may include cured ham, or be served with poached or scrambled eggs, or consist solely of vegetables. Dried beans are often combined with tomato sauce for *Grão com Tomatada* (Chick Peas with Tomato Sauce), *Feijão Branco com Tomatada* (Black-eyed Peas with Tomato Sauce). Use 500 g/1 pound beans, soaked and cooked, to 250 ml/8 fl oz (1 cup) tomato sauce. When the beans are cooked, drain them and heat them through in the sauce. These are very good with pork. Spanish cooks are equally imaginative, combining vegetables with cured ham, or sausages, and garlic.

One of the delights of eating in Portugal is the ever-present salad, an ideal first course that can be left on the table to accompany the rest of the meal. Basically these are tomato, lettuce and onion salads, but they manage to differ amazingly from place to place with small additions or various dressings. Usually olive oil and vinegar are brought to the table to be used as one pleases, just drizzled over the salad. Large and sweet enough to eat like apples, the onions are amazing. They come in quite thick rings in the very simplest salad, a bowl lined wih lettuce leaves topped with sliced tomatoes and onion and perhaps a few black olives. When seasoned with salt and pepper, with oil generously, and vinegar sparingly, they have no equal. Some tomato salads are surprising: generous dishes of sliced tomatoes that are still green yet do not taste at all unripe. Perhaps some sliced onion, and oil and vinegar are all that is added. Grated carrot, chopped cooked red cabbage, or diced beetroot (beets) are used, and sometimes instead of oil and vinegar, a light mayonnaise.

As in Portugal, when serving salads in Spain, cruets with oil and vinegar are presented for the diner to use at his/her discretion. There are other, more elaborate dressings. Salads too can be simple or compound and one, *Pipirrana Jaenera*, with tomato, sweet green (bell) pepper, cured ham and tuna, could be main course.

Potatoes occupy a special place in both countries with a great many excitingly different recipes.

Dried beans of many kinds, though not as popular as potatoes, are nevertheless important in the Peninsula, with an interesting repertoire of dishes.

Judias Verdes Salteadas
Tossed Green Beans

Green beans are one of Mexico's gifts to the world of food and this dish from Murcia and Albacete on Spain's Mediterranean coast, immediately south of Valencia, is exceptionally flavourful. It would be served as a separate course in Spanish restaurant though there is no reason why it should not be served to accompany any main course.

SERVES 4
500g/1 pound fresh young green beans
salt and freshly ground pepper
50g/2oz (4 tablespoons) butter
4 tablespoons lemon juice
1 tablespoon chopped parsley

Cook the beans in boiling salted water for 8 minutes. Drain thoroughly. Heat the butter in a frying pan (skillet), add the beans and cook, stirring from time to time, over moderate heat for 10 minutes. Add the lemon juice, parsley, salt and pepper to taste, and stir to mix thoroughly. Serve immediately.

Variation: This is a popular way of cooking beans in Castille. Cook the beans in boiling salted water until tender. Have ready 3 sweet red (bell) peppers, peeled and thinly sliced (page xx). Make a *sofrito* by mixing together 3 cloves garlic, finely chopped, 1 tablespoon parsley, finely chopped, and 2 tablespoons olive oil. Drain the beans and combine them in a casserole with the *sofrito*. Cook, stirring, over low heat for 2 minutes. Add the peppers and cook for 2 minutes longer, stirring to mix. Serves 4.

Variation: This is a widely popular way of cooking beans. Heat 25g/1oz (2 tablespoons) butter in a frying pan (skillet) and sauté the beans, which should be very fresh and young, over low heat, stirring from time to time until they are tender, 15–20 minutes. Season with salt and 1 clove of crushed garlic, stirring to mix. Serves 4.

Judias Verdes con Jamon
Green Beans with Ham

This attractive vegetable is made special with the addition of cured ham in this Spanish recipe. The cooking time may seem exceptionally long, nevertheless the beans emerge crisp and flavourful. In Spain they would be served as a separate course before the main course, but would make a good accompaniment to many meat and poultry dishes.

SERVES 4
1 tablespoon mild white vinegar
375 g/12 ounces fresh green beans, trimmed
2 tablespoons olive oil
½ medium onion, finely chopped
2 cloves garlic, chopped
125 g/4 ounces cured ham, cut into 1 cm/½ inch pieces
salt and freshly ground pepper

Bring a saucepan of water to the boil. Add the vinegar and the beans. Bring back to a boil and cook for 4 minutes. Drain and refresh the beans in cold water, drain again and pat dry with paper towels.

In a frying pan (skillet) heat the oil and sauté the beans and onion over moderate heat for 4 minutes. Add the garlic and ham and cook 1 minute longer. Season with salt and pepper, cover and cook over low heat for 8 minutes longer. Serve immediately.

Guisantes a la Española
Peas with Ham

Peas, fresh in their green pods, are a favourite vegetable in both Spain and Portugal and are cooked in a number of ways different from our own technique of cooking in boiling salted water. The results are deliciously gratifying.

SERVES 4
2 tablespoons olive oil
1 medium onion, finely chopped
125 g/4 ounces cured ham, chopped
250 g/8 ounces shelled peas, defrosted if frozen
salt and freshly ground pepper
1 tablespoon finely chopped fresh mint

Heat the oil in a medium flameproof casserole and sauté the onion until soft. Add the ham and sauté for 1–2 minutes longer. Add the peas, and salt and pepper to taste. Cover tightly and cook over very low heat until the peas are tender. Frozen peas may take as short a time as 8 minutes. Fresh peas may need 15–20 minutes. Check the casserole and, if necessary, with fresh peas add 125 ml/4 fl oz (½ cup) water. When the peas are tender, sprinkle with the mint and serve.

Variation: Omit the ham. About 5 minutes before the peas are cooked, add 1 peeled and diced cucumber. Finish cooking as in the main recipe. If using hot-house or seedless cucumber, do not peel. Score the skin with a fork, dice and add, using ½ a cucumber.

Guisantes Levantina
Peas, Valencia-Style

This is a more elaborate version of stewed green peas. White wine and saffron make it special.

SERVES 4
2 tablespoons olive oil
1 medium onion, finely chopped
2 cloves garlic, chopped
250 g/8 ounces shelled green peas, defrosted if frozen
50 ml/2 fl oz (¼ cup) dry white wine
50 ml/2 fl oz (¼ cup) water
bouquet garni: sprig each parsley and thyme, and 1 bay leaf, tied together
with thread
salt and freshly ground pepper
⅛ teaspoon saffron threads
sweet red (bell) pepper strips, to garnish

Heat the oil in a casserole and sauté the onion until soft. Add 1 clove garlic and sauté for 1 minute longer. Stir in the peas, then add the wine, water, bouquet garni and salt and pepper to taste. Bring to a simmer, cover and cook over low heat until the peas are tender, 15–20 minutes, or a shorter time for frozen peas. Remove and discard the bouquet garni.

Grind the remaining garlic clove with the saffron threads and stir into the casserole. Cook for a few minutes longer. Serve garnished with the sweet pepper strips.

Variation: Add 1 tablespoon ground almonds to the saffron and garlic mixture.

Ervilhas à Moda do Algarve
Green Peas, Algarve-style

This is served as a main course in the Algarve and would be suitable for lunch or supper. This dish is served as a vegetable accompaniment to plainly cooked meat if the eggs are omitted.

SERVES 4
2 tablespoons olive oil
1 medium onion, finely chopped
1 sweet red (bell) pepper, seeded and cut into strips
125 g/4 ounces *chouriço* or *chorizo* or any garlic flavoured smoked pork
sausage, thinly sliced
750g/1½ pounds shelled green peas, defrosted if frozen
salt and freshly ground pepper
3 tablespoons chopped fresh coriander
4 large eggs
1 teaspoon vinegar

In a saucepan or flameproof casserole heat the oil and sauté the onion, pepper and sausage until the vegetables are soft, about 5 minutes. Stir in the peas and cook for 1–2 minutes, then add 125 ml/4 fl oz (½ cup) water, bring to a simmer, cover and cook over very low heat until the peas are tender, 15–20 minutes. Frozen peas will take less time.

While the peas are cooking have ready a large frying pan (skillet) two-thirds filled with water. Add the vinegar as this helps coagulate the egg whites. Break the eggs into 4 saucers. When the water comes to a boil, slide the eggs into different parts of the pan, add ½ teaspoon salt and simmer, spooning the water over the eggs, for 2–3 minutes. Cover the pan and set aside off the heat while finishing the peas.

Season the peas with salt and pepper. Fold in the coriander and transfer to warmed serving dish. Arrange the poached eggs, lifting them out of the pan with a slotted spoon, on top of the peas. Top each serving of peas with an egg.

Faves a la Catalana
Broad Beans, Catalan-style

Broad beans are usually called *habas* in Spain, but in Catalonia it is more usual to find them called *faves*, a small and recognizable distinction. If they are not available baby lima beans are an acceptable substitute.

SERVES 4–6
2 tablespoons lard
125 g/4 oz smoked bacon, cut into 1 cm/½ inch slices
1 medium onion, finely chopped
1 clove garlic, chopped
250 g/8 oz (2 medium) tomatoes, peeled, seeded and chopped
750 g/1½ pounds shelled broad beans or baby lima beans defrosted if frozen
250 g/8 oz *chorizo* or other garlic flavoured smoked pork sausage, cut into 5mm/¼ inch slices
1 tablespoon chopped fresh herbs, thyme, oregano, mint, parsley
125 ml/4 fl oz (½ cup) dry white wine
1 tablespoon brandy
salt and freshly ground pepper
chicken stock or water

In a flameproof casserole heat the lard and sauté the bacon until lightly browned. Lift out and set aside. In the fat remaining in the pan sauté the onion until soft, add the garlic and saute for 1–2 minutes longer. Add the tomatoes and beans and cook, over low heat, for 5 minutes.

Return the bacon to the casserole. Add the *chorizo*, herbs, wine and brandy. Season to taste with salt and pepper and add just enough chicken stock or water barely to cover, Cover and simmer for about 15 minutes, or until the beans are tender. Serve in a warmed dish or directly from the casserole. This is a good first course.

Favas à Portuguesa
Broad Beans, Portuguese-Style

Broad beans are a much-esteemed vegetable throughout the Iberian Peninsula. One of the most ancient of all European vegetables, there is a surprising similarity in the way these beans are cooked in Spain and Portugal. They seem to have a natural affinity with olive oil, onion, garlic and sausages or bacon. Small differences in ingredients and cooking methods produce enticingly different dishes. This, perhaps the simplest, is one of my favourites.

SERVES 4
50 ml/2 fl oz (¼ cup) olive oil
50 g/2 ounces bacon, chopped
1 medium onion, chopped
1 clove garlic chopped
500 g/1 pound shelled broad beans/or baby lima beans, defrosted if frozen
1 bay leaf
large sprigs each parsley and coriander
salt and freshly ground pepper
pinch of sugar
about 250 ml/8 fl oz (1 cup) water

In a flameproof casserole heat the oil and sauté the bacon, onion, and garlic until the onion is soft. Add the beans, bay leaf, parsley and coriander, salt, pepper and sugar. Cover and sweat over low heat for 5 minutes. Add the water and cook until the beans are tender, about 15 minutes. If the beans are very young, 5 minutes may be long enough. Strain, discarding any liquid, and serve.

Favas com Coentro
Broad Beans with Coriander

This is a simpler recipe than the Algarve broad beans and is transformed by the fresh coriander which lends an exquisite flavour. If broad beans are not available, baby limas are an acceptable substitute.

SERVES 4
1 tablespoon olive oil
50 g/2 ounces lean bacon, diced
1 medium onion, finely chopped
500 g/1 pound shelled broad beans or baby lima beans, defrosted if frozen
250 ml/8 fl oz (1 cup) water
salt and freshly ground pepper
25 g/1 oz (½ cup) chopped fresh coriander

Heat the oil in a heavy saucepan large enough to hold the beans. Sauté the bacon until crisp. Lift out and drain on paper towels, then set aside in a small bowl. Add the onion to the saucepan and sauté until tender. Add the beans, water and salt and pepper to taste. Cover and cook over low heat until the beans are tender, 10–15 minutes. Drain and discard any water from the pan, return the bacon pieces, warm through, add the coriander and stir to mix and serve hot. The beans are usually served with roast meat or poultry.

Favas à Algarvia
Broad Beans, Algarve-style

This is a pleasantly unusual way of serving broad beans. If these are not available, use baby limas.

SERVES 4
500 g/1 pound shelled broad beans or baby lima beans, defrosted if frozen
salt
1 large sprig mint
1 tablespoon olive oil
75 g/3 ounces sliced *morcela* sausage (black pudding, blood sausage)
75 g/3 ounces *chouriço* or *chorizo*, sliced
125 g/4 ounces smoked lean bacon, sliced

In a saucepan combine the beans, salt to taste and mint with water to cover. Bring to a boil and simmer until the beans are tender, 10–15 minutes. Drain thoroughly and discard the mint. Return the beans to the pan.

Meanwhile, heat the oil in a frying pan (skillet) and sauté the sausages and bacon until lightly browned on both sides. Add, with the oil in the pan, to the beans, mix gently, cover and cook over very low heat until the beans are heated through. Serve with *Ensalada de Lechuja* (Lettuce Salad) (page 196) and as an accompaniment to *carapaus*, horse mackerel or scad, simply fried in olive oil. This is a popular fish in Portugal, especially in the Algarve. Any smallish, fried fish can be subsituted for the *carapaus*.

Variation: Use fresh beans instead of broad beans.

Michirones
Spicy Broad Beans

The tiny province of Murcia, just south of Valencia and next door to Andalucía, produces some interesting recipes that are quite distinct from those of its near neighbours. This is a good example of the originality of the cooking.

SERVES 4

500 g/1 pound shelled broad beans or baby lima beans, defrosted if frozen
125 g/4 ounces chorizo sausage, sliced
1 fresh hot red chilli pepper, chopped
salt and freshly ground pepper
1 bay leaf
ham bone
250 ml/8 fl oz (1 cup) water

Combine all the ingredients in a saucepan with a tightly fitting lid, bring to a simmer and cook over low heat for 10–15 minutes, or until the beans are tender. Remove and discard the bay leaf and ham bone. There should not be a great deal of liquid, but strain the beans before serving.

Espinacas con Pases y Piñones
Spinach with Raisins and Pine Nuts

Instead of spinach, silver beet (Swiss chard), collards or kale can all be used for this recipe which makes a delicious first course.

SERVES 4
50 g/2 oz (¹/₃ cup) seedless raisins
salt
900 g/2 pounds spinach, washed and trimmed
3 tablespoons olive oil
3 tablespoons pine nuts
salt and freshly ground pepper
fried bread triangles

Put the raisins to soak in a bowl with warm water to cover. bring a large saucepan of salted water to a brisk boil, drop in the spinach and cook, uncovered, over moderately high heat for 5 minutes. Drain, plunge into cold water and drain again immediately. Squeeze out as much liquid as possible. A convenient way to do this is to roll the spinach in a slatted bamboo mat, or a kitchen towel, and squeeze the water out. Chop the spinach coarsely. Drain the raisins. Rinse out and dry the saucepan.

Heat the oil in the saucepan and add the spinach, raisins and pine nuts. Season with salt and pepper and cook over low heat for 5 minutes. The spinach is now ready to be served, garnished with triangles of bread fried in olive oil, but the flavour improves if the greens are set aside for 30 minutes, then gently reheated.

Variation: For *Espinacas a la Catalana* (Spinach, Catalan-style), cook and drain the spinach as above. Chop it coarsely, and add it to the pan with the oil, 1 clove garlic, chopped, 4 anchovy fillets, chopped, the pine nuts and raisins. Season with salt and pepper and cook over very low heat for 20 minutes. For *Acelgas a la Catalana* (Swiss Chard, Catalan-style), trim away the white part and keep it for another use. Cook as above.

Variation: For *Espinafres à Portuguesa* Spinach, Portuguese-style, cook and chop the spinach as in the main recipe. In a frying pan (skillet) heat 2 tablespoons olive oil and sauté 2 cloves garlic, chopped, until barely golden. Stir in 2 teaspoons plain (all-purpose) flour and cook, stirring, for about 2 minutes. Stir in 125 ml/4 fl oz (½ cup) water and cook until the mixture is smooth. Add the spinach and cook, stirring, until the spinach is heated through. Season with salt and pepper and serve hot.

Variation: Portuguese cooks excel at putting vegetables together in unusual combinations. This one, *Grão com Espinafres* (Chick Peas and Spinach) makes a perfect accompaniment to salt cod, and is good with both meat and poultry. Soak 250 g/8 oz (1 ¹/₃ cups) chickpeas overnight. Drain and put on to cook in cold water to cover and simmer for 1 hour. Drain. Wash and trim 900 g/2 pounds spinach. Slice 1 large onion thinly.

In a casserole make a layer of one third of the spinach, top with half the onion and half the chickpeas. Continue, ending with the spinach. Season the layers with salt and pepper. Pour in 125 ml/4 fl oz (½ cup) beef stock. Pour 4 tablespoons olive oil over the spinach, cover and cook over very low heat until the chickpeas are tender and all the liquid absorbed, about 1 hour. Check during cooking that the mixture is not drying out and add a little more stock if necessary.

Grelos
Sautéed Spring Greens

Grelos comes from the Portuguese verb *grelar*, to sprout, and can apply to almost any young sprouting vegetable – beetroot (beet) greens, collards, kale, Swiss chard, spinach, mustard greens, broccoli and English spring greens so long as they are the tender young shoots of spring. In Portugal turnip greens are the favourite and much used. This makes a pleasantly different way of serving a green vegetable and is very good with any roasted meat or poultry.

SERVES 4
900 g/2 pounds young spring greens
4 tablespoons olive oil
2–4 large cloves garlic, chopped, according to taste
salt and freshly ground pepper

Wash the greens and remove any wilted leaves and coarse stems. Drain in a colander and pat dry with paper towels.

Heat the oil in a large saucepan and sauté the garlic, stirring from time to time, until soft but not brown. Add the greens, stir to mix, season with salt and pepper and cook over moderately high heat for about 4 minutes. Serve immediately.

Pisto Castellano
Vegetable Medley, Old Castille-style

Plainly cooked vegetables are not popular in Spain but combinations of vegetables are. They are usually served as a separate course before the main course. This dish could be eaten as a light lunch or supper as it is quite hearty, especially with the addition of eggs.

SERVES 4–6
2 tablespoons lard
50 g/2 oz (4 slices) bacon, chopped
3 medium onions, chopped
2 medium courgettes (zucchini), trimmed and sliced
3 medium potatoes, peeled and diced
2 tablespoons olive oil
4 medium sweet red (bell) peppers, peeled, seeded and chopped (see below)
500 g/1 pound (4 medium) tomatoes, peeled, seeded and chopped
50 ml/2 fl oz (¼ cup) beef or chicken stock
salt and freshly ground pepper
2 large eggs, lightly beaten

Heat the lard in a frying pan (skillet) and sauté the bacon and onions until the onions are soft. Add the courgettes (zucchini) and potatoes and sauté until the vegetables are almost tender. In another frying pan (skillet) heat the oil and sauté the peppers until soft. Add the tomatoes and when the mixture is well blended and quite thick, about 5 minutes, add the mixture to the pan with the potato mixture.

Season with salt and pepper, pour in the chicken stock, cover and cook over low heat until all the vegetables are tender, about 5 minutes. Pour in the eggs and cook, stirring gently with a wooden spoon, until the eggs are set. Garnish with triangles of bread, fried in olive oil.

Variation: Omit the beaten eggs and serve with poached or fried eggs, cooked separately. Green peppers may be used instead of red ones.

Variation: *Pisto Asturiano* is made with 50 g/2 ounces ham instead of bacon and without courgettes (zucchini) or potatoes. It is garnished with finely chopped hardboiled egg in addition to the 2 eggs scrambled into the vegetable mixture. Only olive oil is used, no lard.

To Peel Sweet (Bell) Peppers

Toasting or grilling (broiling) the peppers brings out their flavour and makes it possible to remove the papery covering skin. Spanish *pimientos morrones* (sweet red peppers) are sold in jars or tins (cans) ready-peeled and can be used instead of the home-made ones.

This is my preferred method for peeling peppers. Spear the peppers at the stem with a long-handled kitchen fork and toast them over a gas flame, turning them to blacken the skins for about 3 minutes. Put them into a plastic bag and leave until cool enough to peel. Or grill (broil) them about 12 cm/5 inches from the source of the heat, turning regularly until they are blackened all over, about 15 minutes. Put them into a plastic bag, cool and peel. Slit the peppers and remove the seeds.

Tomatada a la Navarra
Tomatoes, Navarre-Style

Unlike the Portuguese *tomatada* this is not a sauce but a vegetable dish that could serve as a light main course. The pepper used is a sweet, light green, tapering pepper, called *chile cristal*. Any sweet, light green, tapering pepper can be used, or use sweet green (bell) pepper.

SERVES 2
4 tablespoons olive oil
900 g/2 pounds (8 medium) tomatoes, peeled, seeded and chopped
50 g/2 ounces ham, cut into small strips
50 g/2 ounces *chorizo* sausage, sliced
100 g/4 ounces lean boneless veal, cut into small strips
salt and freshly ground pepper
2 sweet, light green, tapering peppers or sweet green (bell) peppers, peeled, seeded and cut into strips

Heat the oil in a casserole and add the tomatoes, ham, sausage and veal and cook over low heat until the mixture is well-blended and the veal is tender, about 15 minutes. Season to taste with salt and pepper. Add the peppers and cook just long enough to heat them through.

Setas Salteados
Sautéed Mushrooms

This can be served as a first course though in Spain it would probably be served with other *tapas*. The mushrooms might be served as a vegetable to accompany a plainly cooked meat or poultry dish.

SERVES 4
500 g/1 pound mushrooms, stems trimmed
25 g/1 oz (2 tablespoons) butter

3 cloves garlic, chopped
3 tablespoons finely chopped parsley
3 tablespoons fresh white breadcrumbs
salt and freshly ground pepper

Wipe the mushrooms with a damp cloth. If they are small leave them whole, if large either halve or quarter them. Heat the butter in a large frying pan (skillet) and sauté the mushrooms over moderately high heat with the garlic and parsley until they are lightly browned and have given up all their liquid, about 6 minutes. Stir in the breadcrumbs and season to taste with salt and pepper.

Variation: In Catalonia Mushrooms with Ham are called *Bolets am Pernil*, using the large red pine mushrooms of the region. These are not available elsewhere but ordinary mushrooms can be used to make an attractive first course, or in larger servings a light luncheon dish. For 500 g/1 pound mushrooms cut 125 g/4 ounces cured ham into cubes and sauté in 2 tablespoons olive oil. Add the mushrooms left whole if small, quartered or halved if large, and sauté until lightly browned, about 6 minutes. Stir in 2 tablespoons each of breadcrumbs and finely chopped parsley, season with salt, if necessary, and freshly ground pepper. Stir in 125 ml/4 fl oz (½ cup) dry sherry and cook for 5 minutes longer.

Variation: For *Setas a la Riojana* (Mushrooms, Rioja-style), sauté the mushrooms in 2 tablespoons olive oil, season with salt and pepper, and when they have given up all their liquid and are lightly browned, about 6 minutes, pour in 175 ml/6 fl oz (¾ cup) *Salsa a la Riojana* (Sauce Rioja-style) (page 242) and cook for 5 minutes longer.

Variation: For *Setas a la Navarra* (Mushrooms Navarre-style), where the mushrooms are particularly fine, sauté in olive oil as in the previous recipes. Season with salt and a little paprika and when they are cooked pour 175 ml/6 fl oz (¾ cup) *Salsa de Almendras* (Almond Sauce) (page 241) over them and cook just long enough to heat the sauce through.

Patatas/Batatas
Potatoes

Potatoes were first cultivated thousands of years ago in what is now modern Peru, by people we call, for convenience, the Incas, although the cultivators were almost certainly from an older civilization. When the Spaniards arrived the Incas had over a hundred types of potato, some of which still survive in the region. Only a few varieties came to Europe.

I have never been in a country where potatoes are as popular as they are in Portugal. This may be because the potatoes are extraordinarily good, deliciously flavourful. They are served with every main course, often in a dish that also has rice. They are also often served plainly boiled and quartered, and it is worth noting that the Portuguese always cook them in their skins, drain them and peel them. Then they are cut into quarters.

Small potatoes, usually waxy, are peeled and very thinly sliced, then patted dry and fried in olive oil until golden, 3–4 minutes, drained on paper towels and lightly salted. If they are cooked in a deep fat fryer, cook them at 190°C/375°F. These are the *Batatas Fritas* (Potato Crisps, Potato Chips) served in small bowls to accompany drinks.

Potato chips (French fries) are served with many dishes. Small new potatoes are tossed in a mixture of olive oil, butter and chopped fresh coriander instead of the more usual parsley. Fresh mint, finely chopped, can also be used, making the potatoes a wonderful accompaniment to lamb dishes.

A favourite potato dish of mine is equally simple. Potatoes boiled in the Portuguese way in their skins are sliced and arranged in a baking pan. *Salsa Tomate* (Tomato Sauce) (page 244) is poured over them, they are sprinkled with grated cheese and baked in a preheated moderate oven (180°C/350°F/gas 4) until the cheese is lightly browned, about 10–15 minutes. Use about 250 ml/8 fl oz (1 cup) tomato sauce to 500 g/1 pound potatoes and 2 tablespoons grated cheese. Serves 4.

Batatas a Moda do Alentejana
Potatoes, Altentejana-style

In this dish potatoes are combined with one of Portugal's favourite herbs, coriander. Flat-leaved continental parsley can be used instead, but it lacks the exotic flavour of coriander.

SERVES 4
900 g/2 pounds new potatoes, scrubbed and left whole
salt and freshly ground pepper
4 slices smoked bacon, chopped
40 g/1½ oz (3 tablespoons) butter
3 tablespoons olive oil
25 g/1 ounce (½ cup) fresh coriander or parsley, chopped

Put the potatoes on to boil in a large saucepan of salted water and boil for 15–20 minutes, or until just tender. Drain. As soon as the potatoes are cool enough to handle, peel and slice.

Heat the butter and oil in a large frying pan (skillet) and sauté the bacon until it has given up all its fat and is crisp. Add the potatoes and sauté until golden on both sides. Sprinkle with salt, coriander and pepper. Serve immediately.

Patatas a lo Pobre
Poor People's Potatoes

This dish is from Old Castille and probably derives from the early days when the potato reached Spain from its homeland Peru and gifted cooks created new dishes using the exotic root vegetable. It is surprisingly filling, useful for those with limited means. It has become a favourite of mine.

SERVES 6
4 tablespoons olive oil
1.4 kg/3 pounds potatoes, peeled and sliced
2 medium onions, finely chopped
2 teaspoons sweet or hot paprika, or a mixture
1 teaspoon salt, or to taste
250 ml/8 fl oz (1 cup) water

Heat the oil in a flameproof casserole, preferably of earthenware and add the potatoes, onions, paprika and salt mixed together. Turn the mixture in the oil for a minute or two then pour in the water, bring to a simmer, cover and cook over very low heat until the potatoes are tender, about 20 minutes. Stir the potatoes occasionally during cooking to prevent them sticking. Serve by themselves as a first course, or with any plainly cooked meat, poultry or fish.

Alcachofas y Patatas
Artichokes Hearts and Potatoes

This interesting vegetable purée is a Catalan dish served as a garnish for fried brains. The brains are piled in the centre of a platter and surrounded by the purée. Served in this traditional way it makes a fine luncheon dish though in Spain it would probably be a first course. Served by itself as a vegetable it makes a good accompaniment to any plainly cooked meat, poultry or fish. Good-quality tinned (canned) or bottled artichoke hearts can be used instead of freshly cooked ones.

SERVES 6
50 g/2 oz (4 tablespoons) butter
1 medium onion, finely chopped
500 g/1 pound artichoke hearts, sliced (page 194)
500 g/1 pound potatoes, peeled and thinly sliced
350 ml/12 fl oz (1½ cups) chicken stock
125 ml/4 fl oz (½ cup) dry white wine
salt and freshly ground white pepper
⅛ teaspoon grated nutmeg
1 large egg yolk

Heat 25 g/1 oz (2 tablespoons) of the butter in a large frying pan (skillet) with a lid or in a shallow flameproof casserole and sauté the onion until soft. Add the artichoke hearts and potatoes with enough stock barely to cover and the wine. Bring to a simmer, cover and cook until the vegetables are tender, about 15 minutes. Drain and process to a purée in a food processor or blender. Transfer to a saucepan, season with salt, white pepper and nutmeg and beat in the egg yolk. Reheat the purée and serve with *Sesos a la Catalana* (Brains, Catalan-style) (page 171).

Lentejas con Chorizo y Tocino
Lentils with Sausage and Bacon

Lentils are popular in Spain in many forms – soup, salad, or as in this dish which is hearty enough to be a main course. It is also good as an accompaniment instead of potatoes.

SERVES 4
250 g/8 oz (1⅓ cups) brown lentils
1 leek, thoroughly washed, trimmed and sliced
2 medium onions, finely chopped
1 medium carrot, scraped and sliced
1 clove garlic, chopped
125 g/4 ounces *chorizo*, chopped
125 g/4 ounces lean bacon, chopped
salt and freshly ground pepper
3 tablespoons olive oil

Wash and pick over the lentils and put them into a large saucepan with water to cover, about 475 ml/16 fl oz (2 cups). Add the leek, one of the onions, the carrot, garlic, sausage, bacon and salt and pepper to taste. Add 1 tablespoon of the oil, bring to a simmer and cook, covered, over very low heat until the lentils are tender, about 1 hour. The mixture should be quite thick. If it is watery, cook a little longer, uncovered, stirring from time to time.

In a small frying pan (skillet) heat the remaining oil and sauté the remaining onion until lightly browned. Stir the onion and oil into the lentils and serve.

Menestra a la Murciana
Braised Spring Vegetables, Murcia-style

Menestra is usually thought of as a Basque dish, but the tiny province of Murcia, south of Valencia, has its own favourite version, as do other regions. It is a spring dish using the first vegetables of the season.

SERVES 4

3 tablespoons olive oil
4 spring onions (scallions), trimmed and sliced, using some of the green part
375 g/12 ounces (about 3 medium) tomatoes, peeled and chopped
2 small carrots, scraped and sliced
2 small white turnips, peeled and sliced
125 g/4 ounces cured ham, cut into strips
250 g/8 ounces green beans, halved
4 artichoke hearts (page 194)
250 g/8 ounces shelled fresh peas
8 small new potatoes
475 ml/16 fl oz (2 cups) beef stock
salt and freshly ground pepper
8 asparagus tips
2 hardboiled eggs, sliced

Heat the oil in a large flameproof casserole and sauté the spring onions and tomatoes until the mixture is thick and well-blended. Add the carrots, turnips, ham, green beans, artichoke hearts, peas and new potatoes and cook for 5 minutes longer. Pour in the stock, season with salt and pepper, cover and cook for 10 minutes longer or until all the vegetables are tender. Garnish with asparagus tips and sliced hardboiled eggs.

193

Cenouras à Alentejana
Carrots, Alentejo-style

The rich farmlands of the lower Alentejo produce all manner of good things, among them root vegetables. This carrot recipe can be made with a mixture of root vegetables, or with any one of them by itself. Turnips, sweet potatoes and parsnips are all made more interesting when cooked this way.

SERVES 4

1 tablespoon olive oil
1 tablespoon lard or butter
1 medium onion, finely chopped
500 g/1 pound carrots, scraped and cut into 2.5 cm/1 inch slices, or use any other root vegetable, peeled and sliced
1 bay leaf
475 ml/16 fl oz (2 cups) beef stock
3 large egg yolks
2 tablespoons lemon juice
2 tablespoons finely chopped parsley
salt and freshly ground pepper

Heat oil and lard or butter in a saucepan and sauté the onion until soft. Add the carrots and sauté, stirring from time to time, for 2–3 minutes longer. Do not let the onion brown. Add the bay leaf and stock, bring to a simmer and cook, covered, until the carrots are tender, about 30 minutes. Strain, reserving the stock. Keep the carrots warm.

In a bowl beat the egg yolks and lemon juice together. Stir in the parsley and set aside. Pour 250 ml/8 fl oz (1 cup) of the stock into a small saucepan and bring to a simmer. Pour 2 tablespoons of the hot stock into the egg yolk mixture and stir to mix, then pour into the hot stock and cook, stirring, over the lowest possible heat for 2–3 minutes, or until the stock is lightly thickened. It must not boil. Season to taste with salt and pepper and pour over the carrots or other root vegetable, and serve.

To prepare Artichoke Hearts

Good frozen or tinned (canned) or bottled artichoke hearts are often available, though they are not as good as freshly prepared ones. There is a bonus for the cook, in preparing fresh artichoke hearts. Have ready a good vinaigrette, dip the bottom of each leaf in the sauce and eat the tender flesh. When you come to the heart, set it aside for the recipe.

Choose large (300–375 g/10–12 ounce) artichokes. Trim the stem and cut off the top of the centre cone of leaves, then cut the tips off the rest of the leaves. Kitchen scissors are best for this. Drop the artichokes into briskly boiling salted water, then simmer, uncovered, for about 35 minutes or until the leaves pull out easily. Pull out the leaves and nibble the bottoms if you like. Pull out the tender centre cone of leaves, then carefully remove the hairy choke with a spoon. What is left is the heart.

The hearts can be prepared before cooking, though this is not quite as easy. Break off the stem, then bend back and remove all the leaves, starting at the stem end. Carefully cut off the cone of tender leaves at the top. Drop the artichoke into acidulated water while preparing the rest of the artichokes needed for the recipe. Cook in boiling salted water with the juice of a lemon until tender, about 15 minutes. Lift out and remove the chokes.

Do not cook artichokes in aluminium (aluminum) or iron pans as this will discolour them.

Ensaladas/Saladas
Salads

Salads are an integral part of meals in the Peninsula. They are most popular as first courses but are also, less formally, served to accompany a meal, especially family lunches and dinners. They are seldom complicated, relying on the freshness and goodness of their ingredients, usually lettuce, tomato, onion, cucumber, sometimes sweet peppers, and black or green olives. There are some heartier salads that can make the main course. They are usually accompanied by a cruet with olive oil and vinegar, the oil rich with a green cast, the vinegar light and delicate. Combined and seasoned with salt and pepper they make a great vinaigrette, or the oil may be drizzled over the salad and followed by a sprinkling of vinegar. Since summers are long in much of the Peninsula, especially in Spain, salads are refreshing. Served as a first course they stimulate heat-jaded appetites with their cool, crisp freshness. The heartier salads, served as main courses, are perfectly matched with summer weather, but both the simpler salads and the more elaborate ones are good at any time of the year with their mix of textures and flavours.

Ensalada de Lechuga
Lettuce Salad

Salads are popular throughout Spain and are usually served as a first course. They are also served to accompany the main course in family or casual meals. They may also appear as *tapas* and can be as simple as this one, or more complex. They all have one thing in common, which is the superb quality of the ingredients.

SERVES 4

1 small head cos (romaine) lettuce, washed, dried and torn into bite-size pieces
250 g/8 oz (2 medium) tomatoes, cut into eighths
3 tablespoons olive oil
1 tablespoon wine vinegar
1 small clove garlic, crushed (optional)
salt and freshly ground pepper

Arrange the lettuce in a bowl and top with the tomatoes. In a small bowl mix together the vinegar, garlic if using, salt and pepper. Beat in the oil to make a creamy dressing and pour over the salad.

Salada Bacchus
Salad, Bacchus-style

Salads can be quite grand. *Salada Bacchus*, the speciality of the traditional and entirely charming Bacchus restaurant in Lisbon, with its brass-railed circular staircase from bar to dining-room, is an example.

SERVES 1

On a salad plate arrange slender white asparagus, tomatoes, quartered and unpeeled, cooked green beans, button mushrooms, peeled and quartered, lettuce, very young spinach leaves, strips of ham, carrot strips, watercress, celery, cucumber and cheese cut into julienne strips, sliced hardboiled eggs, and oil and vinegar, salt and freshly ground pepper, to be added as liked.

Ensalada de Piperrada
Cucumber, Tomato and Sweet Pepper Salad

This is a popular salad all over Spain though it originated in the Basque country as its name suggests. There is a very similar salad known simply as *Salada à Portuguesa* (Portuguese Salad) that enjoys equal popularity in that country. The combination of cucumber, sweet peppers and tomatoes seems so natural that it is amusing to reflect on the disparate origin of the vegetables; peppers and tomatoes from Mexico, and cucumbers from southern Asia. It was not until the sixteenth century that they were able to unite in this refreshing salad.

SERVES 4
For the vinaigrette
6 tablespoons olive oil
2 tablespoons red wine vinegar
salt and freshly ground pepper
¼ teaspoon sugar

For the salad
½ hot-house cucumber or 1 whole cucumber
375 g/12 oz (about 3 medium) tomatoes, each cut into 8 wedges
1 sweet green (bell) pepper, seeded and cut into 1 cm/½ inch pieces
½ medium onion, finely chopped

In a bowl beat together the oil, vinegar, salt and pepper to taste and the sugar.

Do not peel the hot-house cucumber. Score the skin with a fork, if liked. Peel the cucumber and cut whichever type is used into 1 cm/½ inch cubes. In a salad bowl combine all the ingredients, pour the dressing over them, toss to mix and chill lightly for about 30 minutes before serving.

Variation: for *Salada à Portuguesa* (Portuguese Salad) make a dressing of 6 tablespoons olive oil and 2 tablespoons cider vinegar. Peel and slice a cucumber thinly, or if hot-house, leave unpeeled. Peel, seed and slice 2 sweet green bell peppers (page 187). Spear the tomatoes on a fork and turn them over a moderate flame until the skins are blackened in the same way as the peppers, or put them under a grill (broiler), turning them from time to time until the skins are blackened. Use 500 g/1 pound (about 4 medium) tomatoes. Peel the tomatoes and cut them into medium-thick slices. Combine the vegetables in a salad bowl. Season with salt and freshly ground pepper, pour the dressing over the salad and toss gently. If liked, add a clove of finely chopped garlic to the mixture. Sprinkle, if liked, with 3 tablespoons chopped fresh coriander. Instead of mixing the oil and vinegar to make a dressing, drizzle the salad with the oil, then the vinegar, and toss, adding more oil or vinegar according to taste. Do not chill the salad but let it stand at room temperature for 30 minutes before serving.

Variation: For a simple mixed salad, *salada mista*, served throughout Portugal, line a salad bowl with lettuce leaves, then arrange thinly sliced cucumber, sliced tomato and sliced onion on top of the lettuce. Serve with olive oil and vinegar and drizzle the oil, then the vinegar, over the salad. Season as liked with salt and freshly ground pepper.

Portuguese onions are large and very sweet. For onions that are too sharp to be eaten raw, soak sliced onion for 15 minutes in cold water to cover with 1 tablespoon vinegar, drain, rinse in fresh cold water, drain again and pat dry.

Ensalada a la Andaluza
Salad, Andalucía-style

This is a simple, refreshing summer salad that would make a good first course or part of a buffet. It is typical of this region's approach to hot weather foods.

SERVES 4
500 g/1 pound (4 medium) tomatoes, peeled and sliced
1 medium onion, thinly sliced
2 sweet red (bell) peppers, peeled, seeded and sliced
1 clove garlic, finely chopped
16 small green olives, pitted
salt and freshly ground pepper
125 ml/4 fl oz (½ cup) oil and vinegar dressing
2 tablespoons finely chopped parsley

Combine the tomatoes, onion, peppers, garlic and olives in a salad bowl and season to taste with salt and pepper. Add the oil and vinegar dressing and leave in a cool place for 15 minutes. Sprinkle with the parsley and serve.

Salada de Tomate
Tomato Salad

Portuguese tomatoes are noted for their ripe, red excellence. In summertime when fine tomatoes are available, make this salad from the Algarve.
It is perfect for hot weather with just enough difference from other tomato
salads to make it enticing.

SERVES 4–6
750 g/1½ pounds about 6 medium tomatoes
1 medium onion, finely chopped
salt and freshly ground pepper
2 teaspoons fresh oregano, chopped, or 1 teaspoon dried, crumbled
3 tablespoon olive oil
1 tablespoon mild vineger

Drop the tomatoes into briskly boiling water for 30 seconds, lift out, drop
into cold water and peel. Halve the tomatoes and gently squeeze out the
seeds. Chop the tomatoes and put them into a salad bowl with the onion.
Season with salt, pepper and oregano.

Pour the oil and vinegar over the tomatoes and toss gently to mix. Serve
lightly chilled.

Variation: Add 1 cucumber, peeled and chopped, or ½ a hot-house
cucumber and 1 small sweet green (bell) pepper, seeded and chopped, to
the tomato mixture. The salad will then serve 6.

Variation: For another popular recipe for tomato salad from the Algarve,
Salada do tomate Assado (Grilled Tomato Salad), grill (broil) the tomatoes
and 2 sweet green (bell) peppers until the skins are blackened and blistered. Peel and slice the tomatoes. Peel the peppers, remove the stems
and seeds and slice the peppers. Combine the tomatoes, peppers and 1
thinly sliced medium onion in a salad bowl and season with salt, pepper
and oregano. toss with oil and vinegar as in the main recipe. Serves 6.

Variation: In Portugal a sheep's milk cheese would be used in this salad.
If this type of cheese is not available, use any well-flavoured fairly soft
cheese. Slice 500 g/1 pound (about 4 medium) tomatoes and put them
into a salad bowl. Chop 75 g/3 ounces cheese coarsely or slice it and
sprinkle it over the tomatoes. Toss to mix and serve with a cruet of olive
oil, a lemon, halved, and salt and freshly ground pepper. Season to taste
at the table.

Ensalada Mallorquina
Salad, Mallorcan-style

Tomatoes lend themselves to all manner of culinary treatment. This tomato salad, slightly different from others, confirms that versatility. It is worth the effort to find fresh oregano (or marjoram) for its extra flavour.

SERVES 4
2 large cloves garlic, peeled and left whole
125 ml/4 fl oz (½ cup) olive oil
2 tablespoons mild vinegar
500 g/1 pound (about 4 medium) tomatoes
salt
1 tablespoon chopped fresh oregano (or marjoram) or 1 teaspoon dried
1 tablespoon chopped parsley

In a small saucepan combine the garlic cloves and olive oil and cook, over very low heat, until the garlic is golden. Remove and discard the garlic. Let the oil cool to room temperature. Beat in the vinegar and salt to taste.
    Slice the tomatoes and put them into a salad bowl. Pour the oil dressing over the tomatoes, toss lightly and sprinkle with the herbs.

Ensalada de Melocotones
Peach Salad

This peach salad from Mallorca makes a refreshing beginning to a hot-weather meal.

SERVES 4
500 g/1 pound fresh, ripe peaches
salt
small lettuce leaves, to garnish
250 ml/8 fl oz (1 cup) mayonnaise
50 ml/2 fl oz (¼ cup) single (light) cream
125 g/4 ounces (1 cup) chopped almonds

Drop the peaches into a large saucepan of boiling water for 30 seconds. Lift out and slip off the skins. Cut each peach in half and remove the stone (pit). Cut each half into 4 lengthwise slices. Cook the peach slices in salted water barely to cover until they are tender, about 5 minutes. Drain and cool.

Arrange the small lettuce leaves round the edge of a serving dish. Pile the peach slices in the centre of the dish. Beat together the mayonnaise and light cream and pour over the peaches. Sprinkle with the almonds.

Salada de Favas Frescas
Broad Bean Salad

Salads in Portugal can be light or filling, using cider or white or red wine vinegar, or lemon juice, but there is always the rich, fruity aroma of good olive oil to make the simplest of them into something special.

SERVES 4
500 g/1 pound shelled young broad beans or baby lima beans
salt and freshly ground pepper
3 tablespoons olive oil
1 tablespoon white wine vinegar
1 clove garlic, crushed
1 tablespoon finely chopped parsley

Add the beans to a saucepan of boiling salted water and cook until they are tender, 5–10 minutes according to how young they are. Drain and cool. Put into a salad bowl.

In a bowl mix together the oil, vinegar, garlic, parsley and salt and pepper to taste. Pour the dressing over the beans and toss gently.

Variation: For *Salada de Feijao Verde* (Green Bean Salad), use fresh green beans cut into 1 cm/½ inch pieces instead of broad beans, and substitute cider vinegar for the white wine vinegar and fresh coriander for the parsley.

Variation: For *Salada de Feijão Branco* (Haricot (Dried White) Bean Salad), cook 250 g/8 ounces (1 cup) beans in the usual way, drain and cool. Toss with a dressing as for *Salada de Favas Frescas* (Broad Bean Salad). Black-eyed peas *(feijão frade)* can be used instead of haricot (dried white) beans. Garnish, if liked, with chopped hardboiled egg.

Ensalada de Puerros
Leek Salad

This is a Basque recipe and makes an attractive change of pace from more usual salads.

SERVES 4
16 young leeks
salt
125 ml/4 fl oz (½ cup) Vinaigrette Sauce (page 240)

Choose leeks as equal in size as possible. Wash them thoroughly, then cut off all but about 2.5 cm/1 inch of the green part. Use this green part for stock. Trim the leeks and tie them into a loose bundle with string. Lower them into briskly boiling salted water and cook for 8–10 minutes or until they are tender. Lift them out and let them cool.

Arrange them in a shallow dish and pour the vinaigrette over them. Add more vinaigrette if liked.

Patatas Frias Mallorquinas
Potato Salad, Mallorca-style

This is hearty salad, ideal for summer weather when it could be served as a main course.

SERVES 4–6
750 g/1½ pounds waxy potatoes
salt and freshly ground pepper
1 tablespoon mild vinegar
Salsa Mahonesa (Mayonnaise) (page 238)
6 large sardines, tinned (canned) in oil
2 large eggs, hardboiled and sliced
2 tablespoons chopped parsley

Cook the potatoes in their skins. Let them cool slightly, then peel and slice thinly. Put them into a large salad bowl. Season with salt and pepper and the vinegar. Toss with mayonnaise, the amount according to personal taste. Arrange the drained sardines on top with the sliced eggs and sprinkle with the parsley.

Variation: Add 6 chopped spring onions (scallions), trimmed and sliced, using some of the green part.

Ensalada de Lentejas
Lentil Salad

This is a good way of using leftover cooked lentils. It is worthwhile cooking more than the amount needed to make sure there are some available.

SERVES 4
250 g/8 oz (1 ⅓ cups) lentils, cooked
salt and freshly ground pepper
3 tablespoons olive oil
1 tablespoon red wine vinegar
1 tablespoon finely chopped onion
1 clove garlic, crushed
2 tablespoons peeled, seeded and chopped sweet red (bell) pepper
2 tablespoons chopped parsley

Put the lentils into a salad bowl and season with salt and pepper. Pour in the oil and vinegar, add the chopped onion, garlic and pepper and mix gently. Stand at room temperature for 1 hour and serve sprinkled with chopped parsley.

Salada de Feijão Frade
Black-Eyed Pea Salad

Black-eyed peas are popular in Portugal and have the merit of taking less time to cook than most dried beans. This salad, a hearty one, is good standby, especially for a summer buffet.

SERVES 4
250 g/8 oz (1 ⅓ cups) cups) black-eyed peas
1 medium onion, finely chopped
salt and freshly ground pepper
3 tablespoons olive oil
1 tablespoon mild white wine vinegar or cider vinegar
2 tablespoons chopped parsley

Soak the beans in cold water for about 4 hours. Drain and put on to cook in water to cover by about 5 cm/2 inches. Simmer, covered, for 40–45 minutes, or until the beans are tender. If they seem to be drying out during cooking, add boiling water. Drain and transfer to a large salad bowl. Add the onion, season with salt and pepper. Pour the oil, then the vinegar, over the beans and toss to mix. Sprinkle with parsley and serve.

Variation: For a more robust salad, add 2 hardboiled eggs, coarsely chopped, and 250 g/8 ounces tinned (canned) tuna, drained and flaked.

Ensalada Rusa (Salada Russa)
Russian Salad

This salad, which seems to have nothing to do with Russia, is immensely popular in both Spain and Portugal. It is served as a *tapa* with drinks, or as a first course. The ingredients vary slightly but basically it is a vegetable salad coated with good, home-made *Salsa Mahonesa* (Mayonnaise). I have had it with beetroot (beets) once or twice and this gives it a pretty colour, though it is less traditional.

SERVES 6
500 g/1 pound (4) medium waxy potatoes, boiled, peeled and diced
75 g/3 oz (½ cup) cooked, diced carrots
74 g/3 oz (½ cup) cooked green peas
50 g/2 oz (½ cup) cooked green beans, cut into pieces
50 g/2 oz (¼ cup) cooked, diced beetroot (beet) (optional)
salt and freshly ground pepper
175 ml/6 fl oz (¾ cup) home-made *Salsa Mahonesa* (Mayonnaise) (page 238)
1 clove garlic, crushed
Sweet red (bell) pepper strips, to garnish

Combine all the vegetables in a salad bowl and season with salt and pepper. Mix the mayonnaise with the garlic and gently, but thoroughly, fold it into the vegetable mixture with a rubber spatula. Garnish with the pepper strips. As a *tapa* serve in small dishes.

Variation: Boil and mash the potatoes, season with salt and pepper and stir in the mayonnaise, mixing well. Gently fold in 1 small onion, finely chopped, ½ sweet green (bell) pepper, finely chopped, 1 tablespoon capers, 8 green olives, chopped, 1 tablespoon gherkins, chopped, 75 g/3 oz (½ cup) cooked green peas, and 1 sweet red (bell) pepper finely chopped. Make a mound of the salad on a serving plate and garnish with some strips of sweet red (bell) pepper, and if liked a few peas. Serve lightly chilled.

Salada de Bacalhau
Salt Cod Salad

Both Portugal and Spain esteem salt cod highly and both have a salt cod salad. Both versions are robust dishes and could be served as a main course, or, if served as a first course, followed by something light.

SERVES 3

500 g/1 pound salt cod
2 medium sweet green (bell) peppers, peeled, seeded and sliced (page 187)
55 g/1 pound (about 4 medium) tomatoes, sliced
salt and freshly ground pepper
6 tablespoons olive oil
2 tablespoons lemon juice
1 tablespoon chopped parsley

Soak the cod in cold water overnight, in the usual way, changing the water once or twice. Skin the cod and remove any bones. Put the cod into a saucepan with fresh cold water to cover, bring to a simmer and poach over low heat for 15-20 minutes, or until the fish is tender. Drain and flake coarsely.

Put the cod into a salad bowl with the peppers and tomatoes. Season with salt and pepper. Mix together the olive oil and lemon juice, pour it over the salad and toss to mix. Sprinkle with parsley.

Variation: Omit the peppers. Cook 250 g/8 ounces of chick peas, previously soaked overnight in salted water to cover, until tender. Drain and cool. Combine with the cod in a large salad bowl with 1 large onion, chopped, 1 clove garlic, chopped, 2 large hardboiled eggs, chopped, 2 tablespoons chopped parsley, salt, freshly ground pepper, 1 teaspoon paprika, ⅛ teaspoon cayenne and 6 tablespoons olive oil mixed with 3 tablespoons mild vinegar or cider vinegar. Toss the mixture and add more seasonings, or more oil or vinegar to taste.

Variation: For the Catalan version of the salad, *Ensalada de Bacalao*, soak 125 g/4 ounce white haricot (navy pea) beans for several hours, then cook in fresh salted water to cover until tender. Drain and cool. In a large salad bowl combine the beans with the flaked cod, 1 medium onion, chopped, 125 g/4 ounces (1 medium) tomato, halved and thinly sliced, 16 oil-cured black olives, 2 large eggs, hardboiled and sliced, 3 tablespoons chopped parsley, salt, freshly ground pepper and 6 tablespoons olive oil mixed with 3 tablespoons mild red wine vinegar. Toss the mixture and add more oil and vinegar if needed. Chill lightly and serve.

7

Rice Dishes
Arroz

Both Spain and Portugal are major rice producers as well as being enthusiastic rice eaters. Because the Portuguese are so fond of potatoes, eating them at every main meal, their capacity for rice is often overlooked; quite frequently rice and potatoes appear on the same plate. There are rice dishes that are a meal in themselves though not as many as in Spain where *paella* is the best known. In Portugal both long-grain and short-grain rice are grown in lagoons on the west coast and the paddies (rice fields) make vivid splashes of intense green. Surely there is no green quite as vibrant as that of young rice shoots.

It was the Arabs who introduced rice to Spain, perfecting an irrigation system begun a thousand years earlier by the Romans in Valencia. The rice, which is short-grain, is grown in an area of marshlands on the Mediterranean, an ideal location for rice growing. The short, stubby rice is ideal for *paella*, usually called Paella a la Valenciana after the area where it was created. The word *paella* comes from the dish in which it is cooked, a special metal pan, a *paellera*. The pan is round with shallow sloping sides and two flattened handles. The pans come in many sizes. A 30–33 cm/12–13 inch pan serves 4–6 people according to appetite. It could be said that the rice of Valencía created this most popular of all Spanish dishes, the *paella*. But there are many other rice dishes in the Spanish cuisine.

If imported rice from Valencia is not available, the best substitute is the short-grain pearl rice grown in California and available from Japanese shops. Or use imported Italian risotto or arborio rice. Arborio rice should be rinsed only when the recipe indicates.

Paella a la Valenciana, Tradicional
Traditional Valencian Paella

This is not the *paella* that has won worldwide renown with its mixture of rice, chicken and shellfish, but is the forerunner of that famous dish. The ingredients are all readily available locally, short-grain Valencian rice, snails from local orchards, rabbit, ever-present, or chicken from farms, and green vegetables.

SERVES 4

a 1.4 kg/3 pound chicken or rabbit, cut into 8 serving pieces
salt and freshly ground pepper
125 ml/4 fl oz (½ cup) olive oil
3 cloves garlic, chopped
100 g/4 ounces (about 1 medium) tomato, peeled, seeded and chopped
250 g/8 ounces fresh green beans, cut into 5 cm/2 inch pieces
100 g/4 ounces shelled young broad beans, baby lima beans or fresh green peas
1 tablespoon paprika
⅛ teaspoon saffron threads, crushed in a mortar
16 snails, cleaned and ready for cooking
1.1 litres/2 pints (5 cups) chicken stock
500 g/1 pound (2 cups) short-grain rice

Pat the chicken or rabbit pieces dry with paper towels and season with salt and pepper. Heat the oil in a *paella* pan or flameproof casserole and sauté the chicken or rabbit pieces until golden. Add the garlic, tomato, green beans, and broad beans, lima beans, or peas, and cook for 1 minute. Remove the pan from the heat and mix in the paprika and saffron. Add the snails. Pour in the stock, cover and cook until the chicken or rabbit is tender. Lift out all the solids into a bowl and measure the stock. There should be 1 litre/1¾ pints (4 cups).

Return all the solids to the pan with the rice and the stock. Cover and bring to a simmer over moderately high heat. Reduce the heat to very low and continue to cook until the rice is tender and the liquid absorbed. Let the dish stand, covered, for 10 minutes. Serve straight from the *paella* pan or casserole, accompanied by a green salad. Drink a light, dry red wine.

Variation: For *Arroz al Estilo Barcelonés* (Rice, Barcelona-style), which could be described as Catalan Paella, cook as for traditional *paella* but leave out both types of bean, peas and snails. Add 1 sweet red (bell) pepper, seeded and chopped, 250 g/8 ounces squid, cleaned and cut into 5 mm/¼ inch slices, 250 g/8 ounces *butifarra* sausage, sliced, or use Italian sweet sausage, and 250 g/8 ounces cooked, shelled clams, added at the last minute and left just long enough to heat them through. Any juices from cooking the clams can be added to the rice and other ingredients.

Paella a la Valenciana
Chicken and Shellfish Rice

This is a magnificent party dish, though it can, of course, be scaled down
to family size. It is no wonder that it has come to be Spain's most popular
dish, very nearly a symbol of the cuisine. Really it is only a riched-up
version of the original, but riched-up in the most utterly enticing way.

SERVES 6–8
a 1.4 kg/3 pound chicken, cut into 8 serving pieces
salt and freshly ground pepper
125 ml/4 fl oz (½ cup) olive oil
100 g/4 ounces lean, boneless pork, coarsely chopped
100 g/4 ounces *chorizo* or any garlic-flavoured smoked pork sausage, cut
into 5mm/¼ inch slices
100 g/4 ounces cured ham, coarsely chopped
2 medium onions, finely chopped
4 cloves garlic, chopped
2 sweet red (bell) peppers, seeded and chopped
500 g/1 pound shelled, medium raw prawns (shrimps)
8 raw king prawns (jumbo shrimp), in the shell, or crayfish (langoustines)
or lobster tails, cut into 8 pieces
750 g/1½ pounds (3 cups) short-grain rice
3 tablespoons chopped parsley
1 bay leaf
¼ teaspoon saffron threads, crushed in a mortar
1.4 litres/2⅜ pints (6 cups) chicken stock
100 g/4 ounces shelled green peas, defrosted if frozen
16 clams, scrubbed
16 mussels, scrubbed

For the garnish
lemon wedges
chopped parsley

Pat the chicken pieces dry with paper towels and season with salt and
pepper. Heat the oil in a *paella* pan or flameproof casserole and sauté the
chicken pieces until golden on both sides. Lift out on to a platter and
keep warm.

Add the pork, sausage and ham to the pan and cook, stirring, over
moderately high heat for about 10 minutes. Add to the chicken. Add the
onions, garlic and peppers to the pan and sauté until the onion is soft.

Add the prawns (shrimps) and king prawns (jumbo shrimp) or crayfish or lobster tails and cook over moderately high heat just until they turn pink, no more than 3 minutes. Lift out and reserve.

Return the pork, sausage and ham to the pan. Stir in the rice, add the parsley and bay leaf, and the saffron. Pour in the stock, stir to mix, add the peas, bring to a simmer and cook, uncovered, stirring from time to time, for 10 minutes.

Bury the reserved chicken in the rice together with the prawns and king prawns (jumbo shrimp) or alternatives. Push the clams and mussels into the rice with the side that will open uppermost if possible. Cover tightly and cook over the lowest possible heat until the rice is tender and all the liquid absorbed. Let stand, covered, for 10 minutes. Serve directly from the *paella* pan or casserole, garnished with lemon wedges and sprinkled with parsley. Drink a light, dry red wine or if the weather is hot, *sangria*.

Arroz con Pollo
Rice and Chicken

This Spanish version of chicken with rice is closer to the recipes so dearly loved throughout Latin America, though long-grain is more usual there than short-grain. It is really a simplified form of *paella*. In Latin America it is often cooked in an earthenware casserole instead of a *paella* pan.

SERVES 4

a 1.4 kg/3 pound chicken, cut into 8 serving pieces
salt and freshly ground pepper
4 tablespoons olive oil
2 medium onions, finely chopped
2 cloves garlic, chopped
1 sweet green (bell) pepper, seeded and chopped
1 sweet red (bell) pepper, seeded und chopped
250 g/8 ounces (about 2 medium) tomatoes, peeled, seeded and chopped
1 tablespoon paprika
¼ teaspoon saffron threads, crushed in a mortar
500 g/1 pound (2 cups) short-grain rice
1 litre/1¾ pints (4 cups) chicken stock
2 tablespoons finely chopped parsley, to garnish

Pat the chicken pieces dry with paper towels and season with salt and pepper. Heat the oil in a *paella* pan or flameproof casserole and sauté the chicken pieces until golden. Lift out on to a plate and set aside. In the oil remaining in the pan sauté the onions, garlic and green and red (bell) peppers until the vegetables are soft. Add the tomatoes and cook until the mixture is thick, about 10 minutes.

Stir in the paprika and saffron. Add the rice and stock, then return the chicken pieces to the pan. Bring to a simmer over moderately high heat, cover tightly and cook over very low heat until the chicken is tender and the rice has absorbed all the liquid. Do not worry if the rice seems a little soupy. Let the dish stand, covered off the heat, for 10 minutes when any liquid will have been absorbed. Sprinkle with parsley and serve from the *paella* pan or casserole. Serve with a green salad and drink a light dry red wine.

Frango com Arroz
Chicken with Rice

This is a favourite all over the Iberian Peninsula, and all over Latin America as well. The Spanish version is the best known because of *Paella*, its more elaborate cousin. This Portuguese version is well-flavoured and extremely simple. It works well using long-grain rice.

SERVES 4
3 tablespoons olive oil
1 medium onion, thinly sliced
a 1.6 kg/3½ pound chicken, cut into about 10 pieces
700 g/1½ pounds (about 6 medium) tomatoes, peeled, seeded and chopped
1 bay leaf
1 large sprig each parsley and coriander
salt and freshly ground pepper
475 ml/16 fl oz (2 cups) chicken stock or water
300 g/10 oz (1¼ cups) long-grain rice, washed

Heat the oil in a flameproof casserole and sauté the onion until soft. Add the chicken pieces and sauté until golden, turning frequently. Reduce the heat to very low, cover and cook for 1 hour, or cook in a preheated 150°C/300°F/gas 2 oven until barely tender.

Remove from the heat or oven. Add the tomatoes, bay leaf, parsley, coriander, salt and pepper to taste, and the stock or water. Bring to a simmer over moderate heat, stir, and pour in the rice. Cover and cook for 30 minutes, or until the rice is tender. If all the liquid has not been absorbed, let the casserole stand, covered, for 10 minutes, when the rice will have absorbed the liquid. Serve the dish with the chicken pieces surrounded by the rice, accompanied by a salad. Drink a light dry red wine.

Arroz Abanda
Seafood-flavoured Rice, Alicante-style

Abanda means separate, apart, in the Valencian dialect, and indicates here that the rice should be served as a separate course. The success of the dish depends on the rich flavour of the broth in which it is cooked, which suggests the fish and shellfish that went into its creation. After the rice has been served, a dish of fish and shellfish follows, accompanied by *Allioli* (Garlic Mayonnaise) (page 239). So long as there is plenty of variety in both fish and shellfish it does not much matter what types are used.

SERVES 6

For the broth and second course
375 g/12 ounces raw, unshelled prawns (shrimps)
1.4 litres/2½ pints (6 cups) unsalted fish stock, or clam juice or a mixture
900 g/2 pounds mixed fish such as bass, monkfish, hake, cod or halibut, cleaned and cut into serving pieces
500 g/1 pound mixed shellfish such as mussels, clams, lobster

For the rice
6 tablespoons olive oil
4 cloves garlic, chopped
250 g/8 ounces (about 2 medium) tomatoes, peeled, seeded and chopped
⅛ teaspoon saffron
1 teaspoon paprika
1 dried hot chilli pepper, seeded and chopped
25 g/1 ounce (½ cup) parsley, chopped
salt and freshly ground pepper
500 g/1 pound (2 cups) short-grain rice

In a large saucepan bring the fish stock to the boil, add the prawns (shrimps) and cook for 3 minutes. Lift them out of the stock and let them cool. Shell them and reserve. Return the shells to the stock and simmer, covered, for 15 minutes. Strain and discard the shells. Add the mixed fish and shellfish and cook until the fish is tender and the shellfish have opened. Strain the stock. Take the shellfish out of their shells and arrange with the fish and prawns (shrimps) on a platter and set aside covered lightly so that the seafood will not dry out. Reduce the stock over brisk heat to 1 litre/1¾ pints (4 cups). Season to taste with salt and pepper and set aside.

In a *paella* pan or a frying pan (skillet) heat the olive oil and sauté the garlic just until golden. Add the tomatoes and cook until they are thick. Add the saffron, paprika, chilli pepper, parsley and rice. Stir to mix and pour in the reserved fish stock. Bring to the boil, reduce the heat to low and cook until the rice is almost tender and the liquid almost absorbed. Let it stand, covered, for 10 minutes, then serve.

Serve the reserved, cooked fish and shellfish with *Allioli* (Garlic Mayonnaise) (page 239), crusty bread, a green salad and a crisp, dry white wine.

Arroz Chau-Chau
Rice, Macao-style

This rice dish is from Macao, for long a Portuguese enclave. It is a good first course or can accompany any plainly cooked meat or poultry. There is not a great deal of Chinese influence in Portuguese cuisine. In some ways the influence may be said to be more the other way, that of Portugal on the cooking of China and Japan. *Tempura*, for example, batter-coated fried prawns (shrimp) and vegetables, was inspired by monks in Nagasaki observing the Lenten Fast. *Tempura* is actually a corruption of *Os Temperos*, the Ember, or Fast Days. A number of fruits and vegetables from the New World were also introduced to Asia, including Mexican hot chilli peppers which became a major crop in India, supplanting the culinary use of black peppercorns. This is clearly a Portuguese version of Chinese fried rice.

LUIS MELENDEZ. A display of traditional Spanish earthenware, and the wooden boxes in which
cheese and sweetmeats would be transported.

LUIS MELENDEZ. The luscious text▪
pears h▪

...terranean melon is well captured, while the
...pe quality.

JUAN VAN DER HAMEN. Walnuts and hazelnut-coated sweetmeats.

JUAN VAN DER HAMEN. Almond-coated sweetmeats, displayed on typical thin, wooden cases used for food.

UNKNOWN ARTIST. A study of a man and child eating grapes.

SERVES 6
500 g/1 pound long-grain rice
1 large clove garlic, chopped
4 tablespoons lard or olive oil
125 g/4 ounces *presunto*, or use *serrano* or *prosciutto*, or similar ham, coarsely chopped
125 g/4 ounces *chouriço* or *chorizo* or other garlic-flavoured smoked pork sausage, sliced
250 g/8 ounces sliced cooked prawns (shrimps)
175 g/6 ounces (1 cup) cooked green peas
salt and freshly ground pepper
1 tablespoon soy sauce
4 large eggs, lighty beaten

Put the rice on to cook in a saucepan with a tightly fitting lid in 1 litre/ 1¾ pints (4 cups) salted water, bring to the boil over moderate heat, then reduce the heat to very low and cook the rice for about 20 minutes or until it is tender and the water absorbed. Set aside, covered.

In a large frying pan (skillet) heat the lard or oil and sauté the garlic until golden. Add the ham and sausage and sauté for 2–3 minutes longer. Add the reserved rice and stir to mix well. Cook over low heat for a minute or two to allow the rice to absorb the flavours. Season with salt and pepper, add the prawns (shrimps) and peas and the soy sauce. Stir in the eggs and cook, stirring, just until the eggs are set.

Arroz con Calamares
Rice with Squid

Rice and squid seem to go together naturally and are a Spanish favourite. In Portugal octopus is the shellfish preferred with rice for *Polvo com Arroz* (Octopus with Rice). Whichever is chosen, the results are delicious.

SERVES 8
900 g/2 pounds squid
6 tablespoons olive oil
2 medium onions, chopped
2 cloves garlic, chopped
1 sweet red (bell) pepper, seeded and chopped
250 g/8 ounces (about 2 medium) tomatoes, peeled, seeded and chopped
1 small dried hot red chilli pepper, seeded and chopped
⅛ teaspoon saffron threads, ground
2 tablespoons chopped parsley
salt and freshly ground pepper
125 ml/4 fl oz (½ cup) dry red wine
750 g/1½ lbs (3 cups) short-grain rice
about 1.4 litres/2½ pints (5½ cups) fish stock

Clean the squid, reserving the ink sacs. Cut the squid bodies and tentacles into 1 cm/½ inch slices. In a shallow flameproof casserole heat the oil and sauté the onions until soft. Add the squid and tentacles and sauté for about 5 minutes longer over moderate heat. Add the garlic, sweet pepper, tomatoes, chilli pepper, saffron, parsley and salt and pepper to taste. Cover and cook over low heat for 20 minutes.

Squeeze the ink out of the ink sacs into a bowl. Add the wine, stir to mix. Strain the squid mixture and add the liquid to the wine. Measure and make up the quantity with fish stock to 1.4 litres/2½ pints (5½ cups). Return the squid to the casserole, add the rice and stir in the liquid. Cover tightly and cook over low heat until the liquid is absorbed, about 20 minutes. Let the dish sit, covered, off the heat for 10 minutes, then serve.

Variation: For *Polvo com Arroz* (Octopus with Rice), popular at Christmastime, especially in Minho, choose 900 g/2 pounds small octopus and have the fishmonger clean it, cutting off the tips of the tentacles and discarding them with the eyes and any waste material. Cut the tentacles into pieces. Sauté 2 medium onions, finely chopped, in 2 tablespoons olive oil until soft. Add 1 dried hot red chilli pepper, seeded and chopped, and 1 tablespoon chopped parsley and sauté for about 2 minutes longer. Transfer to a large saucepan, add the octopus, 2 tablespoons white wine vinegar and enough water to cover. Bring to a simmer, cover and cook until the octopus is tender, 2–3 hours depending on the size of the shellfish. When the octopus is tender lift it out and measure the liquid. Make up the quantity to 1 litre/1¾ pts (4 cups). Season with salt and pepper. Pour in

500 g/1 pound (2 cups) long-grain rice, bring to a simmer and cook, covered, over low heat until the rice is tender. Add the octopus and cook just long enough to heat it through. The rice wll be slightly soupy, not dry.

Arroz con Perdiz
Rice with 'Partridge'

There *is* no partridge in this popular Lenten dish from Valencía. A head of garlic adorns the centre of the dish and masquerades as the bird, clearly a joke from the past when the Lenten fast was strictly observed. The garlic is not meant to be eaten. It makes an attractive modern dish to serve with plainly cooked main courses.

SERVES 6–8
175 g/6 oz (1 cup) raw chickpeas or 1 400 g/14 oz tin (can) cooked
4 tablespoons olive oil
½ medium onion, chopped
1 medium tomato (about 125 g/4 oz), peeled and chopped
1 head garlic, left whole, unpeeled
1 medium potato, peeled and cut into 2 mm/⅛ inch slices
½ teaspoon paprika
⅛ teaspoon saffron threads, ground
500 g/1 lb (2 cups) short-grain rice

Soak the chickpeas overnight in cold water to cover. Cook in salted water, covered, for 1½–2 hours or until tender. If using ready-cooked chickpeas omit cooking and add as raw chickpeas.

Heat the oil in a shallow flameproof casserole, preferably earthenware, and sauté the onion until soft. Add the tomato and cook for about 4 minutes longer, or until the mixture is well-blended. Add the garlic, potato, paprika, saffron and rice, stir to mix and sauté for 1–2 minutes. Drain the chickpeas and measure the liquid. Make up the quantity with water to 1 litre/1¾ pints (4 cups). Add the chickpeas and the liquid to the casserole, stir to mix and cook, uncovered, over moderate heat for 5 minutes, stirring from time to time. Put the head of garlic in the centre of the casserole, and bake, uncovered, in a preheated moderate oven 180°C]/350°F/gas 4 for 15 minutes. Remove from the oven, cover loosely and stand for 5 minutes before serving. Serve straight from the casserole.

Porco com Arroz
Pork with Rice

Rice is important in Portuguese cookery and is grown extensively, both short and long-grain types. In this recipe long-grain is used. Portuguese cooks are ingenious in combining rice with meat, fish or vegetables in a number of ways. The dishes are robust and satisfying, needing nothing more than salad as an accompaniment.

SERVES 4
2 tablespoons olive oil
1 large onion, finely chopped
1 clove garlic, chopped
500 g/1 pound lean, boneless pork cut into 1 cm/½ inch pieces
250 g/8 oz (1 cup) long-grain rice
475 ml/16 fl oz (2 cups) chicken stock
salt and freshly ground pepper

In a casserole heat the oil and sauté the onion, garlic and pork until the onion is soft and the pork lightly browned. Add the rice and cook, stirring, over low heat for about 3 minutes or until all the grains are coated with oil. Pour in the stock, season with salt and pepper, bring to a simmer and cook, covered, over low heat for 25–30 minutes or until all the liquid has been absorbed. Cook, uncovered, for the last 5–10 minutes if the liquid seems too abundant after the rice is tender.

Variation: The Algarve has a more elaborate version of the same dish. Use only 250 g/8 ounces pork, but after the pork is browned with the onion and garlic, add 375 g/12 ounces each chopped ham and *chouriço* sausage (or use Spanish *chorizo*), to the rice and finish the dish in the same way.

Arroz Navarro
Rice with Lamb, Navarre-style

It is hardly surprising that the cooks of Navarre with its excellent lamb have created this dish of lamb and rice. The natural affinity between the two has long been recognized in the Middle East, and perhaps the inspiration for the dish came as a result of the Moorish occupation of Spain.

SERVES 6

750 g/1½ pounds lean, boneless lamb, cut into 2.5 cm/1 inch pieces
salt and freshly ground pepper
plain (all-purpose) flour for dredging
4 tablespoons lard or oil
500 g/1 lb (2 cups) rice
1 litre/¾ pints (4 cups) stock from lamb
250 ml/8 fl oz (1 cup) *Salsa de Tomate* (Tomato Sauce) (page 244)

Season the lamb with salt and pepper and dredge with flour, shaking to remove the excess. Heat the lard or oil in a flameproof casserole and brown the lamb on all sides. Pour in enough stock or water barely to cover the lamb and simmer over low heat until the lamb is tender, 1–1½ hours. Lift out the lamb pieces and set aside. Skim the fat from the cooking liquid.

In a saucepan combine the rice with 1 litre/¾ pts (4 cups) of the cooking liquid, making up the quantity if necessary with stock or water. Bring to the boil, cover and cook over very low heat until the rice is almost tender, about 15 minutes. Strain the rice and transfer it to an ovenproof casserole. Gently mix in the lamb, stir in the tomato sauce and bake in a preheated moderate oven (180°C/350°F/gas 4) for 10–15 minutes. Serve with a green salad and drink a light red wine.

Arroz de Manteiga
Buttered Rice

In Portugal rice is often combined with other ingredients to make a main course, but in this recipe it it simply enriched with butter to be served to accompany a main dish. It is richly delicious.

SERVES 4

75 g/3 oz (6 tablespoons) butter
1 medium onion, thinly sliced or chopped
250 g/8 oz (1 cup) short-grain rice
475 ml/16 fl oz (2 cups) chicken stock
salt and freshly ground pepper

In a heavy saucepan with a tight-fitting lid melt the butter and sauté the onion over moderate heat until soft. Stir in the rice and sauté, stirring, until the grains are well-coated with the butter. Do not let the rice brown.

Pour in the stock, season to taste with salt and pepper, bring to a simmer, lower the heat and cook, covered, until the rice is tender and all the liquid absorbed, 25–30 minutes.

Arroz de Tomate
Tomato Rice

This Portuguese rice, which takes advantage of the fine ripe tomatoes available, makes a pleasant accompaniment to any plainly cooked meat or poultry, especially roast meats.

SERVES 6
4 tablespoons olive oil
2 tablespoons lard
2 medium onions, finely chopped
2 cloves garlic, chopped
500 g/1 pound (about 4 medium) tomatoes, peeled, seeded and chopped
700 ml/1¼ pts (3 cups) chicken stock
500 g/1 pound (3 cups) long-grain rice
salt and freshly ground pepper

Heat the oil and lard in a large saucepan and add the onion and garlic. Sauté over moderate heat until the onion is soft and golden. Add the tomatoes, stir to mix, cover and cook over low heat for 15 minutes to blend the flavours.

Add the chicken stock and bring to a simmer. Pour in the rice, season with salt and pepper and stir to mix. Cover and cook over very low heat until the rice is tender and all the liquid absorbed, about 20 minutes. Let stand, covered, for 5 minutes.

Moros y Cristianos
Moors and Christians – Black Beans and Rice

This is a colonial Spanish dish created by the Spanish in Cuba. The black beans, *frijoles negros*, cultivated for centuries in Mexico, were unknown to the Conquerors. They had a lively sense of culinary humour in the sixteen century, for example calling shredded flank steak *Ropa Vieja* (Old Clothes) because the meat went into tatters. When they put the rice they had introduced from Asia together with Mexico's black beans it is inevitable they would have recalled the long, almost eight-century struggle against the Moorish invaders of their country. (Not that they seemed to mind invading the country of others!) The dish is popular in Cuba, in many parts of South America and in Mexico. It is usually served with fried eggs and fried plantains or if plantains are not available, fried, under-ripe bananas. Serve as a separate course, or to accompany a plainly cooked meat or poultry dish.

SERVES 4–6
250 g/8 ounces (1¼ cups) black (turtle) beans
2 tablespoons olive oil
1 medium onion, finely chopped
1 clove garlic, chopped
½ medium sweet green (bell) pepper, seeded and chopped
250 g/8 oz (about 2 medium) tomatoes, peeled, seeded and chopped
salt and freshly ground pepper
250 g/8 ounces (1 cup) short-grain rice

Put the beans on to soak in cold water to cover in a large saucepan for 1–2 hours. Drain. Return the beans to the pot with 175 ml/16 fl oz (2 cups) cold water, bring to a simmer and cook, covered, over low heat until the beans are tender, 1½–2 hours. Check from time to time and if the beans are drying out, and a little boiling water.

While the beans are cooking, heat the oil in a flameproof casserole and sauté the onion, garlic and pepper until the onion is soft. Add the tomatoes and cook until the mixture is smooth and well-blended. Season with salt and pepper. Drain the beans and add to the casserole, stirring to mix. Add the rice and 475 ml/16 fl oz (2 cups) water, stir gently, cover and cook over very low heat until the rice is tender and all the liquid absorbed. Serve topped with fried egg and fried plantain or banana.

Variation: Cook the rice separately. On a warmed platter make a circle of the beans and pile the rice inside. Arrange the eggs on top of the rice and the plantains or bananas round the edge of the dish. Serve with *Salsa de Tomate* (Tomato Sauce) (page 244) handed separately.

A light, dry red wine and a green salad turn this into a main course.

Arroz de Pato à Moda de Braga
Duckling with Rice, Braga-style

This northern dish is popular all over Portugal with slight variations in the cooking method. The one I have chosen is classical and more or less foolproof. Braga, the city that claims the dish, is one of the most ancient in Portugal, founded by the Romans in 279 BC. Now the country's religious centre, it was reconquered early from the Moors.

SERVES 4

a 2–2.3 kg/4½–5 pound duckling, quartered
2 tablespoons olive oil
250 g/8 ounces bacon, chopped
2 onions, thinly sliced
1 clove garlic, chopped
250g/8 ounces smoked garlic sausage, sliced
about 2 litres/3 ½ pints (8 cups), duck or chicken stock or water
500 g/1 pound (2 cups) long-grain rice
3 tablespoons lemon juice

Pull away and discard any surplus fat from the duckling. Prick the pieces all over to help release the fat. In a large frying pan (skillet) heat the oil and brown the duckling pieces all over. Lift out into a large flameproof casserole and spoon off all but 2 tablespoons of the fat. Add the onion to the pan and sauté until soft. Add the garlic, bacon and sausage and sauté until the bacon is cooked. Transfer to the casserole with the duckling. Pour in enough stock or water barely to cover, bring to a simmer, cover and cook over low heat until the duckling is almost tender, 1½–2 hours.

Lift out the duckling pieces and set them aside, covered. Strain and reserve the cooking liquid. Add the solids to the reserved duckling. Skim off as much fat as possible from the stock. Put the rice into the casserole and pour in 1 litre/¾ pints (4 cups) of the reserved stock. There should be enough, but add more stock or water if necessary to make up the quantity. Add the lemon juice and the solids except the sausage. Reserve this. Arrange the duckling pieces on top of the rice, bring to a simmer, cover and cook over very low heat until the rice is tender, 20–30 minutes.

Lift out the duckling pieces, make a layer of rice in an ovenproof serving dish and arrange the duckling on top. Cover with the rest of the rice and arrange the sausage slices in a row down the centre and round the side. Put into a preheated moderate oven (180°C/350°F/gas 4) and bake until the rice is pale golden, 10–15 minutes. Serve from the ovenproof dish. Drink a full-bodied dry red wine.

8

Egg Dishes
Huevos/Ovos

Eggs occupy a large place in the Peninsula's cooking, though not necessarily by themselves. They are more often incorporated into other dishes, especially in cakes, puddings and desserts where they are used lavishly. They are stirred into Portuguese *açordas* (dry soups), they are used in notable omelettes, they may be fried, or stuffed and served cold as *tapas*, and make satisfying lunch dishes such as *Huevos a la Flamenca* (Baked Eggs with Ham, Sausage and Asparagus) and its Portuguese counterpart, *Ervilhas Guisadas à Portuguésa* (Green Peas, Portuguese-style), a name that only partly describes this very good dish. They turn *migas* (fried bread cubes) into hearty lunch or supper dishes, while the Basque dish *Pipperada* (Eggs Scrambled with Sweet (Bell) Peppers) has become a favourite, not just in the rest of Spain, but in half the world as well. The best-known, best-loved, of the egg dishes of the Peninsula is undoubtedly *Tortilla Española*, the Spanish potato omelette, a must when *tapas* are served, and a more than adequate lunch or supper dish with a salad.

Huevos a la Flamenca
Baked Eggs with Ham, Sausage and Asparagus

This dish is said to have originated at Seville in Andalucía. Its name conjures up images of Spanish gypsies. It makes a superb lunch or supper dish, and for very hearty appetites, a first course. The colourful dish is as attractive to look at as it is to eat.

SERVES 4

3 tablespoons olive oil
1 medium onion, finely chopped
2 cloves garlic, chopped
250 g/8 ounces (2 medium) tomatoes, peeled, seeded and chopped
1 teaspoon paprika
salt and freshly ground pepper
75 ml/3 fl oz (¹/₃ cup) chicken stock or water
50 g/2 oz (½ cup) finely diced *serrano* ham or cured ham
125 g/4 ounces *chorizo* sausage, cut into 5 mm/¼ inch slices
8 large eggs
8 freshly cooked asparagus spears
8 tablespoons freshly cooked peas
8 strips sweet red pepper, peeled and seeded, or drained tinned (canned) pimientos
2 tablespoons chopped parsley (optional)

Make a *sofrito*. Heat the oil in a frying pan (skillet) and sauté the onion until soft. Add the garlic and sauté for 1 minute longer. Add the tomatoes, paprika and salt to taste and sauté for a few minutes, stirring from time to time until the mixture is well-blended. Stir in the stock or water, cover and cook for 5 minutes longer.

In a small frying pan (skillet), with enough oil to film the pan, sauté the ham and *chorizo* for 5 minutes.

Pour the sauce into a large flameproof dish. Break the eggs into the dish, keeping them just separated from each other. Arrange the ham and *chorizo* mixture around the edge of the dish. Make little heaps of the peas in between the eggs and arrange the asparagus spears in a decorative pattern. Season the eggs with salt and pepper and garnish with the sweet (bell) pepper or pimiento strips. If liked sprinkle chopped parsley over the dish. Bake in a preheated moderately hot oven (200°C/400°F/gas 6) until the whites of the eggs are lightly set, about 8 minutes. Serve straight from the dish.

If liked, the dish may be cooked in 4 individual flameproof ramekins. Drink a light dry red wine.

Ervilhas Guisadas à Portuguésa
Green Peas, Portuguese-style

This could be said to be the Portuguese version of *Huevos a la Flamenca*. It is a popular lunch or supper dish in Portugal, especially when green peas are at their seasonal best.

SERVES 4

25 g/1 oz (2 tablespoons) butter
100 g/4 ounces bacon, cut into 2.5 cm/1 inch pieces
2 medium onions, finely chopped
1 large clove garlic, chopped
1 bay leaf
4 tablespoons chopped fresh coriander
250 g/8 ounces (about 2 medium) tomatoes, peeled, seeded and chopped
1.4 kg/3 pounds shelled green peas, thoroughly defrosted if frozen
100 g/4 ounces *chouriço* or *chorizo* or any garlic-flavoured smoked pork sausage
salt and freshly ground pepper
250 ml/8 fl oz (1 cup) water
½ teaspoon sugar
4 large eggs

In a shallow flameproof casserole melt the butter and add the bacon, onions, garlic and bay leaf. Sauté over moderate heat until the onions are soft. Add the coriander, tomatoes and peas. Stir to mix, cover and cook over a very low heat for 5 minutes. Add the sausage, pour in the water, season with salt and pepper, cover and cook until the peas are done, about 5–10 minutes according to how young the peas are.

About 5 minutes before serving remove and discard the bay leaf. Lift out the sliced sausage and keep it warm. Stir in the sugar. Arrange the sausage slices round the edge of the casserole. Using a large spoon, make 4 indentations in the peas and slide an egg into each one. Cover and cook for 4–5 minutes over low heat until the egg whites are set. Serve immediately, straight from the casserole. A light dry red wine is pleasant with this, or a crisp dry white wine.

Migas
Fried Bread

Migas, best described as fried bread though they are more than this, make a simple, much-loved family dish in both Spain and Portugal. *Migas* in Spanish translates into the soft part of bread, the crumb, or small pieces of bread. The same word with the same meaning is used in Portugal. They are particularly popular as an accompaniment to fried eggs. It is essential to have good, hearty bread like Portuguese *Pão*, country bread, (page 250) or Spanish *Pan de Pueblo* (page 252), also country bread, though everyone eats them in town or country. Failing these, day-old French or Italian breads are the best substitutes. Some Portuguese *migas* are made with *Broa* (page 251), cornbread. Both Portuguese and Spanish breads are easy to make and it is worth baking a loaf or two so that there is some stale bread for migas. Migas can also be served as a *tapa*.

SERVES 4–6
400 g/14 ounces day-old Spanish or Portuguese country bread, or French or Italian bread
water
100 g/4 ounces (8 slices) bacon, chopped
3 tablespoons olive oil
3 cloves garlic
salt and freshly ground pepper
1 teaspoon paprika
¼ teaspoon ground cumin
1 small onion, finely chopped
50 g/2 ounces chopped *serrano* ham or *prosciutto* or similar ham

Remove the crusts from the bread and cut into 2.5 cm/1 inch cubes. Put the bread into a bowl and sprinkle with a little water, about 2 tablespoons, tossing the bread with the hands so as to dampen all the cubes. Cover the bowl with a cloth and set aside.

Heat 2 tablespoons of the oil in a frying pan (skillet) and sauté the bacon until it has given off all its fat and is quite crisp. Lift out the bacon pieces with a slotted spoon and set them aside. Add 1 of the garlic cloves to the pan and sauté over very low heat until browned. Remove and discard the garlic. Season the bread pieces with salt, pepper, paprika and cumin, tossing to mix. Add to the pan and cook over very low heat, stirring from time to time for about 20 minutes, until crisp but not brown.

While the bread cubes are frying, heat the remaining tablespoon of oil in a small frying pan (skillet) and sauté the onion until soft. Chop and add the remaining garlic and sauté for 1–2 minutes longer. Add the ham and bacon and cook for 1 minute to heat them through. As soon as the bread is ready, add the onion mixture to the bread cubes, stir to mix and serve with *Huevos Fritos a la Española* (Fried Eggs, Spanish-style) (page 229). Served as a light lunch or supper the dish may be accompanied by a full-bodied dry red wine.

Variation: *Migas Andaluzas* (Fried Bread, Andalucian-style), toss the bread cubes in a mixture of 1 tablespoon paprika, ½ teaspoon ground cumin, and salt. Sprinkle with a little water, then fry in hot olive oil. Serve as a *tapa* or with soup.

Migas à Beira Baixa
Migas, Beira Baixa-style

There is often only a thin line dividing *migas* from *açordas* in the Portuguese kitchen. This dish from the province of Beira Baixa is closer to the Spanish *migas* where the bread cubes retain their consistency than to dishes where the bread is cooked to a mush, then fried and rolled up almost like an omelette (see Variation).

SERVES 4
125 ml/4 fl oz (½ cup) olive oil
4 large cloves garlic
500 g/1 pound *Pão* (page 250) or similar hearty country-style bread, cut into 2.5 cm/1 inch cubes
salt
4 large eggs, lightly beaten

In a large, heavy frying pan (skillet) heat the oil. Add the garlic cloves and cook over very low heat until golden-brown. Remove and discard the garlic. Add the bread cubes and cook, stirring, until the bread has absorbed all the oil and is crisp but not brown. Sprinkle the bread with 50 ml/2 fl oz (¼ cup) salted water and cook, stirring, for 1–2 minutes longer. Add the eggs and cook, still stirring, until the eggs are well mixed with the bread and are set. Serve with roast pork or any roasted meat or poultry, or with fried fish.

Variation: For *Migas do Ribatejo* (Migas, Ribatejo-style), use 400g/14 ounces *Broa* (page 251) or other cornbread. Slice the bread and put it into a large frying pan (skillet) and pour in salted boiling water, just enough for the bread to absorb without getting mushy. Cook over low heat, stirring, for about 5 minutes. Mix 3 large cloves very finely chopped garlic with 175 ml/6 fl oz (¾ cup) olive oil and pour gradually into the cornbread, stirring to mix. Cook for about 2 minutes, then, still over low heat, begin to shape the mixture into a roll like an omelette. Two wooden spoons, or wooden spatulas are helpful for this. Continue to cook until the bread has a golden crust and is quite firm. Serve sliced with fried fish or sausages or any roasted meat, especially pork.

Huevos Fritos a la Española
Fried Eggs, Spanish-style

It was in Cuba that I first had eggs cooked in the Spanish style and was delighted by the rich flavour the olive oil bequeaths to the eggs. Cuba has preserved a number of Spanish sixteenth and seventeenth-century recipes while at the same time developing the *cocina criolla*. Recipes have gone back and forth, *Moros y Cristianos* (Black Beans and Rice) is another example of a colonial dish that is also popular in the mother country.

SERVES 2
olive oil
4 large eggs
salt

Into a frying pan (skillet) large enough to hold all 4 eggs at once, pour enough oil to reach a depth of 2.5 cm/1 inch. Heat the oil. Break the eggs into 4 saucers and slide them into the hot oil. With a wooden spoon fold the whites over the yolks. Cook only for about 1 minute over moderately high heat when the whites will have set. Lift out with a slotted spatula on to paper towels. Season with salt and serve immediately. Serve with sausage and fried bread (*migas*) (page 227).

Piperrada
Eggs Scrambled with Sweet (Bell) Peppers and Tomatoes

This is a Basque dish that has become widely popular. It differs little, if at all, from the *Pipérade* of the French Basques and the recipe idea may have been brought to Europe by Basques from Mexico, original home of both peppers and tomatoes.

SERVES 4
4 tablespoons olive oil
1 medium onion, finely chopped
1 clove garlic, chopped
4 sweet red (bell) peppers, or 2 red and 2 green, seeded and finely chopped
500 g/1 pound (about 4 medium tomatoes) peeled, seeded and chopped
salt and freshly ground pepper
4 slices cured ham (optional)
oil for frying ham (optional)
6 large eggs, lightly beaten
fried bread triangles

Heat the oil in a large, heavy frying pan (skillet) and sauté the onion, garlic and peppers until the vegetables are soft. Add the tomatoes, season with salt and pepper and cook over low heat until the mixture is thick and well-blended, about 10 minutes.

In another pan fry the ham slices, if using, in oil, drain and keep warm.

Pour the eggs into the tomato and pepper mixture and cook, stirring with a wooden spoon, until the eggs are lightly set. Serve with the ham and triangles of bread fried in oil or butter.

Variation: Instead of adding the eggs and scrambling them, cooks sometimes top the vegetable mixture with fried or poached eggs.

Tortilla Murciana
Omelette, Murcian-style

This is reminiscent of *Piperrada*, but is made as an omelette instead of the eggs being scrambled.

SERVES 2
3 tablespoons olive oil
1 sweet red (bell) pepper, peeled, seeded and chopped (page 187)
500 g/1 pound (about 4 medium) tomatoes, peeled, seeded and chopped
salt and freshly ground pepper
4 large eggs, lightly beaten

In a 23 cm/9 inch frying pan (skillet), preferably non-stick, heat the oil and sauté the pepper until soft. Add the tomatoes and continue to cook until the mixture is thick and well-blended, about 10 minutes. Season the mixture with salt and pepper and pour in the eggs. Cook over moderate heat, lifting the edges of the omelette with a rubber spatula to let the uncooked mixture run to the bottom of the pan, until the omelette is almost done.

Put a plate over the pan, invert the pan so that the omelette slides on to the plate, then slide it back into the pan to brown the other side lightly. Slide out of the pan and serve immediately. Drink a crisp, dry white wine.

Tortilla Española
Spanish Potato Omelette

This is without doubt one of the best-known and best-loved of Spanish dishes. It can be eaten hot but is best at room temperature; and, accompanied by a green salad and a bottle of wine, a full-bodied dry red, or a crisp white, makes a splendid lunch. Cut into smaller portions it is an excellent *tapa*. For robust appetites it can be served as a first course.

SERVES 4
500 g/1 pound potatoes, peeled and diced, or thinly sliced
250 g/8 ounces (about 3 medium) onions, finely chopped or sliced
salt and freshly ground pepper
250 ml/8 fl oz (1 cup) olive oil
5 large eggs, lightly beaten

Season the potatoes and onions with salt and pepper. Heat the oil in a large, heavy frying pan (skillet), preferably non-stick. Add the potatoes and onions and cook, covered, over low heat, until the vegetables are soft, but not brown, stirring them gently with a wooden spoon from time to time. Drain the potatoes and onions through a sieve set over a bowl. Reserve the oil.

In a large bowl stir the eggs with a little salt and add the potato and onion mixture. Stir gently to mix and let stand for 10–15 minutes.

Wipe out the frying pan (skillet) and add 4 tablespoons of the reserved oil. Heat the oil and pour in the egg mixture, spreading it evenly in the pan. Cook over moderate heat, shaking the pan from time to time to prevent it sticking. When the omelette begins to brown underneath, put a plate over the omelette and invert the pan, sliding the omelette onto the plate. Heat a little more oil in the pan and return the omelette to it, browned side up. Cook just long enough to brown the underside. Transfer the omelette to a warmed plate and serve hot, or at room temperature, if preferred. Serves 4 as a main course, 8 as a first course cut into smaller wedges.

A pale dry *fino* sherry is an admirable accompaniment when the omelette is served as a first course, or as a *tapa*.

Omeleta com Bacalhau
Dried Salt Cod Omelette

It would be extraordinary if Portugal, with its culinary devotion to dried salt cod, did not have an omelette using the fish. Spain has a cod omelette of its own (see Variation), though it does not differ very much from that of its neighbour.

SERVES 2
100 g/4 ounces dried salt cod, skinned and boned
1 tablespoon olive oil and extra oil for cooking omelette
250 g/8 ounces (about 2 medium) tomatoes, peeled, seeded and chopped
4 large eggs
salt

Prepare the cod in the usual way (page 66). Put the cod into a saucepan with water to cover and bring to a simmer over low heat. Simmer for 1 minute. Drain the cod thoroughly, then shred it with the fingers. Set aside.

In a flameproof casserole heat the oil and sauté the tomatoes over low heat, stirring from time to time until they are almost a purée. Add the prepared cod and continue to cook, stirring for 3–4 minutes until very well mixed.

Meanwhile, beat the eggs in a bowl with the salt. Heat enough oil to film the bottom of a frying pan (skillet) and pour in the eggs. When the eggs are almost set, pour the fish and tomato purée on top and cook for a few minutes longer. Fold the omelette over, slide out of the pan on to a warmed plate and serve immediately. A dry white wine is best with this.

Variation: For *Bacalao* (Spanish Salt Cod Omelette), prepare the cod in the same way and set it aside. Heat 2 tablespoons olive oil in a frying pan (skillet) and sauté 1 medium onion, finely chopped, with 1 clove garlic, chopped, until the onion is soft. Add the shredded cod and cook, stirring, for 3–4 minutes. Cool.

In a bowl beat 4 large eggs with salt, freshly ground pepper and 2 tablespoons finely chopped parsley. Add the cooled cod mixture. Heat about 1 tablespoon oil in a frying pan (skillet) and pour in the egg mixture. When the omelette is browned underneath, put a plate over the pan and invert it, sliding the omelette onto the plate. Add a little oil to the pan if necessary and slide the omelette back into it to brown the other side. Slide the omelette out of the pan on to a warmed plate and serve immediately with a dry white wine and a green salad.

Tortilla de Cebollas a la Andaluza
Onion Omelette, Andalucian-style

This onion omelette is not for the cook in a hurry but is more than worth the time involved as the slowly cooked onion has a rich full flavour.

SERVES 2
125 ml/4 fl oz (½ cup) olive oil
900 g/2 pounds (about 6 cups) onions, finely chopped
4 large eggs
salt and freshly ground pepper

In a medium frying pan (skillet) about 23cm/9 inches with a lid, preferably non-stick, heat the oil, and sauté the onions, covered, over moderate heat for about 15 minutes. Stir thoroughly to mix, then reduce the heat to low and continue to cook, covered, until the onions are very soft and lightly browned, stirring from time to time. This will take about 1 hour. Remove the lid from the pan and let the onions cool.

In a large bowl beat the eggs with salt and pepper to taste. Stir in the onion and let stand for about 5 minutes. Wipe out the frying pan (skillet) with paper towels and add about 1 tablespoon oil. Heat the oil and pour in the egg mixture. Cook over moderate heat, lifting the edges with a spatula as the eggs set, to form a rounded edge. When the omelette is almost done, put a plate over the pan and invert it, then slide the omelette back into the pan to lightly brown the other side. Serve with a mixed green salad and drink a fruity, dry white wine, or if preferred, a light dry red wine.

Tortilla Coruñesa
Bacon Omelette, Coruña-style

Great for a meal-in-a-hurry, this omelette is as flavourful as it is easy to make. It is a speciality of the town of Coruña in Galicia which is famous for its omelettes.

SERVES 2
125 ml/4 fl oz (½ cup) olive oil
100 g/4 ounces (8 slices) lean smoked bacon, chopped
25 g/1 oz (½ cup) finely chopped parsley
4 large eggs
salt
1 teaspoon paprika

In a medium frying pan (skillet) heat the oil and sauté the bacon until quite crisp. Add the parsley and sauté for 1 minute longer. Lift the bacon and parsley out of the pan with a slotted spoon into a small bowl and set aside to cool. Beat the eggs with salt to taste and the paprika. Stir in the bacon and parsley.

   Heat the oil remaining in the pan, pour in the egg mixture and cook, stirring, with the flat of a fork until the eggs begin to set; they should then finish cooking in about 20 seconds, and the bottom of the omelette should be lightly browned. Slide the omelette out of the pan on to a warmed plate and serve immediately. A glass or two of light dry red wine is a pleasant accompaniment.

Tortilla Catalana
Onion Omelette, Catalan-style

This is another excellent omelette that is good for the cook who is both hungry and in a hurry. It is from Cataluña.

SERVES 2
1 large onion weighing about 250 g/8 ounces, finely chopped
4 tablespoons olive oil and extra oil for cooking omelette
4 large eggs
salt and freshly ground pepper

Heat the oil in a medium frying pan (skillet), preferably non-stick, and sauté the onion over moderate heat until soft and lightly browned. Pour the contents of the pan into a bowl to cool. Wipe out the pan.

In another bowl beat the eggs with salt and pepper. Add the cooled onion mixture and stir. Heat the pan with enough oil to film the bottom, about 1 tablespoon, and pour in the egg mixture. When the omelette is browned on the underside and almost cooked, put a plate over the pan and invert the omelette on to it, then slide it back into the pan to brown briefly on the other side. Serve immediately. A green salad and a light dry red wine are good accompaniments.

Huevos Rellenos de Gambas
Eggs Stuffed with Prawns (Shrimps)

Stuffed eggs are a favourite almost everywhere and no less so in the Iberian Peninsula. They are good as a *tapa* with drinks, or in a buffet, and if served more generously can make a light luncheon or supper dish when accompanied by salad.

SERVES 2 AS A MAIN COURSE
4 large eggs, hardboiled
Salsa Mahonese (Mayonnaise) (page 238) or *Allioli* (Garlic Mayonnaise)
(page 239)
salt and freshly ground pepper
paprika
250 g/8 ounces small cooked prawns (shrimps), coarsely chopped
1 tablespoon finely chopped parsley

Cut the eggs into halves lengthwise. Scoop out the yolks and put them
into a bowl. Mash with enough mayonnaise or *Allioli* to make a smooth,
light mixture. Season to taste with salt, pepper and paprika. Fold in the
prawns (shrimps) and pile the mixture back into the egg white halves.
Sprinkle with the parsley and serve. A plain sliced tomato salad or a green
salad are both good with the eggs. A rosé or a crisp dry white wine and
some good crusty bread and butter could make this a pleasant summer
lunch or supper.

Variation: For *Ovos Recheados* (Portuguese stuffed eggs), use sardines,
tinned (canned) in oil or in tomato sauce, or tuna, mixed with mayonnaise,
not *Allioli*. Garnish the eggs with slices of black olive and a little finely
chopped parsley, or a sliver of sweet red (bell) pepper.

9

Sauces
Salsas/Molhos

Most dishes from the Iberian Peninsula are cooked with the sauce as an integral part of the dish, it is not added afterwards. Many dishes have a richer flavour as meat or poultry absorb the good things of the sauce in cooking. There are, however, some notable sauces, adopted wherever there is good cooking. Mayonnaise is perhaps the prime example, though there are others.

As for basic recipes, few are needed. Cooks in the Peninsula belong to the cooking traditions with which we are all familiar and very little more needs to be added.

Salsa Mahonesa
Mayonnaise

It is claimed that mayonnaise originated in Mahón, capital of the Balearic island of Menorca, and was adopted with enthusiasm by the French, and later everyone else. It is hard to imagine being without it. It can be made in a food processor or blender in which case use 1 whole egg and 1 egg yolk, adding the oil after the other ingredients have been processed briefly. The oil should be added very gradually, with the motor running. For a lighter mayonnaise use half olive oil, half peanut, sunflower or corn oil, adding the lighter oil when the mayonnaise has emulsified. If the mayonnaise curdles, put an extra yolk into a bowl and beat in the curdled mayonnaise teaspoon by teaspoon, or in a thin stream, beating constantly.

MAKES ABOUT 350 ML/12 FL OZ (1½ CUPS)
2 large egg yolks, at room temperature
2 tablespoons lemon juice or white wine vinegar
½ teaspoon Dijon mustard
salt and freshly ground white pepper
350 ml/12 fl oz (1½ cups) olive oil at room temperature

In a bowl beat the egg yolks with 1 teaspoon of the lemon juice or vinegar, the mustard and salt and pepper to taste, until the yolks are creamy. Beat in the oil drop by drop until the mixture has emulsified and is thick and glossy. Add the rest of the oil in a thin stream, beating constantly. Add the remaining lemon juice or vinegar.

Allioli
Garlic Mayonnaise

Although there are many versions or *Allioli*, Cataluña claims the original classic one as its own. It is undoubtedly the most powerful, consisting solely of garlic, lemon juice or vinegar and oil. Most versions have egg yolks, some have breadcrumbs and potatoes, others mustard or tomatoes. It is not suprising that there should be so many variations, as this is an ancient sauce with recipes going back to the tenth century in Spain. It has been claimed by gastronomic authorities to have been introduced into Spain by the Romans from its original home in Egypt. The name derives from Latin *allium* (garlic) and *oleum* (oil), and turns up in Provence as the famed *Aioli*, a dish of boiled salt cod, boiled potatoes and assorted green vegetables, eggs, snails, and so on, with the accompaning sauce. Use on fish, meat, vegetables and salads.

Allioli a la Catalana
Garlic Mayonnaise, Catalan-style

MAKES ABOUT 250 ML/8 FL OZ (1 CUP)
½ large head of garlic, peeled and crushed
1 teaspoon lemon juice or white wine winegar
250 ml/8 fl oz (1 cup) olive oil, at room temperature
½ teaspoon salt

Put the crushed garlic into a small bowl or large mortar and add the lemon or vinegar, stirring to mix. Gradually add the oil, stirring in the same direction until the oil is absorbed and the mixture as thick as mayonnaise. Stir in the salt, adding more to taste if necessary.

If liked, make the sauce in a food processor or blender, adding the oil very gradually with the motor running.

Variation: This is the more usual form of the sauce as only devoted garlic lovers prefer the strongest version. In a mortar put 8 large cloves garlic, crushed, ½ teaspoon salt, 2 large egg yolks and 1 tablespoon lemon juice or white wine vinegar, or put into a food processor or blender. Add the oil very gradually, stirring constantly in the same direction, or in a food processor with the motor running.

Variation: Make as the recipe using egg yolks, and when the olive oil has all been added and the sauce has the consistency of mayonnaise, stir in 1 teaspoon mixed dry hot mustard, adding more according to taste.

Variation: Make as the recipe using egg yolks, and when all the oil has been added and the sauce has the consistency of mayonnaise, add 375 g/ 12 oz (2 large) tomatoes, peeled, seeded and mashed.

If the sauce fails to emulsify, put an extra egg yolk into a bowl and beat in the curdled sauce teaspoon by teaspoon.

Ajoaceite
Oil and Garlic Sauce

This sauce can be served with meat, poultry, fish, eggs or vegtables, as liked. It is claimed by more than one region in Spain as a native dish, including Andalucía and Extremeña, where breadcrumbs are used instead of potatoes. It is really a form of *Alliolli* (Garlic Mayonnaise).

MAKES ABOUT 475 ML/16 FL OZ (2 CUPS)
3 cloves garlic, crushed
250 g/8 ounces freshly cooked mashed potatoes
salt and freshly ground pepper
2 large egg yolks, lightly beaten
250 ml/8 fl oz (1 cup) olive oil

In a bowl mix together the garlic, potatoes, salt and pepper to taste. Beat in the egg yolks, mixing thoroughly. Gradually add the oil, beating constantly. The sauce should have the consistency of mayonnaise.

Salsa Vinagreta Gallega
Vinaigrette Sauce, Galician-style

This is the universal oil and vinegar sauce used on salads, but with small additions by Galician cooks that transform it into something different. The sauce is very good served with fish or egg dishes.

MAKES ABOUT 150 ML/5 FL OZ (⅝ CUP)
125 ml/4 fl oz (½ cup) olive oil
3 tablespoons mild vinegar
1 clove garlic, crushed
½ teaspoon paprika
salt and freshly ground white pepper

In a bowl combine all the ingredients and beat with a fork until they are thoroughly combined and form a creamy sauce.

Variation: For *Salsa Vinagreta Extremeña* (Vinaigrette Sauce, Extemēna-style), combine in a bowl 1 small onion chopped, 1 clove garlic, crushed, 1 teaspoon finely chopped parsley, a pinch of grated nutmeg, the yolk of 4 hardboiled eggs, mashed, salt, freshly ground white pepper, 1 tablespoon chopped capers, 3 tablespoons mild vinegar and 125 ml/4 fl oz (½ cup) olive oil and mix together thoroughly into a creamy sauce. Add the 4 whites of the eggs, finely chopped, to the sauce and serve with fish or cold meats.

Salsa de Almendras
Almond Sauce

This classic sauce is used to accompany fish as well as eggs, poultry and cold meats.

MAKES ABOUT 250 ML/8 FL OZ (1 CUP)
12 toasted almonds, ground
yolks of 2 large hardboiled eggs
1 tablespoon chopped parsley
475 ml/16 fl oz (2 cups) milk
salt and freshly ground white pepper

Combine the almonds, egg yolks and parsley in a food processor or blender and process while slowly adding the milk to make a smooth mixture. Season with salt and pepper and pour into a saucepan. Simmer over very low heat until reduced to half.

Massa de Pimentão
Sweet Red (Bell) Pepper Paste

This is a useful seasoning mixture that Portuguese cooks keep on hand for adding to meats and poultry dishes, often as a marinade. It has a lovely vermillion colour and is easy to make. It is salty, so care should be taken not to add salt to any dish in which it will be used.

MAKES ABOUT 250 G/8 OZ (1 CUP)
3 large sweet red (bell) peppers, seeded and cut into quarters lengthwise
1 tablespoon coarse sea salt (kosher salt)
2 cloves garlic, chopped
4 tablespoons olive oil

In a shallow bowl combine the peppers with the salt, mixing thoroughly. Stand, uncovered, at room temperature for 24 hours. Pour off the liquid that will have accumulated, rinse the pepper strips in cold water to remove excess salt, drain and pat dry with paper towels.

Arrange the peppers skin-side up on a baking sheet. Place under a preheated grill (broiler) and cook until the skins are blackened and blistered, about 10 minutes. Cool slightly, then peel off and discard the skins. Combine with the garlic in a food processor or blender and process to a purée, adding the oil gradually. Use as a marinade for meat and poultry according to recipe directions. The paste will keep, refrigerated, in a glass jar with a lid for about 2 weeks.

Though it is unorthodox I have found that a tablespoon or so of pepper paste added to a fresh tomato sauce gives it an exciting flavour.

Salsa a la Riojana
Sauce, Rioja-style

This is quite a complicated sauce from the tiny province of Rioja in the north of Spain. It is really two sauces combined, one of them the famed *Salsa Española* (Spanish Sauce) (see below) a version of which, *Sauce espagnole*, is much used in French cooking. As this sauce is also used independently in Spanish cooking it is worth the effort of making Rioja Sauce, reserving the extra Spanish Sauce for another use. The sauce is essential for *Setas a la Riojana* (Mushrooms, Rioja-style) (page 189).

2 tablespoons olive oil
6 spring onion (scallions), chopped
600 ml/20 fl oz (2½ cups) dry red wine
250 ml/8 fl oz (1 cup) *Salsa Española* (Spanish Sauce) (see below)

Heat the oil in a saucepan and sauté the spring onion (scallions) until soft. Pour in the wine and simmer, uncovered, over low heat until the liquid is reduced to 150 ml/5 fl oz (⅝ cup). Stir in the *Salsa Española* (Spanish Sauce) and cook for 15 minutes longer over very low heat. Use as directed.

Salsa Española
Spanish Sauce

6 tablespoons olive oil
1 medium carrot, scraped and chopped
1 medium onion, chopped
1 leek, trimmed, washed and thinly sliced
250 g/8 ounces lean, boneless beef or veal, chopped
4 tablespoons plain all purpose flour
500 g/ 1 lb (4 medium) tomatoes, peeled and chopped
250 ml/10 fl oz (1½ cups) each dry white and dry red wine
½ teaspoon ground black pepper
¼ teaspoon thyme
½ bay leaf
1 litre/¾ pints (4 cups) water

In a frying pan (skillet) heat the oil. Add the carrot, onion and leek and sauté until the vegetables are soft. Lift out into a saucepan. Add the meat to the pan and sauté until lightly browned, then add to the saucepan. Add the flour to the fat remaining in the frying pan (skillet) and cook, stirring, until lightly browned. Add to the saucepan, stir to mix.

Add the tomatoes to the saucepan and cook, stirring, for about 5 minutes. Add the wine, bay leaf thyme and pepper and the water. Simmer uncovered, over a very low heat stirring from time to time, for 1 hour. Strain through a fine sieve lined wih dampened cheesecloth, pressing down on the solids to extract all the flavour. Add to the *Salsa Riojana* (Sauce, Rioja-style) and cook, uncovered, for 20 minutes longer over very low heat. Adjust the seasoning, adding salt as necessary.

Tomatada
Tomato Sauce

This is a most useful sauce and takes advantage of the fine, flavourful tomatoes available in Portugal. Whenever red, ripe tomatoes are in the market, make this sauce to serve with eggs, meat, poultry, fish or vegetables.

MAKES ABOUT 600 ML/1 PINT (2¼ CUPS)
125 ml/4 fl oz (½ cup) olive oil
2 sweet red (bell) peppers, seeded and cut into strips
900 g/2 pounds (8 medium) tomatoes, peeled, seeded and chopped
2 medium onions, finely sliced
1 fresh hot red chilli pepper, seeded and chopped
salt and freshly ground pepper

Heat the oil in a saucepan and add the pepper strips. Cook them over very low heat until soft. Add the tomatoes, onion, chilli pepper, salt and pepper and simmer over low heat, stirring from time to time, until the mixture is well-blended and has the texture of a sauce.

Salsa de Tomate a la Castellana
Tomato Sauce, Spanish-style

Tomatoes came to Spain from their original home, Mexico, after the Conquest. They grow splendidly in both Spain and Portugal as they do in Mexico, sweet and richly flavoured. This very simple sauce from New Castille brings out the fresh taste of the fruit and enhances meat, poultry, fish, egg and vegetable dishes. It is widely used.

MAKES ABOUT 600 ML/1 PINT (2½ CUPS)
3 tablespoons olive oil
1 medium onion, finely chopped
1 clove garlic, chopped
900 g/2 pounds (about 8 medium) tomatoes, peeled, seeded and chopped
½ teaspoon sugar
salt and freshly ground pepper

Heat the oil in a saucepan and sauté the onion until soft. Add the garlic and sauté for 2 minutes longer. Add the tomatoes, sugar and salt and pepper to taste and cook until the mixture is thick and well-blended, about 15 minutes. For a very smooth sauce, rub through a sieve. Serve hot.

Salsa Romesco
Romesco Sauce

I am convinced that there are as many version of Romesco Sauce as there are cooks in Cataluña, home of this most delicious cold sauce for fish and shellfish. There is a problem for those outside Spain in finding an equivalent for the type of dried sweet or slighly hot red pepper used, and it would be possible to write a thesis just on peppers.

Peppers (chillics), sweet, pungent, and hot all originated in Mexico from whence they have spread around the world. It is interesting that Mexico's most popular dried sweet pepper, the mild, wrinkled, full-flavoured, dark red *ancho*, did not migrate to Spain, though many other peppers did, including *pimientos* which are simply sweet, fresh red peppers, often sold ready-roasted and peeled in tins (cans) or jars. They are the peppers from which the Hungarians made *paprika*, now universally available. Whenever my recipes specify paprika the sweet type is meant, and not hot paprika which is also available and is always labelled hot. Another ground hot pepper, cayenne, is made from small dried hot peppers. A combination of some of these peppers can approximate to the Spanish *romesco* or *ñora* peppers used in this sauce. These closely resemble the Mexican *guajillo*, a tapering, smooth-skinned, red-brown pepper which gives a beautiful red colour to food. A variety of *guajillo* turns up in U.S. markets as New Mexico pepper, interesting because this chilli was taken by Captain General Juan de Oñate to the region in 1597 from Mexico. A millionaire gentleman farmer, he introduced cattle into what later became part of the United States.

If *Guajillo* peppers, *ñoras*, *romesco*, or New Mexico are not available, use a recipe for the sauce made with sweet red (bell) peppers plus fresh or dried small red chilli peppers. (see Variation). Mexican peppers and their descendants are legion but they are often adaptable, very accommodating to the cook. The sauce is named after the *romesco* pepper cultivated in the region. The sauce should be hot, *picante*, but not excessively so. It is primarily served with fish and shellfish, but is also good with meats, poultry and vegetables where a cold sauce is appropriate. It is also good with snails.

MAKES ABOUT 475 ML/16 FL OZ (2 CUPS)
2 New Mexico-style dried sweet peppers, or 2 Mexican *guajillos*, or
Spanish *ñoras or romesco* peppers
1–2 hot dried red chillies, seeded, according to taste
250 ml/8 fl oz (1 cup) olive oil
2 slices French type bread, 5mm/¼ inch thick
250 g/8 ounces (about 2 medium) tomatoes, peeled, seeded and chopped
4 cloves garlic, chopped
50 g/1 oz (¼ cup) toasted blanched almonds, ground
salt and freshly ground pepper
125 ml/4 fl oz (½ cup) red wine vinegar

Soak the peppers in warm water until they are soft, about 30 minutes. Drain, pat dry, and chop coarsely. Heat 50 ml/2 fl oz (1/4 cup) of the oil in a small frying pan (skillet) and fry the bread until golden on both sides.

Lift out on to paper towels to drain, then chop coarsely. Add the tomatoes and garlic to the pan and sauté for 3–4 minutes. Cool.

In a blender or food processor combine the peppers, fried bread, tomatoes, garlic and any oil remaining in the pan, almonds, salt and pepper, the rest of the oil and the vinegar. Process until well-mixed. The sauce should retain some texture. Let sit for 2 hours, then beat lightly before serving. Some cooks prefer a smoother sauce and put the finished sauce through a sieve.

Variation: If the sweet, slightly hot dried red peppers are not available, use a large, peeled, seeded and coarsely chopped fresh sweet red (bell) pepper (page 187) and 2 hot dried red chillies, seeded, soaked and choppped. Sauté the peppers with the garlic and tomatoes in 2 tablespoons of the oil and make the sauce as above.

Variation: Some cooks make the sauce simply with fresh sweet red (bell) peppers, seeded garlic, and fresh hot chillies, seeded, seasoned with salt, and puréed in a food processor or blender with equal amounts of oil and vinegar. The proportions are varied to suit the taste of the cook.

Molho de Piri-piri
Hot Red Chilli Pepper (Piri-piri) Sauce

Piri-piri Sauce is without any doubt Portugal's best loved sauce and is the hottest hot pepper sauce I have ever encountered. It has an interesting history. The small, fresh hot peppers migrated south from Mexico to what is now Brazil. En route they seem to have become hotter than when they started off. After the arrival of the Portuguese, they crossed over to Africa with their new masters, still acquiring heat. They changed their name and became, back home in Brazil, *malaguéta* peppers, and in the new homeland of Angola, *piri-piri*. They are used when red and ripe.

Piri-piri Sauce, like other hot sauces such as Tabasco, is sold bottled, commercially. However, it is possible to make piri-piri at home, and recipes are legion. The simplest consists of filling a jar one-third full of very hot dried red chilli peppers, then filling up the jar with olive oil, closing it tightly and leaving it in a cool place for 1 month before using. The oil will be impregnated with the heat and flavour of the peppers. Other cooks say the peppers should be chopped, and put into a jar with salt, olive oil and vinegar, in the proportion of twice as much oil to vinegar and enough to cover the peppers. I have worked from store-bought Piri-piri Sauces to create what I think is a near equivalent. It is wickedly hot.

MAKES ABOUT 250 ML/8 FL OZ (1 CUP)
25 g/1 ounce hot dried red chilli peppers, stems removed
250 ml/8 fl oz (1 cup) warm water
salt, about 1 teaspoon
1½ teaspoons potato flour (starch) or cornflour (cornstarch)
2 tablespoons red wine vinegar

Put the peppers into a bowl with the warm water and soak for 30 minutes. Transfer the contents of the bowl to a blender or food processor and process until smooth. Put through a sieve and discard any seeds. Season with salt. Pour into a small saucepan.

Dissolve the flour or starch in a little water and stir it into the pepper mixture. Cook, stirring, over low heat until the mixture is lightly thickened. Allow to cool, stir in the vinegar, and measure. If necessary, make up the quantity to 250 ml/8 fl oz (1 cup) with warm water. Bottle and use with caution.

10

Breads and Pastry
Panes y Pastelaría/Pães e Pastelaría

A meal would not be considered a meal in Spain or Portugal without the good solid crusty bread available everywhere. It is not difficult to reproduce, given the right type of flour, and is worth the small effort required to make it. Spain has, in addition to its ordinary bread, many sweet breads that are enjoyed especially for breakfast, and at any other time of day.

Iberian cooks are noted for their pastry-making and while all probably have their own pastry recipes, the Shortcrust Pastry (Basic Pie Dough) and the puff pastry, both in this chapter, are good standard recipes.

Pão
Portuguese Country Bread

This is the everyday bread of Portugal, crusty and firm. Country women take their loaves to the local bakery where they are baked to a rich brown in brick ovens. Much of the fine taste and goodness of this bread comes from the strong, unbleached bread flour that is used, and from thorough kneading, so that good results can be obtained from cooking the bread in an ordinary domestic oven. It is well worth making.

MAKES A 20CM/8 INCH ROUND LOAF
1 tablespoon active dry yeast
1 teaspoon sugar
500 g/1 pound (4 cups) unbleached, strong, plain white bread flour
250 ml/8 fl oz (1 cup) lukewarm water
1 teaspoon salt

In a small bowl prove the yeast with the sugar in 50 ml/2 fl oz (¼ cup) of the water until frothy, about 5–10 minutes.

In a large bowl sift the flour with the salt. Make a well in the centre and pour in the yeast and the rest of the water. Mix to a firm dough and add a little more water if necessary. Form into a ball and turn out on to a lightly floured surface. Knead until the dough is smooth and satiny, 10–15 minutes.

Rinse out and dry the bowl and oil it lightly. Return the ball of dough to the bowl, turn it to coat with the oil, cover and stand in a warm, draught-free place until it is doubled in bulk, about 1–1½ hours. Punch the dough down and turn it on to the floured surface. Knead again until it is smooth and elastic, about 5 minutes. Form into a ball and put into a lightly oiled 20 cm/8 inch round cake tin (layer-cake pan), cover and let it rise again until doubled in bulk, about 45 minutes. Bake in a preheated moderately hot oven (200°C/400°F/gas 6 for 15 minutes, then lower the temperature to 180°C/350°F/gas4) and bake for 15–20 minutes longer, or until the loaf is richly browned and sounds hollow when tapped on the bottom. Transfer to a wire rack and cool.

Broa
Portuguese Cornbread

This cornmeal (maize) bread is popular in the north of Portugal, especially in the country districts. It is usually served with robust soups. A chewy bread as hearty as the soups, it is easy to make and delicious to eat.

MAKES 1 LOAF
1 sachet (package) (¼ ounce/2½ teaspoons) active dry yeast
1 teaspoon sugar
300 ml/½ pint (2¼ cups) lukewarm water
250 g/8 oz (2 cups) fine yellow cornmeal (maize meal)
1½ teaspoons salt
1 tablespoon olive oil
about 375 g/12 oz (3 cups) plain flour
175 ml/6 fl oz (¾ cup) lukewarm milk

In a small bowl mix the yeast and sugar with 50 ml/2 fl oz (¼ cup) of the water to prove the yeast. Let it stand for about 15 minutes or until frothy.

In a large bowl mix the cornmeal and salt with the oil, remaining water and milk, mixing thoroughly. Add the yeast, stir to mix, then gradually add the flour to make a soft but manageable dough. Turn out on to a floured board and knead until smooth and elastic, about 5 minutes. Form into a ball and put into a greased bowl. Cover with a cloth, and set in a warm, draught-free place to rise until doubled in bulk, about 1 hour.

Punch the dough down and turn it out on to a floured board. Knead the bread for 5 minutes, then form it into a round loaf. Place the loaf in a round 23 cm/9 inch greased pie plate, cover and allow to rise a second time until doubled in bulk, about 1 hour. Bake in a preheated moderate oven (180°C/350°F/gas 4) for about 40 minutes or until the loaf sounds hollow when tapped on the bottom.

Pan de Pueblo
Basic Spanish Bread

This recipe will give a good approximation of everyday Spanish bread which is very good indeed and well worth the trouble of making.

MAKES 1 LOAF
3 teaspoons active dry yeast
½ teaspoon sugar
250 ml/8 fl oz (1 cup) warm water
250 g/8 oz (2 cups) bread flour or unbleached plain flour
2 teaspoons salt, preferably coarse
cornmeal (maize meal) for baking sheet

In a small bowl mix the yeast and sugar with 50 ml/2 fl oz (¼ cup) of the water to prove the yeast. Stand in a warm place until frothy.

Combine the flour and salt in a large bowl. Make a well in the centre and add the yeast and remaining water. Mix to form a soft dough. Turn out on to a lightly floured surface and knead until smooth and elastic, 10–15 minutes, adding a little more flour if the dough is sticky. Form into a ball.

Rinse out and dry the bowl and oil it lightly. Add the ball of dough, turning to coat all over with oil. Cover loosely with a cloth and stand in a warm, draught-free place to rise until double in bulk, about 3 hours. Punch the dough down and knead again until smooth, about 5 minutes.

Sprinkle a baking sheet with a little cornmeal (maize meal).

Roll or pull the dough into a rectangle about 15 x 40 cm/6 x 16 inches and roll up, pinching to seal the ends and seam. Place on the prepared baking sheet. Using a very sharp knife, make 3 diagonal slashes in the dough at regular intervals. If necessary, put the loaf on the baking sheet diagonally according to the size of the oven. (British ovens are smaller than ovens in the United States.) Place in a warm, draught-free place and let the dough rise again until doubled in bulk, 1–2 hours. Brush the bread with cold water, using a soft pastry brush. Bake in a preheated hot oven (230°C/450°F/gas 8) for 25 minutes, brushing again with cold water after the bread has been baking for about 5 minutes. The bread is done when it is lightly browned and sounds hollow when the bottom is tapped.

Milho Frito
Fried Cornmeal (Maize Meal)

This is a popular nibble in Madeira, served with drinks before dinner. It is also popular as an accompaniment to meat dishes, especially pork. Curiously it is not unlike a dish from Barbados, *Coo-coo*, though this combines okra, of African origin, with New World corn (maize). There the maize meal (cornmeal) is not fried but served as a vegetable alterative to rice or potatoes.

SERVES 4–6
1 litre/¾ pints (4 cups) water
1 teaspoon salt or to taste
15g/½ oz (1 tablespoon) butter or lard
250 g/8 ounces (2 cups) yellow cornmeal (maize meal)
100 g/4 ounces cabbage, shredded/or other greens
vegetable oil for frying

In a large saucepan combine the water, salt and butter or lard and bring to a boil over moderate heat. Pour the cornmeal (maize meal) into the water in a thin, slow, steady stream, stirring constantly with a wooden spoon. Stir in the cabbage or other greens and cook, stirring, until the mixture is very thick and smooth, about 5 minutes. Oil a 20 cm/8 inch square baking dish, 5 cm/2 inches in depth, and pour in the cooked mixture. Let it cool to room temperature, then chill until very firm.

Cut into 5 cm/2 inch squares and fry in oil in a medium frying pan (skillet) over moderate heat until lightly browned. Drain on paper towels and serve.

Ensaimadas
Snail-shaped Sweet Rolls

These are much-loved breakfast bread in Mallorca, and an equally loved sweet bread to accompany dessert. Legend has it that the snail shape is an imitation of the Moorish turban. The rolls may be filled with cream for special occasions. Bakeries make them to order for family-size eating on Sundays and holidays.

MAKES 16

125 ml/4 fl oz (½ cup) warm milk
½ teaspoon sugar, plus 2 tablespoons
2 teaspoons active dry yeast
250 g/8 ounces (2 cups) unbleached plain (all-purpose) flour
½ teaspoon salt
1 large egg, lightly beaten
25g/1 oz (2 tablespoons) melted lard or butter
icing (confectioners') sugar for dusting

In a small bowl mix the milk and sugar together. Sprinkle on the yeast, then stir to mix. Stand in a warm place until frothy.

Sift the flour and salt into a large bowl. Stir the egg into the yeast with the sugar. Make a well in the centre of the flour and add the yeast mixture. Mix to a soft dough. Turn out on to a lightly floured surface and knead for about 5 minutes until the dough is smooth and shiny. If necessary, add a little more flour.

Rinse out and dry the bowl in which the dough was mixed and lightly oil it. Form the dough into a ball, return it to the bowl and turn to coat with oil. Cover with a cloth and leave in a warm, draught-free place to rise until doubled in bulk.

Turn the risen dough out on to a work surface. The next part is a bit tricky but a Mallorcan friend assures me it is the best and simplest way, though he did add that most of his countrymen and women buy their *ensaimadas* from the local bakery! Divide the dough into 8 equal pieces. Roll each piece between the palms until it is 1 cm/½ inch thick. Now roll out with a rolling pin until each piece is about 76 cm/30 inches long and 5 cm/2 inches wide. Have ready the melted lard or butter. Using a pastry brush, brush the strips of dough with the fat just short of the edges. Roll up tightly like a Swiss (jelly) roll. Cut each roll exactly in half, then form each half into a loose spiral or snail-shape. Pinch the dough to seal this spiral. Leave the prepared rolls in a warm, draught-free place to rise again, about 2 hours or longer, until they are doubled in bulk. Put the rolls on to a greased baking sheet and bake in a preheated moderate oven (180°C/350°F/gas 4) until golden brown, 10–15 minutes. Dust with icing (confectioners') sugar before serving. Serve warm from the oven.

Variations: A simpler way, though perhaps a little less traditional, is to cut the dough into 8 pieces, then roll the pieces between the palms into a long thin rope, 1 cm/½ inch wide and about 50.5 cm/20 inches long. Brush with butter or lard and roll up loosely. Bake as above.

Bolo Rei
Kings' Day Bread

This is a special holiday bread baked to celebrate 6 January, the Day of the Three Kings (Epiphany), when the Three Wise Men came to visit the Infant Jesus bearing gifts for him. This is the principal day for gift-giving, especially to children, in all the Latin countries, and all have a version of the bread, which is baked in a ring and contains either a bean, or a coin, or a small figurine or small trinket. Tradition varies from country to country about the fate of whoever gets the token in his or her piece of cake. In Portugal it imposes a penalty on the finder, who must buy next year's *bolo rei*. In Spain it means the finder will have good luck all year. The Portuguese bread is probably the richest of all the versions with its lavish use of nuts and crystallized fruits.

MAKES 1 LARGE RING, ABOUT 25 CM/10 INCHES
50 ml/2 fl oz (¼ cup) lukewarm water
½ teaspoon sugar
3 teaspoons active dry yeast
625 g/1¼ pounds (5 cups) unbleached plain (all-purpose) flour
½ teaspoon salt
100 g/4 ounces (1 cup) crystallized fruits (dried mixed candied fruits), chopped
50 g/2 ounces (⅓ cup) sultanas (seedless golden raisins)
75 g/3 ounces (¾ cup) mixed pine nuts, almonds and walnuts, chopped
126 ml/4 fl oz (½ cup) tawny port
100 g/4 ounces (1 stick) unsalted butter
grated rind of 1 orange and 1 lemon
100 g/4 ounces (½ cup) sugar
50 ml/2 fl ounces (¼ cup) lukewarm milk
2 large eggs, lightly beaten

For the glaze
1 egg, lightly beaten with 1 teaspoon water

For the decoration
10 slices candied citron (lemon and orange peel)
10 crystallized (candied) red cherries, halved
10 whole blanched almonds
2 tablespoons pine nuts

Sprinkle the yeast over the water and ½ teaspoon sugar in a small bowl.

Set aside in a warm place until frothy, 10–15 minutes. Sift the flour and salt into a large bowl. In a small bowl macerate the crystallized (candied) fruits, sultanas (seedless golden raisins) and mixed nuts in the port.

Cream the butter, orange and lemon rind and sugar together until light and fluffy. Stir in the milk, then whisk in the eggs. Add the macerated fruit and nuts with the port.

Make a well in the centre of the flour and pour in the yeast mixture together with the egg, milk, nut and fruit mixture and mix to form a soft, rather sticky dough. Turn out on to a lightly floured surface and knead until smooth and elastic, adding more flour as necessary, for about 5 minutes. Clean and lightly oil the bowl in which the dough was mixed. Form the dough into a ball and add to the bowl, turning to coat with oil. Cover with a cloth and stand in a warm, draught-free place until doubled in bulk.

Punch the dough down, turn out on to the floured surface and knead again, for about 5 minutes. Push a coin, bean or trinket, into the dough at this point. Form the dough into a large ring and pinch the ends to seal. Place on a greased baking sheet. Put a 10 cm/4 inch jar or similar utensil in the centre of the ring to keep it open. Leave to rise in a warm place until again doubled in bulk, about 1 hour.

Brush with the egg, to glaze, and decorate with the crystallized (candied) fruits and nuts. Sprinkle, if liked, with a little sugar. Remove the jar. Bake in a preheated moderate oven (180°C/350°F/gas 4) until golden-brown and the bottom sounds hollow when tapped, 35–40 minutes.

Serve cut into wedges as a breakfast bread, or eat whenever liked.

Variation: The Spanish *Rosca de Reyes* (King's Day Ring) is fundamentally the same, though a smaller amount of nuts, fruits and raisins are used. Do not macerate any mix of fruit and nuts. Omit these, as in the Spanish version they are not added to the dough. Add 1 tablespoon brandy, preferably Spanish, to the egg–yeast mixture when adding it to the flour to make the dough. After shaping the ring and glazing it, decorate it with slices of crystallized (candied) fruits and sprinkle with 1 tablespoon sugar before baking. Push the fruit lightly into the dough and let the bread rise again, then bake as in the *Bolo Rei* recipe.

Shortcrust Pastry
(Basic Pie Dough)

Most cooks have their own favourite pastry recipes both for shortcrust and puff pastry. Use them, or use these. Sometimes frozen pastry of good quality can be bought and there is no reason why this should not be used. This makes enough pastry for a 20–23 cm/8–9 inch pie case (shell), or for 6–10 cm/4 inch patty tins (tartlet tins).

MAKES ABOUT 250g (8 OUNCES)
150 g/5 ounces (1½ cups) plain (all-purpose) flour
¼ teaspoon salt
65g/2½ oz (5 tablespoons) chilled butter, diced
40g/1½ oz (3 tablespoons) lard or vegetable shortening, diced
2–3 tablespoons very cold (iced) water

Sift the flour and salt into a large bowl. Rub the butter and lard or vegetable shortening into the flour with the fingertips until it resembles a coarse meal or breadcrumbs. Sprinkle with 2 tablespoons of the water, mix quickly and form into a ball. If necessary add the remaining tablespoon of water to hold the dough together. It should be soft but not sticky. Turn the dough out on to a floured surface and knead with the heel of the hand for 30 seconds to distribute the fat evenly. Form into a ball, dust with flour, put into a polythene (plastic) bag or wrap in clingfilm (plastic film) and refrigerate for 1 hour before using.

Pastry dough will keep, refrigerated, for about 3 days. It freezes successfully.

Use according to recipe instructions.

Sweet Shortcrust Pastry
(Sweet Pie Dough)

This is used for dessert tarts and fruit pies. One recipe makes a 20–23 cm/8–9 inch pie shell. Omit the salt from the Shortcrust Pastry (Basic Pie Dough) and use all butter instead of a mixture of butter and lard. When sifting the flour add 3 tablespoons sugar. Instead of mixing the dough with cold water, use 1 medium egg, lightly beaten.

For a 25–28 cm/10–11 inch tart increase the sugar to 4 tablespoons, the flour to 225 g/8 ounces (2 cups) and use 1 large or 2 small eggs, lightly beaten.

Puff Pastry

MAKES ABOUT 500 G/1 POUND
250 g/8 ounces (2 cups) plain (all-purpose) flour
1 teaspoon salt
250 g/8 ounces (2 sticks) chilled unsalted butter
200 ml/8 fl oz (1 cup) very cold (iced) water

Sift the flour and salt together in a large bowl. Dice 50 g/2 oz (4 tablespoons) of the butter and work into the flour with the fingertips until the mixture resembles a coarse meal or breadcrumbs. Add 125 ml/4 fl oz (½ cup) of the water, work the dough quickly, form into a ball, dust with flour and put into a polythene (plastic) bag. Refrigerate for 1 hour.

With the fingers, work the rest of the butter into a square. Put it between two sheets of greaseproof (wax) paper and roll it out to make a 10 cm/4 inch square. Peel off the paper, sprinkle the butter with flour on both sides, wrap in fresh paper and refrigerate until the butter is firm.

On a lightly floured surface roll out the dough to an 18 cm/7 inch square. Put the butter diagonally into the centre. Fold the dough over the butter, as if making an envelope, to enclose it thoroughly. Turn it over. Dust the work surface and the dough lightly with flour and roll the dough out into a rectangle 15 × 25 cm/6 × 10 inches. Fold the top over all but the bottom third of the rectangle, then fold the bottom third over the top as if folding a letter into thirds.

Turn the dough so that one of the open ends faces you. With the rolling pin, roll the dough away from you from the centre almost to the edge. Turn it around and roll the other half away from you, again almost to the edge, to make a rectangle 25 cm/10 inches long, always taking care to stop about 1 cm/½ inch from the edge to stop the butter oozing out. Fold the dough once more into thirds as for a letter, flouring the dough and the work surface as necessary. This completes two turns. Wrap the dough in greaseproof (wax) paper and refrigerate for 30 minutes.

Tuke out the dough, peel off the paper and again flour the dough and work surface lightly. Roll out as before with an open end facing you. Fold up again into thirds. Roll out again and fold up. Chill the dough, wrapped in greaseproof (wax) paper, for at least 30 minutes. It is now ready to be used.

The dough can be kept, refrigerated, for about 1 week. It can be kept frozen, wrapped in foil. Defrost before using.

Empanadillas
Small Turnovers

These small turnovers are tremendously popular in Spain, especially as a *tapa*. They are equally popular throughout Latin America. They are of Middle Eastern origin but as with everything they adopt, Spanish cooks transform them into their own. Full-size pies are *empanadas* and in Portugal turnovers are *empadas*

MAKES 20 TURNOVERS
1 recipe Shortcrust pastry (Basic Pie Dough) (page 256)

Roll out the pastry thinly and cut out 7.5 cm (3 inch) circles.

For the fillings
For a **fish filling**, sauté 2 tablespoons finely chopped onion in 1 tablespoon olive oil until the onion is soft. Add 75 g/3 ounces (½ cup) flaked salmon, tuna, any white fish or mashed sardines, 2 tablespoons sweet red (bell) pepper, finely chopped, 2 tablespoons peeled, seeded and chopped tomato, 1 tablespoon finely chopped parsley, salt, freshly ground pepper. Cook, over moderate heat for 5 minutes. Add enough tomato sauce to moisten, about 2 tablespoons. Remove from the heat and add 1 small hardboiled egg, finely chopped. Let the mixture cool slightly, then put about 2 teaspoons in the centre of each circle of pastry. Fold over to form a turnover, seal the edges by pressing with a fork or crimping with the fingers and fry in hot oil in a skillet (frying pan) until browned on both sides. The oil should be 5 cm/2 inches deep. Drain on paper towels and serve warm. Do not overfill the turnovers.

For a **meat filling**, sauté 2 tablespoons finely chopped onion in 1 tablespoon olive oil until the onion is soft. Add 1 clove garlic, chopped, 2 tablespoons cured ham, chopped, 2 tablespoons cooked veal, pork, lamb or chicken, 1 tablespoon chopped parsley, salt, freshly ground pepper and 2 tablespoons dry white wine. Simmer the mixture over low heat for 5 minutes. Cool slightly, then stir in 1 small hardboiled egg, finely chopped. Stir to mix and put about 2 teaspoons in the centre of each pastry circle. Fry as for the fish filling.

Although there are certain classic fillings, imagination and what is in the refrigerator can dictate what goes into an *empanadilla* filling. Prawns (shrimp), mussels, salt codfish, chopped green olives, chopped chorizo or other sausage are all suitable.

Empadas de Galinha à Moda do Alentejo
Chicken Pies, Alentejo-style

These little pies differ from the simpler turnovers more favoured in Spain. They are not fried, but baked, and are served as a first course. Brazil copies this style, making little pies instead of turnovers like the rest of Latin America.

MAKES 12 (SERVES 6)
a 1.1 kg/2½ pound chicken
75 g/3 ounces (3 slices) bacon, chopped
75 g/3 ounces *presunto* or smoked ham, chopped
1 medium onion, coarsely chopped
1 clove garlic, chopped
1 large sprig parsley
⅛ teaspoon each ground sage and oregano or 1 leaf fresh sage, 1 sprig fresh oregano
1 tablespoon white wine vinegar
salt and freshly ground pepper
1 egg
1½ recipes Shortcrust Pastry (Basic Dough) (page 256)

Put the chicken into a casserole that will hold it comfortably, an oval one is best. Add all the rest of the ingredients, except the egg and pastry. Add enough water barely to cover. Bring to a simmer, cover and cook until the chicken is tender, about 30–45 minutes. Lift out the chicken, bacon and ham on to a plate. Allow to cool. Strain and reserve the stock. Skin and bone the chicken and cut the meat into bite-size pieces. Put into a bowl with the ham and bacon and moisten with a little of the stock.

Roll out the pastry and cut about half of it into 12 × 7.5 cm/3 inch circles. Use it to line greased patty tins (tartlet shells) of that size. Spoon in the chicken mixture. Cut 12 slightly smaller pastry circles and cover the pies, seal the edges and cut a slit in the top of each. Brush with egg and bake in a preheated moderate oven (180°C/350°F/gas 4) for about 30 minutes or until golden-brown. Serve 2 pies per person, either as a first course or as a light lunch.

Variation: If liked, the stock used to moisten the chicken may be thickened. Pour 250 ml/8 fl oz (1 cup) of the stock into a small saucepan and bring it to a simmer. Beat 2 egg yolks in a bowl and stir in 2 tablespoons of the hot stock. Pour the mixture into the saucepan and cook, stirring, over low heat, without letting it boil, until the mixture is lightly thickened. Mix with the chicken, bacon and ham.

Variation: If liked, make 1 large pie. Use two recipes of pastry and line a 23 cm/9 inch pie plate with half the rolled-out pastry. Cut another circle and cover the filling, sealing the edges. Cut 3 diagonal slits in the top and bake for about 40 minutes. Serve as a luncheon dish.

11

Puddings and Desserts
Pudines y Postres/Pudínes e Doces

It is natural that with such an abundance throughout the Iberian Peninsula, fresh fruits are often served to conclude a meal. There are many fruit desserts including Portuguese fruit salads which are enlivened with wine. Both Spain and Portugal also have a Moorish inheritance of very sweet egg-rich desserts, some ingeniously using up the egg whites left over from a pudding using only egg yolks – *Pudim Molotoff* (Molotoff Pudding), for example. *Flan*, caramel custard, the *Crème Renversée au Caramel* of the French, is universally popular. It may be flavoured with orange, if liked, but it is the traditional caramel custard that enjoys such popularity and is an equal favourite throughout Latin America. In Portugal, where it is called *Pudim Flan*, it may be flavoured with vanilla, coffee or chocolate. Quite literally everyone loves *flan*. They also, especially in Portugal, love rice pudding which is creamy and rich in whichever part of the Peninsula it is cooked. Cakes, small and large, are legion – *Bolos Grandes* (Large Cakes) are regarded with much affection in Portugal – and many of them make a fine dessert.

Peras con Vino
Pears in Wine

This is a delicious and popular way of cooking pears in Spain and works very well also for peaches.

SERVES 4
4 medium slightly under-ripe pears
350 ml/12 fl oz (¾ cup) dry red wine
350 ml/12 fl oz (¾ cup) water
100 g/4 ounces (½ cup) sugar
½ lemon, thinly sliced, seeds removed
1 cinnamon stick, about 5 cm/2 inches

Cut a thin slice off the blossom end or top of each pear and peel them, leaving the stem on. Do not core the pears. In a shallow saucepan large enough to hold the pears in a single layer combine the pears, wine, water, sugar, lemon and the cinnamon stick. Bring to a simmer, cover and cook until the pears are tender, 10–15 minutes.

Lift the pears with a slotted spoon into a serving dish. Boil the liquid over fairly high heat for 5 minutes until it is slightly reduced and syrupy. Pour it over the pears. Cool, then refrigerate until the pears are chilled. Serve in individual dishes with some of the syrup.

Melocotónes en Vino
Peaches in Red Wine

This is the simplest way of serving peaches as an elegant dessert.

SERVES 4
4 medium fresh, ripe peaches
50 g/2 ounces (¼ cup) sugar, preferably caster (superfine)
250 ml/8 fl oz dry red wine (1 cup)

Drop the peaches into a saucepan of briskly boiling water for 1 minute. Lift out and slip off the skins. Halve the peaches then remove and discard the stones (pits). Arrange them in a serving bowl. Sprinkle with the sugar, pour in the wine and chill in the refrigerator for at least 2 hours before serving.

Variations: Prepare the peaches as in the main recipe but do not add any wine. Chill the peaches and sugar thoroughly. Have ready 250 ml/8 fl oz (1 cup) chilled dry Spanish champagne or other sparkling Spanish wine, and pour over the peaches when ready to serve.

Salada de Frutas
Fruit Salad

This is a typical Portuguese fruit salad using the best fruits available. There are no strict rules for making salads though there are common-sense ones like not adding bananas or any fruit that may discolour, until the last minute. Delicate soft fruits like strawberries should be added just before serving as these tend to go mushy.

SERVES 4
500 g/1 pound fresh fruits such as peaches, pears, plums
75 g/3 ounces (½ cup) seedless raisins
100 g/4 ounces (½ cup) sugar
50 ml/2 fl oz (¼ cup) dry white wine
125 ml/4 fl oz (½ cup) ruby or tawny Port

Combine the fresh fruits and raisins in a bowl. Sprinkle with the sugar. Mix the white wine and Port together and pour over the fruit mixture. Toss gently to mix and refrigerate until well chilled before serving.

Variation: If a non-alcoholic version is preferred, use lemon juice for the dry white wine and orange juice in place of the Port.

Variations: If liked, a single fruit may be used instead of a mixture. For *Ananas com Vinho do Porto* (Pineapple with Port) cut a small pineapple, peeled, into bite-size pieces and put into a serving bowl. Sprinkle with 100 g/4 ounces (½ cup) sugar and 125 ml/4 fl oz (½ cup) ruby or tawny Port and decorate with chopped mint. Strawberries can be used for this, or a mixture of strawberries and pineapple.

Tarta de Melocotón
Peach Tart

The fresh fruit contrasts deliciously with the rich custard topping in this tart, which can be made with other fruits like apricots or apples. Fruit tarts of this kind are popular in both Spain and Portugal.

MAKES A 20–23 CM/8–9 INCH TART
For the pastry case/shell
1 recipe Sweet Shortcrust Pastry (Sweet Pie Dough)
(page 257).

For the filling
3–4 fresh ripe peaches
½ teaspoon ground cinnamon

For the custard
3 medium eggs
50 g/2 ounces (¼ cup) sugar
250 ml/8 fl oz (1 cup) warm milk
1 teaspoon cornflour (cornstarch)

Line a flan (tart, pie) tin (dish) with the pastry. Prick the bottom of the pastry all over with a fork and chill for 1 hour. Line the pan with foil and half-fill with dried beans or rice. Bake in a preheated hot oven (220°C/425°F/gas 7) for 15 minutes. Remove from the oven, take out the beans or rice and keep them to use again. Remove and discard the foil. The pie shell is now ready to be filled.

Drop the peaches into boiling water for 30 seconds. Lift them out and slip off the skins. Halve the peaches and discard the stones (pits). Arrange the peach halves in a circle on top of the pastry, cut side down. Put another peach half in the centre if there is room, or cut a peach half to fit. Sprinkle with the cinnamon. The number of peaches needed will vary with size. If the peaches are slightly under-ripe cook them for a few minutes until they are tender.

Make the custard. In the top of a double boiler, off the heat, beat the eggs with the sugar until they form a ribbon when the whisk is lifted. Set the double boiler over moderate heat and gradually stir in the warm milk. Cook, stirring constantly, until the custard has thickened enough to coat the spoon. Stir in the cornflour (cornstarch) mixed with a little water and continue stirring until the custard has thickened, a few minutes. Pour over the peach halves.

Bake the tart in a preheated moderate oven (180°C/350°F/gas 4) for about 30 minutes, or until the pastry is lightly browned. Serve warm or chilled.

Variation: For *Tarte de Maçã e Creme* (Portuguese Apple Tart with Custard) make the pastry and have the unbaked pie shell ready to be filled. Peel and core 500 g/1 pound (about 3 medium) tart, crisp cooking apples and cut them into thin slices. Arrange them on top of the pastry in an overlapping pattern as decoratively as possible. Bake in a preheated moderate oven (180°C/350°F/gas 4) for 20 minutes. Have ready a custard as in the main recipe and pour it over the apples. Return the tart to the oven and bake for about 15 minutes, or until the pastry is golden-brown. Serve warm or chilled, with cream if liked.

Variation: For *Tarte de Amendoa* (Almond Tart) prepare the pastry shell as in the main recipe. In a bowl mix together 100 g/4 ounces (1 cup) sliced (slivered) almonds, 100 g/4 ounces (½ cup) sugar, 100 g/4 ounces (1 stick) butter, diced, and 50 ml/2 fl oz (¼ cup) milk. Stir to mix, transfer to a small saucepan and simmer, stirring, until the ingredients are well blended. Cool slightly, then pour into the pastry shell. Bake in a preheated hot oven (210C/425°F/gas 7) until the top is very lightly browned, about 8 minutes.

Flan de Leche
Caramel Custard

This is Spain's most popular dessert, with Portugal's richer version not far behind. Latin America loves it, as does France, and since it is blissfully easy to make, so does most of the world.

SERVES 6

For the caramel
175 g/6 ounces (¾ cup) sugar

For the custard
3 whole large eggs
3 large egg yolks
100 g/4 ounces (½ cup) sugar
½ teaspoon vanilla essence (extract)
475 ml/16 fl oz (2 cups) milk

Put the sugar into a small, heavy saucepan (enamelled cast-iron is best), and set it over moderate heat. Cook, stirring constantly, until the sugar melts and turns a rich golden colour. Remove from the heat and immediately pour into 6 × 250 ml/8 fl oz (1 cup) custard cups or a 1.5 litre (2½ pint) mould (mold). Take care doing this as the caramel is very hot. Set aside.

In a large bowl beat the eggs and egg yolks until well-mixed. Beat in the sugar. Add the vanilla to the milk and whisk into the egg and sugar mixture. Pour into the prepared cups or mould (mold). Set in a baking pan and pour in enough hot water to come halfway up the sides. Bake in a preheated moderate oven (180°C/350F/gas 4) for about 30 minutes, or until a knife inserted into the custard comes out clean. Remove from the oven and the water bath and cool, then refrigerate. To serve, run a knife between the edge of the custard and the mould (mold) and invert on to dessert plates.

Variation: For *Flan de Naranja* (Orange Custard) caramelize the moulds (molds) in the same way as in the main recipe. In a saucepan combine the peel from 1 small orange and a 5 cm/2 inch piece stick cinnamon with the milk. Simmer over low heat for 2–3 minutes, then let the milk stand, off the heat, for about 30 minutes until well-flavoured. Strain the milk and use it to make the custard as in the main recipe. If liked, omit the milk altogether and instead make the *flan* with an equivalent amount of orange juice plus 1 teaspoon grated rind. Use 6 whole large eggs instead of eggs and egg yolks and make as in the main recipe. Adjust the amount of sugar to personal taste as the orange juice can be slightly tart or very sweet.

Variation: To make 8 servings of *Porto Pudim Flan* (Portuguese Caramel Custard), make the caramel in the usual way but with only 100 g/4 ounces (½ cup) sugar. Set it aside and keep it warm. In a heavy saucepan heat 350 ml/12 fl oz (1½ cups) each double (heavy) cream and milk to scalding point, when small bubbles appear at the edge. Remove from the heat and pour in the caramel, stirring constantly until it is dissolved.

Beat 8 large egg yolks until frothy. Pour them into the caramel, milk and cream mixture, then stir in 2 tablespoons tawny Port. Strain the mixture through a fine sieve and pour into eight 250 ml/8 fl oz (1 cup) custard cups or into a 2 litre/3½ pint (8 cup) mould (mold). Set in a baking pan with hot water to come about halfway up the sides, and bake in a preheated moderate oven (180°C/350°F/gas 4) for 40 minutes or until a knife inserted in the custard comes out clean. Remove from the oven and the water bath and cool, then refrigerate until thoroughly chilled. To unmould the custard, run a knife round the edge, then invert on to dessert plates.

Pudim Molotoff
Molotoff Pudding

This oddly named pudding, which is sometimes spelled Molotov, is a great favourite in the Algarve. It is often served with *Ovos Moles* (Sweet Egg Sauce), creating a cheerful and economical kitchen situation as the egg sauce requires 8 egg yolks and the pudding 8 egg whites.

SERVES 6
butter and 1 tablespoon sugar for mould (pan)
8 large egg whites
½ teaspoon salt
2 teaspoons cornflour (cornstarch)
100 g/4 ounces (½ cup) sugar

For the sauce
1 recipe *Ovos Moles d'Aveiro* (sweet Egg Sauce) (page 271)

For the decoration (optional)
50 g/2 ounces (½ cup) chopped toasted almonds

Butter a 23 cm/9 inch ring mould (tube pan), add the sugar and turn the pan to coat all the surfaces. Invert and discard any excess sugar.

In a large bowl beat the egg whites with the salt until they stand in peaks. Sift the cornflour (cornstarch) over the egg whites and beat until it is incorporated. Add the sugar gradually and continue beating until it is incorporated and the whites stand in soft peaks.

Pour the mixture into the prepared (pan) and tap lightly on a work top to get rid of any bubbles. Stand in a large baking pan and pour in 2.5 cm/ 1 inch hot water. Bake in a preheated moderately hot oven (200°C/400°F gas 6) for 5 minutes, turn off the oven and let the pudding stand in the closed oven for 15 minutes. It should be a delicate light brown. If it seems to be browning too fast, cover with foil.

Remove from the oven, lift out of the water bath and loosen both edges with a spatula dipped in hot water. Cover with a large, decorative plate and invert the pudding on to it. Cool to room temperature and spoon some of the egg custard over it. Serve the rest of the custard separately. If liked, garnish with toasted almonds.

Variation: This version of the pudding is a little harder to make but is just as popular. It could be described as Caramel Meringue. Omit the cornflour (cornstarch). Prepare the ring mould (tube pan) in the same way. In a small, heavy saucepan, preferably enamelled cast iron, heat 250 g/8 ounces (1 cup) sugar over very low heat, stirring with a wooden spoon until melted and a rich amber colour. Remove from the heat and pour in 175 ml/6 fl oz (¾ cup) hot water. The caramel will harden and splutter. Return the pan to low heat and simmer, stirring from time to time, until the sugar has dissolved, making a syrup. Cover and keep warm.

Beat the egg whites with the salt until they stand in peaks. Beat in the sugar. Gradually pour in 125 ml/4 fl oz (½ cup) of the syrup, beating constantly to incorporate it into the eggs. Pour the mixture into the prepared mould (pan) and cook as in the previous recipe.

Warm the reserved caramel: it should not be very thick. Add a very little water if necessary to make it runny. Unmould the pudding on to a decorative plate and pour the caramel syrup over it. Cut into wedges and serve.

Ovos Moles d'Aveiro
Sweet Egg Sauce, Aveiro-style

Aveiro, on the coast of Beira Litoral, is the home of this rich egg yolk dessert. In the town of its birthplace it is sold in little wooden barrels or in white, shell-like cases, and is eaten by the spoonful. It is a favourite dessert throughout the country and is used in a great many ways, making it multi-purpose. It appears as a topping and as a filling for sponge cakes and tarts, as a custard sauce for puddings, notably *Pudim Molotoff* (page 269), and as a filling for marzipan sweets (candies). Originally the only ingredients were egg yolks, sugar and water. Nowadays rice flour, or water from cooking short-grain rice until very soft, is added, the rice being discarded or used for another purpose. Some cooks purée the cooked rice and use it instead of the rice water. The use of rice improves the texture of the finished sweet egg sauce which keeps for 2–3 weeks in a covered container in the refrigerator.

SERVES 4
50 g/2 ounces (¼ cup) short-grain rice
475 ml/16 fl oz (2 cups) water
250 g/8 ounces (1 cup) sugar
8 large egg yolks, lightly beaten

Combine the rice and water in a saucepan and simmer, covered, until the rice is very soft, about 30 minutes. Strain, reserve the water, and discard the rice or keep it for another use.

Put the sugar into a saucepan with 125 ml/4 fl oz (½ cup) of the rice water and cook over moderate heat, stirring from time to time, to make a thin syrup. Remove the pan from the heat and cool slightly, then gradually whisk the syrup into the egg yolks, beating vigorously. Pour the mixture into the saucepan and cook over very low heat, whisking or stirring constantly until the mixture is thick. Be careful not to let it boil. When it is like a thick custard pour it into a dish and let cool. Serve it in small dishes and eat with a spoon, or use with other sweets.

Variation: If using rice flour, make in the same way as above, using plain water for the syrup. Mix 4 tablespoons rice flour with 4 tablespoons water and stir it into the egg yolk/syrup mixture, off the heat, as soon as the eggs and syrup have been beaten thoroughly together. Cook the mixture over very low heat, stirring, until it is thick and the bottom of the pan is briefly visible when a spoon is drawn across it. Pour into a dish and cool before serving. If the custard is to be used as a sauce, cook for a shorter time, only until the mixture is of medium-thick pouring consistency.

Pão-de-Ló
Sponge Cake

I suppose this could best be described as a Portuguese *genoise*, the French sponge cake, though the Portuguese version has no butter, containing just eggs, sugar and a little flour. Traditionally it is baked in a ring mould (tube pan) lined with baking parchment paper, a rather tricky business involving cutting squares of paper and fitting them into the pan. A round cake tin, though less traditional, is quite acceptable. There is also an acceptable method of making the cake that reduces the amount of egg-beating needed. The cake is popular all over the country and especially so in the northern provinces. It us always on hand at tea-time, and can be used in other desserts.

MAKES A 20 CM/8 INCH CAKE
butter for greasing
8 large eggs, separated
pinch of salt
100 g/4 ounces (½ cup) sugar
75 g/3 ounces (¾ cup) plain (all-purpose) flour, sifted

Prepare the ring mould (tube pan) or round cake tin. Grease generously with butter and line with baking parchment paper to cover the sides and base of the tin (pan). Set aside.

In a large bowl beat the egg whites and salt until they stand in peaks. Gradually beat in the sugar until the whites are shiny and stiff. Beat the egg yolks until they are light and lemon-coloured, and gradually beat in the flour. Fold the whites into the yolk mixture gently but thoroughly and pour into the prepared tin (pan). Do this as quickly as possible.

Bake in a preheated moderate oven (180°C/350°F/gas 4) for 15–20 minutes or until golden and springy to the touch. Be careful not to overcook or the cake will toughen. Remove from the oven. Carefully lift the cake out in its paper lining and place on a cake rack to cool. It can be served as soon as it has cooled completely.

Toucinho do Céu
Bacon from Heaven Almond Cake

The origin of this oddly named almond cake is obscure but it is so well liked that it is enjoyed all over Portugal and is an equal favourite in Brazil. Some authorities say it came from the Convent of Odivelas in a Lisbon suburb and may go as far back as the fifteenth century. Others claim it came from a convent near Guimaräes in Minho, still others that it came from Murca in the province of Tras-os-Montes and Alto Douro. Some say it originally contained bacon, others that this is just a metaphor implying that in heaven simple foods like bacon are transformed into foods of heavenly richness like this cake, all eggs and almonds. Some recipes include *abóbora*, a type of pumpkin (winter squash), and in others candied *chila*, a vegetable rather like spaghetti squash. A very similar cake turns up in Yucatán in Mexico as *Torte de Cielo* (Heavenly Cake), where eggs and almonds are used lavishly and flour positively stingily, if at all. Whatever its origin it deserves its title of heavenly. This is a version of the cake that I like very well.

MAKES A 20 CM/8 INCH ROUND CAKE

For preparing the cake tin (pan)
25 g-1 oz (2 tablespoons) butter, softened at room temperature
1 tablespoon sugar

For the cake
500 g/1 pound (2 cups) sugar
125 ml/4 fl oz (½ cup) water
225 g/8 ounces (2 cups) finely ground blanched almonds
4 whole eggs and 6 egg yolks
½–1 teaspoon ground cinnamon, according to taste
⅛ teaspoon ground cloves (optional)

For the decoration (optional)
sugar
chopped almonds

Use a 20 cm (8 inch) round cake tin (pan) with a removable base (spring-form pan) and grease the bottom and sides generously with the butter. Add the tablespoon of sugar, tipping the tin (pan) from side to side to coat it all over. Turn the tin (pan) upside-down to tip out excess sugar.

To make the cake, combine the sugar and water in a heavy saucepan

273

and cook, stirring, over moderate heat, to dissolve the sugar. Stir in the ground almonds and continue to cook, stirring, for 5 minutes, when the mixture will be thick and translucent. Set aside to cool.

Beat the eggs and egg yolks together, beat in the cinnamon and cloves, then beat the egg mixture into the almond mixture. Return the saucepan to the lowest possible heat and cook, stirring, until the mixture is thickened, about 10 minutes. Do not allow it to boil.

Pour the mixture into the prepared tin (pan) and bake in the middle of a preheated moderate oven (180°C/350°F/gas 4) for 15–20 minutes, or until the cake is firm to the touch. Allow the cake to cool before removing from the tin (pan). Serve the cake at room temperature. Sprinkle, if liked, with a little sugar and a few chopped almonds.

Variation: This version from the Alentejo uses some flour but more eggs. In a bowl beat together 750 g/1½ pounds (3 cups) sugar, 16 egg yolks, 11 egg whites, 1 teaspoon ground cinnamon, and ⅛ teaspoon ground cloves. Mix 500 g/1 pound (2 cups) finely ground blanched almonds and 4 tablespoons plain flour and gradually beat them into the egg and sugar mixture. Pour into the prepared tin (pan) and bake as above. This version should be popular with the owners of poultry farms.

Arroz Doce à Portuguesa
Rice Pudding, Portuguese-style

Rice pudding is greatly loved throughout the Iberian Peninsula. It is always made with short-grain rice and is cooked on top of the stove. Cinnamon and lemon peel are the preferred seasonings and the pudding is cooked in milk to a creamy consistency. There are surprisingly few differences between the *Arroz Duce* of Portugal and the *Arroz con Leche* of Spain. Portuguese cooks decorate the pudding with ground cinnamon, often in fanciful designs of hearts, sometimes with the name of a birthday girl, or even flowers. There is no end to the inventiveness of cooks, or to the steadiness of their hands.

SERVES 4–6
250 g/8 ounces (1 cup) short-grain rice
475 ml/16 fl oz (2 cups) water
5 cm/2 inch strip lemon peel
½ teaspoon salt
600 ml/1 pint (2½ cups) milk
1 cinnamon stick
100 g/4 oz (½ cup) sugar
15 g/½ oz (1 tablespoon) butter
4 large egg yolks, lightly beaten
ground cinnamon

Put the rice into a saucepan with the water, lemon peel and salt. Bring to a boil and simmer, uncovered, until the rice has absorbed all the water, about 10 minutes. Remove and discard the lemon peel.

In another saucepan bring the milk to scalding point and pour it into the rice, stirring to mix. Add the cinnamon stick. Cook, uncovered, over very low heat, stirring from time to time, until the milk is almost absorbed. Then add the sugar, butter and egg yolks and continue to cook, stirring from time to time, until the sugar, butter and eggs have also been absorbed by the rice and the mixture is creamy. Remove and discard the cinnamon stick. Turn the pudding out into a serving dish and cool. Decorate, as liked, with ground cinnamon and refrigerate until thoroughly chilled, about 2 hours.

Variation: For *Arroz con Leche Gallego* (Rice Pudding, Galician-style) cook as above. When it is done, put it into an ovenproof dish and cover with 6 tablespoons sugar. There should be a good coating. Put under a hot grill (broiler) just until the sugar caramelizes and eat the pudding hot, or at room temperature.

Queijadas de Sintra
Sintra Cheesecakes

Sintra is an enchanting small town in the wooded hills above Estoril. The vegetation is lush and the gardens of Montserrat are famed for their collection of ferns. There is a Gothic palace dominating the town centre and a ruined Moorish castle high on the hills above the town and it is altogether no wonder that Lord Byron fell in love with it, writing part of *Childe Harold's Pilgrimage* here. Apart from its architecture, and its natural beauties, Sintra is famous for its cheesecakes made from sheep's milk cheese and baked in paper-thin pastry shells. Curd cheese or ricotta are both excellent substitutes.

MAKES 24 SMALL TARTLETS

For the filling
250 g/8 ounces curd or ricotta cheese
250 g/8 ounces (1 cup) sugar
3 large egg yolks
½ teaspoon ground cinnamon
25 g/1 oz (¼ cup) plain (all-purpose) flour

For the pastry
250 g/8 oz (2 cups) plain (all-purpose) flour
¼ teaspoon salt
25 g/1 oz (2 tablespoons) butter or lard
125 ml/4 fl oz (½ cup) cold water

To make the filling, combine the cheese, sugar, egg yolks, cinnamon and flour in a food processor and process until smooth. Scrape out into a bowl and set aside.

To make the pastry, sift the flour and salt into a bowl. Dice the butter or lard and rub into the flour with the fingertips until it resembles coarse meal or breadcrumbs. Sprinkle enough of the water over the flour to make a dough. Form into a ball and roll out as thinly as possible. Cut into 9 cm/3½ inch rounds, use to line small patty tins (tartlet tins) and half-fill with the cheese mixture.

Bake in a preheated moderately hot oven (200°C/400°F/gas 6) for 15–20 minutes, or until the cheesecakes are puffed and a rich brown. Allow to cool, then lift carefully out of the tins. Serve cold or at room temperature.

Variation: In Sintra 25 g/1 oz (¼ cup) desiccated (grated) coconut is sometimes added to the filling. The same amount of ground almonds may also be added.

Variation: The pastry casing may be omitted and the cheese filling baked in very well-buttered tins.

Barriga de Freira
Nun's Belly

Portuguese nuns are to be thanked for the many delicious sweet things, puddings and cakes, they created during the sixteenth and seventeenth centuries. It was a time when the sugar plantations in the New World made sugar cheap and available for the first time in Europe's history and the nuns took full advantage of its abundance. Eggs were plentiful and there was the Moorish influence of rich sweets. Nuns sold their sweet things to raise money for their convents and they also enjoyed them at gatherings, perhaps to celebrate the election of a new Superior, when the sweets, accompanied by wine, would punctuate music and poetry recitals – a little like the Middle Eastern custom of serving visitors with sweet things and coffee. The sixteenth century was also a time when very strange names were given to foods, like *Ropa Vieja* (Old Clothes), a very good beef dish made with flank steak. Call it by its Portuguese name if you prefer, or soften it into Nun's Tummy; it is just as delicious and just as easy to prepare.

SERVES 4
250 g/8 oz (1 cup) sugar
250 ml/8 fl oz (1 cup) water
25 g/1 oz (2 tablespoons) unsalted (sweet) butter
250 g/8 oz (8 cups) fresh white breadcrumbs
8 egg yolks, well-beaten

For the decoration
ground cinnamon, toasted slivered almonds, chopped walnuts, crystallized fruits, glacé (candied) cherries.

In a saucepan combine the sugar and water and simmer to make a fairly thick syrup. Remove the pan from the heat, add the butter and stir until it has melted into the syrup. Stir in the breadcrumbs, mixing thoroughly. Set the pan over very low heat (the mixture must not boil) and gradually stir in the beaten egg yolks. Cook, stirring, just until the eggs thicken the mixture and are cooked.

Put the mixture into a serving dish. Sprinkle with ground cinnamon then decorate, as liked, with nuts and crystallized fruits and glacé (candied) cherries. Serve at room temperature, or chilled.

Papos de Anjo
Sweet Egg Cakes in Syrup

The name of this sweet translates into Angel's Breasts and they are indeed
as soft and light as one would imagine ethereal breasts to be. I have also
seen this as Angel's Double Chins.

SERVES 4
butter for greasing
4 large egg yolks
1 large egg white
pinch of salt
250 g/8 ounces (1 cup) sugar
125 ml/4 fl oz (½ cup) water
½ teaspoon vanilla essence (extract)

Generously butter the sides and bottoms of 12 × 5 cm/2 inch patty tins
(muffin-tin cups).

Beat the egg yolks until they are thick. Beat the egg white separately
until it forms a stiff peak. Fold the egg white into the yolks gently but
thoroughly. Divide the mixture equally among the prepared tins (cups)
and set in a large, shallow baking pan. Pour in enough hot water to come
halfway up the sides of the tins (pans). Bake in a preheated moderate oven
(180°C/350°F/gas 4), for 15–20 minutes, or until a cake tester comes out
clean and the cakes are firm to the touch. Cool in the tins for a few
minutes, then turn out on to a large plate.

While the cakes are baking, make the syrup. In a small saucepan
combine the sugar, water and vanilla and cook, stirring, until the mixture
forms a thick syrup. Allow to cool a little, then dip each cooled cake into
the syrup and transfer to a shallow bowl. Pour the rest of the syrup over
them and chill thoroughly before serving.

Churros
Fried Batter Cakes

These doughnut-like fritters are another of the Spanish dishes that have
become favourites throughout Latin America. Wonderful for breakfast
with coffee or chocolate, they are also sold from street stalls at carnivals
and fairgrounds, where they are made to order, quickly fried and as
quickly eaten.

MAKES ABOUT 16
475 ml/16 fl oz (2 cups) water
1 teaspoon salt
250 g/8 ounces (cups) plain (all-purpose) flour
oil for frying
sugar

In a saucepan combine the water and salt and bring to a boil. Add the flour, all at once, and stir with a wooden spoon until the mixture forms a ball. Cool slightly. Fill a pastry bag fitted with an 5 mm/¼ inch fluted tube and pipe the dough into 10 cm/4 inch lengths. Fry in a frying pan (skillet) in 5 cm/2 inches hot vegetable oil. Fry about 4 *churros* at a time, turning them once until they are golden, or fry in longer strips and cut into 10 cm/4 inch pieces when they are cooked. Drain quickly on paper towels, dip in sugar and eat.

Variation: For a slightly richer *churro*, beat 1 large egg into the dough, off the heat, after it has formed a ball in the saucepan.

The Spanish use a special *churro* maker, not likely to be readily available, to shape the *churros*. At a pinch a large funnel can be used but the *churros* will not have their familiar fluted look.

Morgados
Marzipan Sweets

The Arabs planted almond trees in both the Algarve in Portugal and Andalucía in Spain and marzipan sweets in Portugal are one of the end results of this agricultural initiative. They are easy enough to make even starting with unpeeled almonds but since both ground almonds and ready-made marzipan are both available, advantage can be taken of them. The sweetened almond paste, which is marzipan, can be made into any number of shapes, vegetable or animal, coloured as liked with natural food colourings and served in little paper cakes like chocolates. The paste can be made into round balls stuffed with *Ovos Moles* (Sweet Egg Sauce) (page 271), flavoured with cocoa powder, or indeed used in any way imagination demands.

250 g/8 ounces (½ cup) sugar
4 tablespoons water
250 g/8 ounces (1 cup) finely ground almonds

Combine the sugar and water in a small saucepan and simmer over low heat to make a light syrup. Stir in the ground almonds and mix well. Cook, stirring, until the mixture is very thick and quite dry. When cool, mould into any shape you like and set aside to dry for about one day, then colour with vegetable dye.

Variation: Mix the ground almonds with caster (superfine) sugar, then add 1 medium egg white, lightly beaten, to the mixture, working it until it is smooth and pliable. Let it rest, then mould it into miniature fruits and vegetables, and colour.

Sangría
Red Wine and Fruit Punch

It seems appropriate to include a recipe for that favourite hot weather drink, *sangría*, since it goes so well with Iberian food. Most people have a preferred recipe, some making the drink more alcoholic, others less. This is a standard recipe to be varied as you please.

SERVES 4–6
1 bottle full-bodied dry red wine, preferably Spanish, chilled
2–3 tablespoons caster (superfine) sugar
2 fl oz (¼ cup) Spanish brandy or orange liqueur (optional)
250–475 ml/8–16 fl oz (1–2 cups) soda water (club soda, Seltzer)

For the decoration
orange and lemon slices, apple and peach wedges, ice cubes

In a large jug combine the wine, sugar, brandy or liqueur, if using. Stir to mix, pour in the soda water (club soda), decorate to taste with the fruit and add the ice cubes. The drink should be served well-chilled. Serve in large wine glasses. If preferred, omit the ice cubes from the drink and fill the glasses with ice cubes before pouring in the *sangría*.

Variation: There is a Portuguese version that uses Portuguese red wine and adds 50 ml/2 fl oz (¼ cup) each brandy and tawny port and 250 ml/ 8 fl oz (1 cup) each lemonade and soda water (club soda), but no sugar. Decorate with fruit, using halved strawberries when they are in season.

Bibliography

Dr Jean Andrews, *Peppers, The Domesticated Capsicums*, University of Texas Press, 1984

George Henry Borrow, *The Bible in Spain*

Ann Maria Alera, *La Cocina Regional Española*, Mundo Actual de Ediciones, Barcelona, 1985

Jose Castillo, *Recetas de Cocina de Abuelas Vascas*, Imprenta Ondarribi, Spain, 1983

Cofradia Extremeña de Gastronomia, *Recetario de Cocina Extremeña*, Universitas Editorial, 1985

Columbia Encyclopedia, Third Edition, Columbia University Press, 1968

Alfred W. Crosby Jr., *The Columbian Exchange*, Greenwood Press, Westport, Connecticut, 1972

Alvaro Cunqueiro and Araceli Filgueira Iglesias, *Cocina Gallega*, Editorial Everest, Spain, 1985

Alan Davidson, *North Atlantic Seafood*, Macmillan, London, 1979

Alan Davidson, *Mediterranean Seafood*, second edition, Penguin Books, 1981

Mark Ellingham, John Fisher and Graham Denyon, *The Rough Guide to Portugal*, Routledge and Kegan Paul, New York and London, 1986

J. H. Elliot, *Imperial Spain (1469–1716)*, St Martin's Press, New York, 1964

Nina Epton, *Spanish Fiestas*, Cassell, London, 1968

Claire Shaver Haughton, *Green Immigrants, The Plants That Transformed America*, Harcourt Brace Jovanovich, New York and London, 1978

Dr Alex .Hawkes, *A World of Vegetable Cookery*, Simon and Schuster, New York, 1968

U.P.Hedrick (ed.), *Sturtevant's Edible Plants of the World*, Dover Publications Inc., New York, 1972

Melvenna McKendrick, *The Horizon Concise History of Spain*, American Heritage Publishing Company, New York, 1972

Maria de Lourdes Modesto, *Cozinha Tradicional Portuguesa*, Editorial, Verbal, Lisbon, 1982

Joseph F. O'Callaghen, *A History of Medieval Spain*, Cornell University Press, Ithaca and London, 1975

Simone Ortega, *Quesos Españoles*, Alianza Editorial, Madrid, 1987

Juan B. Serra Padrosa, *Catalogo de Quesos Españoles*, Publications del Ministero de Agricultura, Madrid, 1973

Elvira Pinto, *La Bonne Cuisine Portugaise*, Édicions Garancière, Paris, 1985

Elizabeth Schneider, *Uncommon Fruits and Vegetables*, Harper and Row, New York, 1986

Maria Odette Cortes Valente, *Cozinha Tradicional Portuguesa*, Editorial Organizacões, Lisbon,

List of Illustrations

Index